Green Keynesianism and the Global Financial Crisis

It is widely accepted that limiting climate change to 2°C will require substantial and sustained investments in low-carbon technologies and infrastructure. However, the dominance of market fundamentalism in economic thinking for the past three decades has meant that governments have generally viewed large spending programs as politically undesirable. In this context, the Global Financial Crisis (GFC) represented a huge opportunity for proponents of public investment in environmental projects or "Green Keynesianism."

This book examines the experience of Australia, Canada, Japan, Korea, and the United States with Green Keynesian stimulus programs in the wake of the GFC. Unfortunately, on the whole, the cases do not provide much optimism for proponents of Green Keynesianism. Much less funding than was originally allocated to green programs was actually spent in areas that would produce an environmental benefit. Furthermore, a number of projects had negligible or even detrimental environmental outcomes. While the book also documents several success stories, the research indicates overall that more careful consideration of the design of green stimulus programs is needed. In addition to concrete policy advice, the book provides a broader vision for how governments could use Keynesian policies to work toward creating an "ecological state."

This book will be of great interest to students and scholars of environmental politics, environmental economics, political economy, and sustainable development.

Kyla Tienhaara is an Assistant Professor in the School of Environmental Studies and the Department of Global Development Studies at Queen's University, Canada and a Visiting Fellow at the School of Regulation and Global Governance, Australian National University.

Routledge Studies in Environmental Policy

Green Keynesianism and the Global Financial Crisis

Kyla Tienhaara

LONDON AND NEW YORK

First published 2018
by Routledge

2 Park Square, Milton Park, Abingdon, Oxfordshire OX14 4RN

52 Vanderbilt Avenue, New York, NY 10017

Routledge is an imprint of the Taylor & Francis Group, an informa business

First issued in paperback 2019

British Library Cataloguing-in-Publication Data
A catalogue record for this book is available from the British Library

Library of Congress Cataloging-in-Publication Data
Names: Tienhaara, Kyla Susanne, 1978- author.
Title: Green Keynesianism and the global financial crisis / Kyla Tienhaara.
Description: Abingdon, Oxon; New York, NY: Routledge, 2018. |
Series: Routledge studies in environmental policy | Includes bibliographical references and index.
Identifiers: LCCN 2017055875 | ISBN 9781138551756 (hbk) |
ISBN 9781315147710 (ebk)
Subjects: LCSH: Environmental policy–Economic aspects. | Keynesian economics–Environmental aspects. | Global Financial Crisis, 2008-2009 . |
Economic policy–Environmental aspects.
Classification: LCC HC79.E5 T5235 2018 | DDC 333.7–dc23
LC record available at https://lccn.loc.gov/2017055875

ISBN: 978-1-138-55175-6 (hbk)
ISBN: 978-0-367-43021-4 (pbk)

Typeset in Times New Roman
by Deanta Global Publishing Services, Chennai, India

This book is dedicated to my daughters and to all the rainbow warriors fighting for their future.

Contents

Figures

Tables

Acknowledgments

This book took much longer to write than it was supposed to. The inspiration for it first came in 2009, when Fiona Haines was visiting the Regulatory Institutions Network (RegNet), where I was one year into my post doc. Fiona organized a seminar series where she asked RegNet staff and students to reflect on what the Global Financial Crisis (GFC) meant for the area of governance that they focused on in their work. Having spent the previous five years immersed in the arcane world of investor-state disputes, this was a refreshing opportunity to look at something new in my broader field of environmental politics. By the time I presented the seminar, I was hooked. After railing against a system for such a long time, it felt refreshing to be researching something seemingly positive. Of course, the GFC itself was disturbing and frightening, but the opportunity for change that it seemed to present was exhilarating.

A lot has changed in the eight years that have passed since that initial seminar, including much of my optimism about the opportunity presented by the crisis. After one failed attempt to get a grant to fund a project on a green recovery from the GFC, I was lucky enough to win an Australian Research Council (ARC) Discovery Early Career Researcher Award (DECRA) in 2011 (project number DE120102787). I took up this three-year fellowship in early 2012, only to press pause ten months later to welcome my first child to the world. After almost a year of maternity leave, I returned to work part-time. The fieldwork for the project proved to be somewhat more challenging as a new mother, but I was lucky enough to have a very supportive partner who was happy to take leave from work and traipse around Korea and Japan with a toddler. My parents, Nancy and Martti, and brother Johann would do the same in Canada and the United States. I honestly do not know what I would have done without this support. Suffice to say, my daughter's passport is remarkably full for someone of her age, and she continues to display a strong preference for Japanese cartoons.

Other, less adorable, distractions also prevented my full commitment to the project at times. Given my expertise on investor-state disputes, I found it impossible to ignore the ongoing negotiations of the Trans Pacific Partnership (TPP). The activist in me could not resist any opportunity to try to inform the public and the Australian government of the dangers of that agreement. Eventually, the DECRA funding ran out, and I decided to take some time out from the academy to devote more time to activism. I worked with Greenpeace Australia Pacific as a researcher on their campaigns to end coal exports and to prevent oil drilling in the Great Australian Bight. Finishing this book thus became a project for evenings and the occasional weekend. To be clear, all quotes from Greenpeace in this book were included in the text prior to my brief stint as a rainbow warrior. However, I do acknowledge that my interest in a just transition (see Chapter 8) developed during my time there.

Along the way, there were many people that made the project and this book possible. My colleagues at RegNet, particularly Neil Gunningham, Val and John Braithwaite, and Veronica Taylor, suffered through multiple drafts of the original grant proposal and convinced me that I should not drop the idea just because it got knocked back once. Throughout the project, I was assisted by a number of talented research assistants. When a sudden opportunity to travel to Korea arose a few weeks after I returned from maternity leave, I doubted that it would be possible to arrange interviews in time. Clare Kim not only made it possible, but also accompanied me to Seoul and conducted a number of interviews in Korean. Her presence made what could have been a very stressful experience one of the most enjoyable fieldwork trips I have ever done. I also had a lot of help with my Japanese case study, first from Suzuka Sato and then from my wonderful colleague and good friend Jill Mowbray-Tsutsumi. Of course, I am also greatly indebted to all the interviewees who took the time to share their knowledge and experience with me.

In between field trips, I organized the 2015 Earth System Governance (ESG) Conference in Canberra. This conference would not have been a success without the enormous help I received from one of my Masters students, Ryan Joseph. Toward the end of the project, I relied quite heavily on two further assistants to help me pull a lot of loose ends together. Meredith Edelman was particularly helpful with my United States research and with some overall editorial advice. And I can't thank Alexis Farr enough for, among other things, helping me sort out my excessively long list of references!

I benefited from discussions of some the issues covered in this book with colleagues at a number of conferences and seminars. In particular, I learned a great deal from a semi-plenary on growth that I organized for the ESG conference, and I appreciate the contributions made in that session by Peter Dauvergne and Jennifer Clapp. But most importantly, I will never forget the magnanimity of the keynote speaker – John Barry – when I stuffed up his travel plans, resulting in him having to present by videoconference (late at night) from Belfast. He kindly wrote off the snafu as an intervention from Gaia to help him keep his carbon footprint small!

I also am also indebted to the editors and anonymous reviewers at *Environmental Politics*, the *Journal of Australian Political Economy*, and *Global Policy*. Parts of articles that I published in these outlets are included, with permission, in Chapters 2, 3, and 4. I also value the constructive comments on my book proposal that I received from two anonymous reviewers, and the enthusiasm of my commissioning editor at Routledge, Annabelle Harris.

There are a number of others who have provided invaluable moral support over the years. Of particular note is the infamous "B team" – my beloved colleagues Kate Henne and Ben Authers and their wonderful partners Kent Weyand and Patrick Bugeja. And, although they were in far-flung cities throughout most of this period, I also appreciated the support from a distance that my favorite Canadian-Australians – Russ Brewer, Natasha Tusikov, and Blayne Haggart – have provided. When I was a visiting fellow at the University of New South Wales, I greatly benefited from lunchtime discussions with Pichamon Yeophanton. I also enjoyed the opportunity to catch up regularly with Christian Downie, even if most of our chats ended with the depressing conclusion that the Australian political system is broken and catastrophic climate change is inevitable.

As this book goes to press, I am embarking on new chapter in life with the birth of my second child and an amazing opportunity to continue to pursue my interest in Green Keynesianism as a Canada Research Chair (CRC) in Economy and Environment. For the latter opportunity (and their flexibility in accommodating the former), I must thank both Alice Hovorka and Marc Epprecht at Queen's University as well as the CRC Program.

Last, but absolutely not least, my immense thanks to Kyle, a wonderful partner and father to our girls. In the time that this book has occupied a big chunk of my attention, my first-born often dominated the rest. Despite my neglect of him, his support has never wavered, nor has his willingness to disrupt his own career so that I can answer the door when opportunity knocks. For this, and so many other reasons, I am eternally grateful.

List of abbreviations

ACEEE	American Council for an Energy-Efficient Economy
ARRA	*American Recovery and Reinvestment Act*
ARENA	Australian Renewable Energy Agency
ARPA-E	Advanced Research Projects Agency-Energy
ASCE	American Society for Civil Engineers
AUD	Australian dollar
BC	British Columbia
BCTC	British Columbia Transmission Corporation
CAD	Canadian dollar
CAFE	corporate average fuel economy
CARS	*Consumer Assistance to Recycle and Save Act*
CCC	Civilian Conservation Corps
CCPA	Canadian Center for Policy Alternatives
CCPI	Clean Coal Power Initiative
CCS	carbon capture and storage
CELA	Canadian Environmental Law Association
CEO	chief executive officer
CO_2	carbon dioxide
CO_2-e	carbon dioxide equivalent
CO_2-e/yr	carbon dioxide equivalent per year
COP	Conference of the Parties
DARPA	Defense Advanced Research Projects Agency
DOE	Department of Energy (United States)
EPAct	*Energy Policy Act*
EIA	environmental impact assessment
FIT	feed-in-tariff
FDR	Franklin Delano Roosevelt
G7	Group of Seven
G8	Group of Eight
G20	Group of Twenty
GAO	Government Accountability Office (United States)
GATT	General Agreement of Tariffs and Trade
GDP	gross domestic product
GEC	Global Economic Council

GFC	Global Financial Crisis
GGGI	Global Green Growth Institute
GNDG	Green New Deal Group
HIP	Home Insulation Program
HSBC	Hong Kong Shanghai Banking Corporation
HSR	high-speed rail
IGCC	integrated gasification combined cycle
IISD	International Institute for Sustainable Development
ILO	International Labour Organization
IPE	International Political Economy
IPEE	International Political Economy of the Environment
IMF	International Monetary Fund
IUCN	International Union for Conservation of Nature
JPY	Japanese yen
KRW	South Korean won
km/h	kilometers per hour
kV	kilovolt
kW	kilowatt
kWh	kilowatt hour
LED	light-emitting diode
METI	Ministry of Economy Trade and Industry (Japan)
MIT	Massachusetts Institute of Technology
MIAC	Ministry of Internal Affairs and Communications (Japan)
MLITT	Ministry of Land Infrastructure Transport and Tourism (Japan)
MLTM	Ministry of Land Transport and Maritime Affairs (Japan)
MOE	Ministry of Environment (Japan)
mph	miles per hour
MMT	million metric tons
MT	metric tons
MT CO$_2$e/yr	metric tons of carbon dioxide equivalent per year
mpg	miles per gallon
MW	megawatt
NDP	New Democratic Party (Canada)
NGO	nongovernment organization
NHTSA	National Highway Traffic Safety Administration (United States)
NRCAN	Natural Resources Canada
NTL	Northwest Transmission Line
OECD	Organization for Economic Co-operation and Development
PEI	Prince Edward Island
POMAC	Professors' Organization for Movement against the Grand Korean Canal
PM&C	Prime Minister and Cabinet (Australia)
PV	photovoltaics PVC polyvinyl chloride
R&D	research and development
SCM	subsidies and countervailing measures

TRIMs	trade-related investment measures
UK	United Kingdom
UN	United Nations
UNEO	United Nations Environment Organization
UNEP	United Nations Environment Programme
UNFCCC	United Nations Framework Convention on Climate Change
UNCSD	United Nations Conference on Sustainable Development (Rio +20)
US	United States
USD	United States dollar
WAP	Weatherization Assistance Program
WEO	World Environment Organization
WRI	World Resources Institute
WTO	World Trade Organization
WWF	World Wildlife Fund

Part I

Introduction

1   Too big to fail

Maybe Wall Street was, in fact, too big to fail. Maybe an injustice had to be done in defense of the common good. I wasn't convinced by this argument, but I understood the logic of interventionism. I wonder, though, why this same logic doesn't apply to the planet. Is the Earth not too big to fail?

Sean Illing (2015)

On May 2, 2008, Cyclone Nargis swept into the low-lying Irrawaddy River Delta in central Myanmar. Storm experts had been tracking the cyclone for days, but at the last moment it unexpectedly turned and adopted a much more devastating path. Winds upward of 119 miles an hour pounded the impoverished country and set off a storm surge that reached 25 miles inland. Families sleeping in simple shacks within the Delta were caught unawares and swept out to sea. Whole villages and townships were laid to waste. More than 140,000 people were killed in the worst disaster the country had ever seen (UNEP 2009a). As Casey (2008) remarks, Nargis "was Asia's answer to Hurricane Katrina … [but] many times more deadly."

A few days later, on the other side of the world, with reference to a crisis of a very different nature, United States (US) Treasury Secretary Hank Paulson remarked that he believed that following the failure of investment bank Bear Sterns, "the worst is likely to be behind us" (Phillips and Palleta 2008). But Paulson, like the experts tracking Nargis before it turned, was wrong. Four months after his optimistic prediction, Paulson was bailing out Fannie Mae and Freddie Mac, two huge mortgage firms (Irwin and Goldfarb 2008). What became known as the Global Financial Crisis (GFC), which would lead to the Great Recession (or by some accounts, the "Lesser Depression"), had begun in earnest by early September 2008.

In both cases, experts failed to anticipate the devastation that would be wrought by the impending crises, and the warnings of those sounding the alarm bells were not heeded. In the case of Nargis, there were limited data for experts to rely on, as Myanmar has no radar network to help predict the location and height of storm surges. Further, the military junta in power failed to act on the information available and evacuate those in low-lying areas. In the US, economic analysts did not lack information, but were blinded by an ideological belief that the economic system could not fail. Presidential candidate John McCain famously declared that the "fundamentals of the economy are strong" mere hours before global financial services firm Lehman Brothers filed for bankruptcy protection under federal law, sending markets into a tailspin (*Time Magazine* n.d.; Stein 2011). It is not possible to know whether drastic action at an earlier time might have averted the GFC or limited the loss of life in Myanmar, but each provides a stark lesson about the consequences of complacency.

At first glance, these events may appear to be entirely unrelated, but they are not. The devastating impacts of Cyclone Nargis cannot be divorced from the broader environmental crisis that the world has been facing for several decades. There is no definitive evidence that this cyclone was amplified by climatic changes. However, it is widely believed that in the future, the frequency and magnitude of storms, and the vulnerability of low-lying areas, will increase worldwide as temperatures and sea levels rise (UNEP 2009a). Further, the heavy loss of life from Nargis is primarily attributable to the extensive removal of mangrove forest in the Irrawaddy River Delta, which could have served as a buffer from the storm surge (UNEP 2009a).

In turn, the forces that have driven the environmental crisis also created the GFC. Fundamentally, both crises have largely emerged because of an economic system that promotes overconsumption (leading to unsustainable consumer debt) and infinite (but inequitably distributed) growth (Green New Deal Group 2008). Further, as Ayres (2014) points out, the simplification of the global economic system in recent decades, driven by demands for economic efficiency, has led to instability. As trade barriers have fallen and a select few large-sized firms have come to dominate the market, the complexity and the subsequent resilience of the global economy has been reduced. This loss of resilience is mirrored in ecosystems around the world, which have been simplified through land clearing and species extinctions, also driven largely by demands for the efficient production of goods. The environmental sustainability of any model of capitalism is the subject of ongoing debate. However, there appears to be widespread acceptance that the form that has held sway since the early 1980s, variously referred to as "neoliberalism" or "free-market fundamentalism," and the globalization that has attended it, has been devastating for the global environment (Christoff and Eckersley 2013). The demands of the global economy have accelerated climate change and driven significant changes in land use around the world, leaving people in countries like Myanmar extremely vulnerable.

The connections between the causes of the crises are critical to understanding the broader context of this book; however, they are not its central focus. Nor is this book about ways to simultaneously solve both crises, although others who address the same topic often frame their work as providing solutions. This book is primarily concerned with the opportunities that emerged in 2008 for environmentalists – activists, government officials, scholars, or businesspeople – to advance an environmental agenda by piggybacking state-led responses to the GFC. The book focuses on government measures aimed at promoting an economic recovery after September 2008, rather than efforts to reform the financial system to prevent future crises. It discusses the extent to which these measures were harnessed to produce the double dividends of employment and environmental benefits, such as emissions reductions.

It is an old adage that in every crisis there is an opportunity. Cyclone Nargis presented an opportunity for the world's leaders to acknowledge the stark realities of a warming world and the consequences of environmental destruction. However, if Hurricane Katrina's devastating impact in the US could not provide an impetus for action on climate change, then a disaster – no matter how horrific – in a far-flung corner of the world, remote from the halls of power, was highly unlikely to do so. Conversely, the GFC was not a phenomenon that major economies could afford to ignore. Several firms were deemed "too big to fail" and bailed out, but that was not enough to avert disaster. Greater government intervention in the market was required, which flew in the face of the prevailing economic orthodoxy. The state, once thought to be in "retreat" (Strange 1996), was back at center stage and the much-neglected and frequently derided English economist John Maynard Keynes was resurrected and restored to his place as the most influential economic thinker of the last hundred years (Skidelsky 2009). Naomi Klein (2008) argued at the time that the GFC should be for neoliberalism what "the fall of the Berlin Wall was for authoritarian communism: an indictment of ideology."

This disruption of the status quo created an opening for a substantial improvement in the relationship between capitalism and nature, and significant state-led action on climate change and other environmental issues. Presumably trying to channel Winston Churchill,[1] US President Barack Obama's Chief of Staff Rahm Emmanuel was quoted, with reference to the GFC, as saying "you never want a serious crisis go to waste. And what I mean by that it's an opportunity to do things you think you could not do before" (quoted in Seib 2008). This book examines the degree to which governments, in 2008 and 2009, pursued action they believed difficult to undertake under the constraints of neoliberalism to address the global environmental crisis. In particular, it explores the extent to which governments embraced "Green Keynesianism," which is defined here as government intervention in the economy through public policies that aim to achieve full employment and environmental sustainability.

This opening chapter first provides a brief introduction to the twin crises of environment and economy. It then discusses the twin opportunities that the GFC presented to the environmental movement. Subsequently, key literature that informs this study on the international political economy of the environment and comparative environmental politics is introduced. Next, the qualitative case study approach and the selection of countries whose policies are examined in the book are explained. The political, economic, and environmental context in each country is then outlined. Finally, an overview of the remainder of the book is provided.

The crises

The GFC started as the US subprime mortgage crisis that resulted from the bundling and repackaging of "toxic" assets as "safe" investments (Kamin and

DeMarco 2010; Duca 2013). The initial crisis appeared relatively contained, affecting only countries outside the US that were exposed to the subprime market (particularly the United Kingdom [UK] and European countries). However, in the last quarter of 2008, the crisis escalated dramatically with the collapse of Lehman Brothers and the bailout of American International Group, the largest insurance company in the US. On the heels of these events came similar collapses and rescues of financial institutions in other advanced economies. As the knock-on effects of the credit crunch sank in, emerging economies also began to suffer. What began as a crisis in one sector in one country eventually became "the world's first truly global financial crisis" (Omarova 2009, 157).

Most advanced economies suffered deep recessions as a result of the GFC. The International Monetary Fund (IMF) reported a 0.8 percent decline in global economic output in 2009 (IMF 2010). Global trade in manufactured goods fell sharply, with repercussions for East Asian economies in particular (IMF 2009). At the same time, plummeting commodity prices severely affected countries in Africa, Latin America, and the Middle East. The International Labour Organization (ILO) estimates that 212 million people were unemployed in 2009, almost 34 million more than in 2007 (ILO 2010). The Great Recession is considered the most severe economic downturn since the Great Depression.

While the world was experiencing the worst economic crisis in a generation, it was also faced with an environmental crisis of similar magnitude. In 2008–2009, research findings indicated that climate change was occurring far more rapidly than previously projected. Specifically, the arctic sea ice was shown to be disappearing at a far greater rate than scientists had predicted (UNEP 2009b). The World Wildlife Fund (WWF) released its Living Planet Report in 2008, which showed that biodiversity had declined by 30 percent over the previous 35 years. The WWF (2008) found that, in a business-as-usual scenario, the world's fisheries were projected to decline by more than 90 percent by 2050.

These startling figures are only a few of the many that could be catalogued here, and the data accumulated since 2009 have demonstrated that the situation is worse than originally predicted. A group of researchers, led by Johan Rockström from the Stockholm Resilience Centre and Will Steffen from the Australian National University, developed the planetary boundaries framework in 2009, which "defines a safe operating space for humanity based on the intrinsic biophysical processes that regulate the stability of the Earth System" (Steffen et al. 2015, 1). According to their research, as of 2015, four of the nine planetary boundaries (climate change, loss of biosphere integrity, land-system change, and altered biogeochemical cycles) had been crossed.

If government intervention to rescue Wall Street was justifiable by the importance of financial institutions in maintaining stability in the global economy, the same logic should apply with respect to these critical biophysical processes. As Illing (2015) puts it, "the Earth is too big to fail."

The opportunities

In his pithy remarks about not wanting to waste the crisis, Rahm Emmanuel effectively categorized the GFC as what historical institutionalists call a "critical juncture." In a critical juncture, the structural (i.e., economic, cultural, ideological, organizational) constraints on political actors are "significantly relaxed for a relatively short period" (Capoccia and Kelemen 2007, 343). As a result, political actors have a greater range of options for action and leaders have "greater latitude in shaping policy than might be available in more stable periods" (Peters 2011, 76).

There was the potential for the GFC to be a critical juncture for the environmental movement. First, there was a need for governments to respond quickly to the crisis, which opened opportunities to direct government spending to environmental projects. Deficit-funded public spending (Keynesian fiscal stimulus) became not only politically acceptable, but also popular in many countries and was even promoted by international financial institutions like the IMF (2009). There was broad agreement among economists that fiscal stimulus should be "timely, targeted, and temporary" (known as the three Ts) (Elmendorf and Furman 2008; Stone and Cox 2008; Summers 2008). "Timely" means that spending plans should be implemented quickly. "Targeted" means that funds should be directed primarily at lower-income brackets and sectors of the economy most affected by the recession (thus, increasing the likelihood of the injection of money into the economy through further spending), creating a "multiplier effect." Finally, "temporary" means that any stimulus should have a fixed end date. Other than the three Ts, there was no consensus on how public money should be spent.

It is widely accepted that limiting climate change to an average temperature rise of 2°C (or, even more ambitiously, 1.5°C) will require substantial and sustained investments in low-carbon technologies and infrastructure (OECD n.d.a). Some of these investments will of course be made by the private sector, independent of government action, or spurred on by the introduction of a price on carbon. However, in recent years, a consensus has emerged among environmental policy scholars that the transition to a low-carbon economy and the greening of basic infrastructure cannot be left to market forces alone. As Gore (2010, 732) notes:

> Whilst markets might allocate resources effectively between existing activities, they are not effective in allocating resources between new and old activities, in generating structural change and in dealing with the social impacts of the associated creative destruction of economic activities and livelihoods.

In other words, government intervention in energy markets and government-administered rebuilding of basic infrastructure will be necessary regardless of the use of other strategies for achieving sustainability (whether market-based or regulatory) or the form of "new economy" that societies eventually transition to. Eskelinen (2015, 102) describes this conclusion as the "minimum common denominator in politics of environmental sustainability."

The potential to direct Keynesian stimulus to environmental projects was recognized early by a small number of individuals and organizations (e.g., Green New Deal Group 2008; Pollin et al. 2008). The number of proposals for "green stimulus" or a "Green New Deal" grew throughout 2009 (Bowen et al. 2009; Houser, Mohan, and Heilmayr 2009; UNEP 2009c). At first glance, the benefits of coupling environmental protection with economic recovery appeared axiomatic. Then-United Nations (UN) Secretary-General Ban Ki-Moon and Al Gore (2009) wrote in the *Financial Times* that "continuing to pour trillions of dollars into carbon-based infrastructure and fossil-fuel subsidies would be like investing in subprime real estate all over again." Proponents have argued that green investments create more jobs than "brown" ones (Pollin et al. 2008; Robins, Clover, and Singh 2009a) and achieve considerable economic savings for individuals and businesses through lower fuel bills, reduced congestion, and improvements in health (less air pollution) (Houser et al. 2009).

The GFC was also a critical juncture in a second, more abstract, respect. The economic orthodoxy of market fundamentalism was implicated in creating the crisis and thus, was largely discredited. There was a sense, at least in the early days of the GFC, that neoliberalism could be replaced with a new economic model or paradigm. This created an opening for environmentalists to propose some form of "green" economic system as the way forward (Spies-Butcher and Stilwell 2009). Harris (2013, 71) suggests that the GFC represented:

> A major opportunity for a new kind of macroeconomics to emerge – one that is "old" in that it returns to some traditional Keynesian principles, but "new" in that it incorporates the ecological realities of the twenty-first century.

This book focuses on the ways in which the GFC provided environmentalists with an opportunity to steer government investment to environmentally beneficial technologies and infrastructure. However, ultimately, the case studies demonstrate that promoting a Green New Deal was inextricably intertwined with the opportunity to push for change in the macroeconomic paradigm. A successful program of green investments across the G20 countries could have laid the groundwork for the adoption of the kind of framework envisioned by Harris and others. Conversely, a lackluster performance by governments in stimulating the economy through purportedly green projects would not only undermine the environmental agenda, but also renew public distrust in the state. In other words, if done well, a Green New Deal could have paved the way for more radical changes in economics but, if done poorly, could help breathe life back into neoliberalism.

Approach

The approach adopted for this study is highly interdisciplinary. Some chapters, particularly Chapters 2 and 8, draw on post-Keynesian and ecological economics literature. Others include insights from fields such as life-cycle analysis and urban planning. However, the research is primarily situated at the intersection of two rapidly developing fields: the international political economy of the environment (IPEE) and comparative environmental politics.

International political economy of the environment

In a seminal article published in 2012, Clapp and Helleiner map out IPEE as a subfield of International Political Economy (IPE). IPE emerged in the 1970s as a response to dramatic international events, including the 1973 oil shock and the breakdown of the Bretton Woods monetary system. The pioneers of IPE came from a variety of different fields, such as international relations and comparative politics, and shared a commitment to interdisciplinarity (O'Brien and Williams 2013). They drew on the writings of political economists, including Keynes.

Environmentalism was a burgeoning movement in the 1970s and the connections between economics, politics, and ecology were understood early on. For example, the 1972 Club of Rome report, *The Limits to Growth*, concluded that Earth could not sustain high rates of economic growth indefinitely (Meadows et al. 1972). However, scholarly interest in such interconnections was limited prior to the publication of the 1987 Brundtland Commission Report, which introduced the concept of "sustainable development" as "development that meets the needs of the present without compromising the ability of future generations to meet their own needs" (World Commission on Environment and Development 1987, 44). This policy agenda, also promoted at the 1992 Earth Summit in Rio de Janeiro, has been the dominant focus of IPEE scholarship in the intervening period (Clapp and Helleiner 2012).

Within IPEE, there are a variety of worldviews expressed. The dominant view, held by what Clapp and Dauvergne (2005) refer to as "market liberals," is that economic growth is not only compatible with sustainable development, it is in fact a pre-requisite for it. Market liberals believe that poverty is a key driver of environmental degradation, which is best addressed by improving the protection of property rights and ensuring that markets are open and globally integrated. On the other end of the spectrum is a "critical camp" comprising ecological economists and other radical thinkers who argue that economic growth is the key driver of, rather than the solution to, the environmental crisis (Clapp 2014). "Institutionalists" occupy the middle ground between these two extremes. Like the market liberal approach, institutionalism assumes that economic growth can be a positive force for the environment. However, institutionalists emphasize that positive outcomes are not assured and that the global economy must to some extent be constrained and directed by states as well as by strong global institutions (Clapp and Dauvergne 2005). Much of the optimism of institutionalists is premised on the theory of ecological modernization, which suggests that environmental harm can be decoupled from economic growth (see Chapter 2).

While many Green Keynesian proposals that emerged in the wake of the GFC could be categorized as institutionalist, and the notion of a Green New Deal has often been conflated with the broader "green economy" and "green growth" discourses (see Chapter 2), this book adopts a more critical approach. Although any green stimulus proposals would be expected, by design, to contribute to economic growth, Green Keynesianism can be conceived as part of a transitional project with the ultimate objective of achieving of a steady-state economy. Therefore, this book pays close attention to issues such as rebound effects (see Chapters 2 and 5), which are typically ignored by market liberals and institutionalists. However, unlike other critical accounts, the objective here is not to dismiss Green Keynesianism as oxymoronic. The stimulus measures discussed in subsequent chapters are not deemed to be environmentally harmful solely on the basis that they helped revive economic growth in the short term. Instead, the aim is to learn from the case studies and identify what type of green stimulus measures would best fit a progressive transitional Green Keynesian project.

Comparative environmental politics

As Clapp and Helleiner (2012) note, while a rich body of research has emerged in IPEE, it has focused primarily on treaties, institutions, and regimes. Although this study addresses the role played by global institutions in helping or hindering the advancement of Green Keynesianism (see Chapter 3), it goes beyond the traditional confines of IPEE by incorporating a comparative case study analysis.

Comparative environmental politics is the "systematic study and comparison of environmental politics in different countries around the globe" (Steinberg and VanDeever 2012, 5). Comparing the experiences of different countries with particular policies or other endeavors brings to the fore the importance of political and cultural context. The GFC was a perfect opportunity to conduct comparative research because it was a unique moment in which many countries enacted similar policies with the same general impetus for action.

While comparative environmental politics can involve the comparison of behaviors of any number of different actors across different countries, this study is focused primarily on national governments (referred to hereafter as simply "states"). States have received surprisingly little attention in studies of comparative and global environmental politics, particularly in comparison with private entities, non-governmental organizations, and political organizations or movements. Much of this neglect seems to result from a lack of faith in the state's capacity to address environmental problems (Wurzel 2012; Bäckstrand and Kronsell 2015). However, as Barry and Eckersley (2005, xii) argue:

> Despite the changes wrought by globalization, democratic states still have more steering capacity and legitimacy to regulate the activities of corporations and other social agents along ecologically sustainable lines in more systematic ways than any nonstate alternative.

Furthermore, while much interest has been directed at the capacity of local actors and institutions to respond to the global environmental crisis, what is often neglected is the fact that supportive national policy is one of the few consistently necessary ingredients for successful local environmental initiatives (Ostrom 1990).

As noted above, the GFC appeared to mark what could have been a "return of the state" in terms of an increased engagement in directing the economy. According to Meadowcroft (2012, 70), "although neoliberalism has a wide range of meanings, it is typically associated with policies to promote market-based solutions to societal problems and to roll back the 'interferences' of the state." As such, the purported "death of neoliberalism" and a resurgence of interest in Keynesianism could have marked the beginning of a new era of increased state action in several areas, including environmental protection. While interest in Keynesianism turned out to be quite short-lived in many parts of the world, Brexit and the election of Donald Trump as US president suggest that neoliberalism is again on the back foot, even if the new model of the state in those contexts is quite different from that envisioned here.

Methodology

There are two levels of comparison employed in this study. First, the overall green stimulus packages in five case study countries are introduced and compared, in rather broad terms, in the next section. Chapters 4–7 present a more substantial comparative analysis, which focuses on individual stimulus measures in the case countries, grouped by theme (e.g., weatherization and green infrastructure). The primary method employed is qualitative inductive content analysis (Mayring 2000). Data were collected from a mix of sources, including other academic work, government documents, government audits and commissions of inquiry, media reports, and semi-structured interviews with experts.[2] Data were then organized into categories and themes that emerged organically, rather than being forced into a pre-defined framework (Teräväinen-Litardo 2014).

The case countries

At the outset of this research, a decision was made to limit the pool of prospective case countries to the G20 member states, because these states developed the most substantial responses to the crisis (Prasad and Sorkin 2009). Further, it was determined that only states with market economies would be selected. Most significantly, this ruled out the inclusion of China, despite its substantial investments in green projects following the GFC (see Figure 1.2), because it has a hybrid (socialist market) economy. Within the remaining pool, the aim was to select countries to represent diverse responses to the GFC, in terms of the absolute amount of green spending and green spending as a percentage of the total stimulus package. The initial selection was aided by an analysis of spending estimates from a team at HSBC Global Research (Robins et al. 2009a, 2009b).

The HSBC report claimed that over USD 470 billion out of a total of nearly USD 3 trillion (15.7 percent) of fiscal stimulus promised by governments as of May 2009 was allocated to green investments (Robins et al. 2009b). It is important to note that HSBC's very broad definition of green stimulus encompasses several categories of spending, such as carbon capture and storage (CCS) and nuclear power, that many environmentalists refuse to categorize as green. Further, in practice, much of the "green" spending counted by Robins et al. (2009a, 2009b) had dubious environmental benefits (as detailed in Chapters 4–7). However, despite the problems with the HSBC figures, they are a useful starting point, particularly because they have been so heavily relied on by academics and the media (e.g., Bernard et al. 2009; Schepelmann et al. 2009; Barbier 2010).

The countries selected for this study are Australia, Canada, Japan, Korea, and the US. In terms of absolute spending, the US is at the high end of the spectrum, while Canada is at the low end (see Figure 1.1). Japan is mid-range on total spend, but low on green measures as a proportion of the overall package (see Figures 1.1

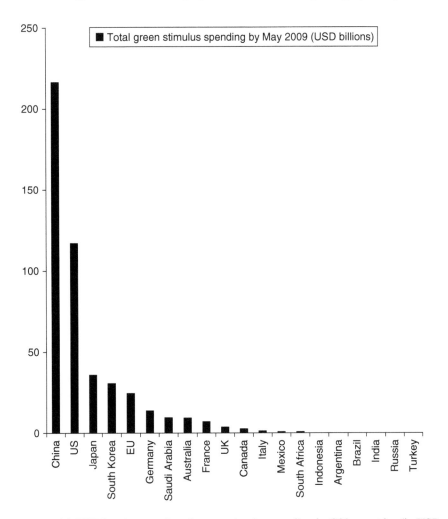

Figure 1.1 HSBC estimates of total green stimulus spending in G20 countries (in USD billion)

Sources: Compiled from data in Robins et al. (2009a, 2009b).

and 1.2). Conversely, Korea has the highest ratio of green stimulus measures (see Figure 1.2). Australia is in the middle of the range for spending in absolute terms and as a percentage of the total package (see Figures 1.1 and 1.2).

A broad overview of each country's stimulus package is provided below. Not every green stimulus measure adopted in the target countries is explored in detail in subsequent chapters of the book. Fiscal stimulus can come in the form of tax cuts or direct spending (investment) measures – this book focuses on the latter. Investment measures that dominated each country's stimulus package, both in terms of dollars spent and public and media interest, are given principal attention. This ensures coverage of the projects likely to have the greatest impact in strict environmental terms and on the public's perception of green stimulus. Nuclear projects were excluded from the study (as discussed in Chapter 2). Upgrades to traditional infrastructure (e.g., wastewater and sewage, and non-high-speed trains)

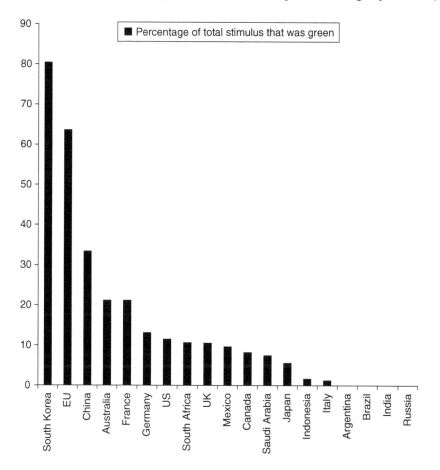

Figure 1.2 HSBC estimates of green stimulus as a percentage of total stimulus in G20 countries

Sources: Compiled from data in Robins et al. (2009a, 2009b).

were also eschewed in favor of more innovative projects that suggested a shift in government approach to a new kind of economy. While it would have been impossible to track every penny spent on environmental projects in five countries, the narrow focus is acknowledged as a shortcoming of the research. Another limitation is that due to the difficulty of acquiring information on actual stimulus spending, it was not possible to always verify whether the pledged spending reported by the HSBC team translated into actual spending. Where such information was readily available, it is provided in the country summaries below.

A final note concerns employment data and quantitative environmental data, such as emissions reductions estimates. While this type of data is reported in the empirical chapters, every effort is made to provide multiple (often competing) estimates; all numbers should be viewed with a degree of skepticism. As Ladislaw and Goldberger (2010) highlight, measurements of this nature are inherently difficult to make. For example, the creation of a green job may be offset by the loss of a job in another industry, resulting in no net increase in employment. Tracking these interconnections is challenging. As such, the quantitative data cited are meant to provide only one part of the broader picture and alone are quite limited in value.

Australia

In 2007, the Australian Labor Party, led by Kevin Rudd, was elected to government. Climate change had been a key election issue and Rudd had dubbed it "the great moral challenge of our generation" (Rudd 2007). The first official act of the new government was to ratify the Kyoto Protocol to the UN Framework Convention on Climate Change (UNFCCC).

While Rudd's approach to climate change was a marked departure from that of his predecessor, John Howard, his position on economic issues was not. During the election, Labor was eager to shed its reputation for excessive spending and attempted to brand itself as a party of "economic conservatives" (Taylor and Uren 2010, 2, 81). However, the onset of the GFC radically changed the economic discourse in Australia, at least for a brief moment. In early 2009, Rudd wrote a lengthy piece in the *Monthly* deriding neoliberalism as the cause of the crisis and proposing a social-democratic (Keynesian) response. He appeared to regard the GFC as a critical juncture that could result in a paradigm shift in economic policy: "from time to time in human history there occur events of a truly seismic significance, events that mark a turning point between one epoch and the next, when one orthodoxy is overthrown and another takes its place" (Rudd 2009).

Australia's stimulus came in several waves. Unlike most OECD countries, Australia gave priority to boosting government spending rather than tax cuts (OECD 2009a). The first tranche of spending came relatively early in October 2008 and consisted mainly of direct cash payments to pensioners and families, and a boost in the First Home Owner Grant. The second package in December 2008 delivered funds to rail and infrastructure in the tertiary education sector. The 2008 stimulus combined to just over AUD 15 billion (USD 12 billion)[3] (Taylor and Uren 2010, appendix B).

When Rudd signaled that another round of spending would come in early 2009, a coalition of environmental groups, the country's peak union body, the Property Council of Australia, and several other groups made a joint statement, calling on the government to include substantial investments in green home renovations and green infrastructure (Australian Conservation Foundation et al. 2008). The government's AUD 42 billion (USD 33 billion) Nation Building and Jobs Plan arrived in February 2009, including AUD 3.9 billion (USD 3.1 billion) for an Energy Efficient Homes Package. Within this package, the Home Insulation Program (HIP) was noteworthy, both for its stated environmental objectives and its political impact. This program is discussed in Chapter 4.

Finally, the May 2009 Budget included a further AUD 22.5 billion (USD 17.8 billion) in infrastructure investments, which is included in some estimates of the country's total stimulus (Taylor and Uren 2010; see appendix B). While the opposition, a Liberal-National Coalition, derided the government for what it viewed as excessive spending, the stimulus was praised outside the country by organizations such as the IMF and the OECD (Wettenhall 2011, 81).

The HSBC report estimated Australia's green stimulus at USD 9.3 billion, which was approximately 21 percent of the 2009 stimulus and 17 percent of total stimulus spending during 2008–2009 (Robins et al. 2009b). This placed the country in the middle of the G20 spectrum in terms of the green proportion of the stimulus package, ahead of the US, Canada, and the UK but behind China, the European Union, and South Korea (see Figure 1.2). The HSBC report included AUD 4.6 billion (USD 3.6 billion) in upgrades to metro rail networks from the 2009 Budget because of the anticipated positive effects on emissions reductions. Setting aside the fact that the environmental impact of such investments is highly context dependent (Bowen and Stern 2010), one can question whether environmental objectives were a critical factor in the government's decision to allocate funding to metro rail. In the 2009 Budget, the upgrades to rail links are justified largely on the basis of alleviating urban congestion. Although the benefit of reducing greenhouse gases is mentioned, it is clearly a peripheral goal at best (Commonwealth of Australia 2009, 4). It is likely that that these investments would have been tabled even in the absence of environmental concerns.

If we remove metro rail upgrades from the green stimulus calculation for Australia, and all funding that was pre-existing or redirected from other environmental programs, this leaves approximately AUD 7.4 billion (USD 5.8 billion) in new funds. According to available information, only about 35 percent of that funding was actually spent (see Table 1.1).

The CCS Flagships and Solar Flagships programs increased funding for Renewables Australia, and the Solar Homes and Communities Plan, and the NEEI were both funded in the May 2009 Budget. Although the budget was "forged in the fire of the most challenging global economic conditions since the Great Depression" (Swan 2009), it does not follow that every major project announced in the budget was a stimulus measure per se. None of the projects under the Clean Energy Initiative had the potential to create a substantial number of jobs in the short term. Further, the funding (which was to be spread out over nine years in

Table 1.1 Major green programs funded in Australia in 2009

Program	Funding in 2009 (AUD M)	Funding spent by 2017 (AUD M)	Outcomes
HIP	2,800	1,450	See Chapter 4
Low Emissions Assistance Plan for Renters (LEAPR)	487.4	14.5	19,591 rental properties insulated, rolled into HIP in Aug 2009
Solar Hot Water Rebate (SHWR)	262.2	173	255,000 households assisted (since 2007), rolled into the Renewable Energy Bonus Scheme in 2010 (ended 2012)
CCS Flagships	2,000	271–299	See Chapter 7
Solar Flagships	1,365	167	See Chapter 7
Renewables Australia (renamed Australian Centre for Renewable Energy)	100	100	Funded a portfolio of small projects in renewables sector
Solar Homes and Communities Plan	245.3	245.3	Installation of 107,752 PV systems from 2000 to 2010
National Energy Efficiency Initiative (NEEI)	100	100	Smart Grid Smart City Project (trial of smart-grid technologies) ran from 2010 to 2014
Total	7,360	2521–2549	

Sources: Tienhaara (2015) and Browne and Swann (2017).

the case of the CCS Flagships) failed to meet the "temporary" criterion typically applied to stimulus measures. These programs were in the works prior to the GFC and formed a part of the Rudd government's broader strategy to tackle climate change rather than a specific response to the crisis. Nevertheless, the Solar and CCS Flagships programs provide a useful comparison to those adopted in Canada and the US and are, therefore, addressed in Chapter 7.

Overall, Australia's stimulus package does not represent a paradigm shift in environmental policymaking. This is even more apparent if one considers the brown aspects of the stimulus and 2009 Budget, such as the AUD 4.8 billion (USD 3.8 billion) allocated to road projects, touted as part of "the biggest road investment program in the nation's history" (Commonwealth of Australia 2009, 14).

Canada

Canada has a long history of environmental stewardship and, in the two years preceding the GFC, opinion polls showed that Canadians considered ecological protection to be the most important political priority for the country (MacNeil 2014). Despite this, the Conservative Party of Canada (which does not have a strong record on environmental issues) won general elections in 2006 and 2008, forming a minority government each time. Prime Minister Stephen Harper's "Made in Canada" plan for environmental protection included the 2006 announcement that the country could not meet its commitments under the Kyoto Protocol to the UNFCCC. Although the Conservatives have attempted at various times to project a green image, it has been abundantly clear that the Harper government, as MacNeil (2014, 176) asserts, chose "to focus on resource cultivation as the key to Canada's economic future."

Ideologically, the Conservatives were also not predisposed to Keynesian economics. In fact, it took the threat of the formation of a coalition by other major parties (which would have toppled the government) to prompt Harper's administration to address the GFC. When the stimulus package was announced in January 2009, it amounted to nearly CAD 40 billion (USD 35 billion). The green portion of the plan, as estimated by the HSBC team, was CAD 3.3 billion (USD 2.9 billion) or 8.3 percent, which was very low in comparison with the US and other G20 countries, where the average was 15 percent. According to UNEP (2009a), Canada's green stimulus funding amounted to only 0.17 percent of gross domestic product (GDP) – far below the organization's target (1 percent of GDP).

The largest green elements of Canada's Economic Action Plan were CAD 1 billion (USD 880 million) over five years to support clean energy technologies (CAD 650 million [USD 572 million] for large-scale CCS demonstration projects, CAD 200 million [USD 176 million] for other small-scale technological demonstration projects, and CAD 150 million [USD 132 million] for research and development); the creation of a Green Infrastructure Fund, with CAD 1 billion (USD 880 million) to be spent over five years; CAD 351 million (USD 309 million) in funding for the nuclear energy sector; CAD 300 million (USD 264 million) for the existing ecoENERGY Retrofit program; and CAD 407 million (USD 358 million) for investments in passenger rail.

In terms of what was spent, CAD 275 million (USD 245 million) of the Green Infrastructure Fund was transferred to other departments (Infrastructure Canada 2016). This left CAD 725 million (USD 638 million) (see Chapter 6 for more details on how this money was spent). CAD 205 million (USD 180 million) was shifted out of the Clean Energy Fund into the very popular ecoENERGY Retrofit program (discussed in Chapter 4). To accommodate this, the research and development (R&D) budget was slashed to CAD 24 million (USD 21 million) and small-scale clean technology projects only received CAD 146 million (USD 128 million), of which CAD 140.5 million (USD 123.6 million) was spent on 18 projects (NRCAN 2014, 2016c). CAD 610 million (USD 537 million) remained available for large-scale CCS projects but, as of mid-2017, only CAD 150 million (USD 132 million) in actual spending had occurred (see Chapter 7).

Most Canadian environmental organizations were dismayed with the overall stimulus package, even at its original funding level in 2009. For example, Greenpeace Canada (2009) noted that it "considers the Harper government's budget a miserable failure at seizing a golden opportunity to provide long-term investment for a green economy." The key critiques were excessive funding for CCS (the technology is not considered feasible or green by most environmental groups); too much funding for the nuclear energy sector (similar reasoning); inadequate funding for passenger rail; and a complete absence of funding for renewable energy, marine issues, or parks (Canadian Centre for Policy Alternatives 2009; David Suzuki Foundation 2009; Greenpeace Canada 2009). While the additional funds directed to housing retrofits under the ecoENERGY program were supported, it was argued that the Home Renovation Tax Credit included in the stimulus package should have included green conditions.

As shown in Table 1.2, actual spending was at least CAD 706 million (USD 621 million) lower than what was allocated (due to funding changes in the largest programs). This means that even if all smaller green stimulus programs were fully funded, Canada's overall investment was only CAD 2.6 billion (USD 2.3 billion). If CCS and nuclear investments were removed, this figure would be reduced to CAD 2.2 billion (USD 1.9 billion).

Another major issue that arose in relation to the Canadian stimulus package concerned the government's decision to streamline the approval process for funded infrastructure projects by eliminating the requirement for a federal environmental impact assessment (EIA). Provincial assessments would still, in some cases, be necessary. The government's aim was to allow projects to progress quickly and thereby have a more immediate economic effect. In a November 2010 report, the Canadian auditor-general found that 93 percent of the 7,000 project proposals reviewed under the CAD 4 billion (USD 3.5 billion) Infrastructure Stimulus Fund were excluded from environmental assessment (Office of the Auditor General of Canada 2010, 17). A limited sample of projects was examined in greater detail; the auditor-general found that, in most cases, the federal government lacked adequate information to determine whether an exclusion from the EIA process was warranted.

Table 1.2 Green aspects of Canada's Economic Action Plan

Program		*Funding allocated in 2009 (CAD M)*	*Funding actually spent (CAD M)*
Clean energy technology	CCS	650	150
	Small-scale demos	200	176
	R&D	150	24
Green Infrastructure Fund		1,000	725
Nuclear		351	285
ecoENERGY Home Retrofit*		300	585
Passenger rail		407	407
Total		3,058	2,352

(*As noted in Chapter 4, ecoENERGY received several more top-ups and extensions after 2010.)

Source: Compiled by the author with data from NRCAN (2016a, 2016c), Infrastructure Canada (n.d.) and Government of Canada (2009, 2012).

Four Canadian stimulus measures are examined in this book: the ecoENERGY Home Retrofit program (see Chapter 4), the Green Infrastructure Fund's largest project – the Northwest Transmission Line (see Chapter 6), and the programs for CCS and renewable energy under the Clean Energy Fund (see Chapter 7).

Japan

Japan has often sought to portray itself as a leader in green technology, and it has a crucial role to play in climate politics. In 1997, Japan hosted a meeting of the UNFCCC in Kyoto. This meeting resulted in the Kyoto Protocol, which finally came into force in February 2005. However, unlike Australia and Canada, the country is energy-poor and heavily reliant on nuclear power and imported fossil fuels. Much of the focus on energy efficiency in Japan is driven by a desire for energy security. Japan's mode of governing is also quite different from that in the other case countries. Power lies primarily in the bureaucracy rather than in the parliament or with the prime minister and there are very strong ties between industry and government, which affect the development of economic and environmental policy (Sofer 2016).

Japan has had a great deal of experience with economic crises in the past two decades. Although there is now some debate about whether the country's economic stagnation and so-called "lost decades" of economic growth since the early 1990s are a reality or media myth, there is no doubt that the Japanese government has been employing Keynesian fiscal policy for some time (Krugman 2013). As a result, the government entered the GFC period with considerable debt and a revenue shortage, so developing a large stimulus package was politically difficult (Katada 2013).

Japan was relatively sheltered from the preliminary stages of the GFC because its banking sector was not highly exposed to toxic financial assets (Kawai and Takagi 2011; Katada 2013). However, after Lehman Brothers collapsed, the country was hit hard by a severe decline in exports. Thus, the GFC is more often referred to as the "Lehman shock" in Japan (Horie 2015). In 2009, the economy contracted 6.3 percent, the sharpest drop of any OECD country and nearly two-and-a-half times the contraction of the US (IMF 2011).

Japan's response to the GFC came through several stimulus packages, introduced by several different administrations. First, in August 2008, under Prime Minister Yasuo Fukuda and the Liberal Democratic Party, a JPY 11.7 trillion (USD 117 billion) package was introduced. This was followed by a second stimulus package of JPY 26.9 trillion (USD 269 billion) to take effect in October 2008. This contained mostly non-spending measures, such as toll road fee reductions (with the environmentally negative impact of increasing road traffic) and loan promotions for small businesses. Under Prime Minister Tarō Asō, who took over leadership of the Liberal Democratic Party following Fukuda's resignation, a third stimulus package was released in December 2008, containing JPY 43 trillion (USD 430 billion) for the employment safety net. According to the HSBC report, the only environmental component of this package was USD 12.4 billion in tax cuts, some of which could have spurred investment in energy efficiency equipment (Robins et al. 2009a).

In April 2009, Asō released a much bigger stimulus package – the largest in Japan's postwar history – of JPY 56.8 trillion (USD 568 billion), including JPY 15.4 trillion (USD 154 billion) of public investment, against the wishes of some in his own party (Fukada 2009; Katada 2013). In August 2009, the election returned the Democratic Party of Japan to power under Prime Minister Yukio Hatoyama. The new government questioned some of the stimulus investments and suspended JPY 2.7 trillion (USD 27 billion) worth of expenditure from the April package and allocated it to other purposes.

Japan's economically important automotive and electronics industries were hit hard by the GFC, as they are highly "income-elastic" (non-essential items that consumers forgo purchasing when they experience a decline in income) (Kojima 2009; Katada 2013). Unable to boost exports in a global downturn, the Japanese government focused its 2009 fiscal stimulus on boosting domestic demand for these products. This is also where the largest "green" investments in Japan were made. Chapter 5 discusses the Eco-Points program that subsidized the purchase of energy efficient appliances and the Eco-Cars scheme that did the same for fuel-efficient vehicles. Combined, these made up USD 6.6 billion of the USD 23.6 billion categorized as green by the HSBC report (Robins et al. 2009b). As noted in Chapter 5, the Japanese government spent nearly JYP 1.3 trillion (USD 13 billion) – or nearly double the figure reported by HSBC in May 2009 – on these programs over the course of 2009–2010. Another program not analyzed in this book provided USD 1.1 billion in grants for solar panels on residences, schools, and offices. The HSBC report does not delve into further detail on Japan's spending; most of the remaining green stimulus was likely in the form of tax cuts.

Korea

According to the Presidential Committee on Green Growth (2010, 7), "Korea is the only country in the world to have transformed itself from an aid recipient into a donor country within the span of a single generation." This rapid economic development almost doubled Korea's greenhouse gas emissions between 1990 and 2005. Under a business-as-usual scenario, it is estimated that emissions will increase by a further 30 percent by 2020 (Jones and Yoo 2010; UNEP 2010a). The country is heavily reliant on foreign fossil fuels supplies, importing 97 percent of its energy. It is also particularly susceptible to climate change. During 1912–2008, average surface temperatures in Korea rose 1.74°C, which is above the world average (UNEP 2010a). The increased risks of flooding and droughts in a warmer world have become a significant concern for the Korean government in recent years.

In 2007, Lee Myung-bak, former mayor of Seoul and former chief executive officer (CEO) of Hyundai Engineering and Construction, campaigned to become president. He had been a well-liked mayor largely because of the successful Cheonggyecheon Creek Restoration Project, which created an attractive greenspace in the center of Seoul that is very popular among residents (Normille 2010). Lee was elected president in December 2007.

It is traditional for Korean presidents, who are elected for five-year terms and cannot stand for re-election, to lay out the plan for their administration in a public speech on the country's independence day. In the case of Lee Myung-bak, this speech fell on the country's 60th anniversary (i.e., August 15, 2008). On this occasion, President Lee announced that Korea would adopt a new development path – low-carbon green growth. Green growth was not initially a priority for Lee, whose agenda was built around a platform of "747" growth targets (increasing South Korea's GDP to seven percent, per capita income to USD 40,000, and making South Korea the world's seventh-largest economy). Considering these initial goals, the new focus on green growth was a striking change in narrative (Connell 2013). The announcement took many in the government by surprise (Mazzetti 2012; confidential interview with a government official, Seoul, December 2013).

As an export-oriented country heavily focused on medium- and high-technology products, Korea's economy was severely affected by the GFC. The Lee administration was quick to respond (Jun 2010). In November 2008, a KRW 14 trillion (USD 10.9 billion) package was introduced, focused largely on tax cuts, infrastructure, and support for the construction industry (Nanto 2009). This was followed by a KRW 50 trillion (USD 38.1 billion) "Green New Deal" in January 2009.

In the HSBC report, Korea's green stimulus up to May 2009 was calculated to be USD 30.7 billion. The report does not mention the first Korean stimulus, although it does mention the stimulus plans of other countries developed in 2008. Consequently, Korea's proportion of green stimulus was reported as 80.5 percent (see Figure 1.2). Had the earlier stimulus been included (bringing the total stimulus to USD 49 billion), the green percentage would have fallen to 63 percent, placing Korea on par with the European Union. This raises questions regarding claims made in early 2009 that Korea had the greenest stimulus package in the world (e.g., Bernard et al. 2009).

The centerpiece of the Green New Deal – the Four Major Rivers Project – was originally allocated almost KRW 14.5 trillion (USD 11.3 billion) or 29 percent of the total budget for the Green New Deal (see Table 1.3). By the time the project was completed in late 2011, costs had ballooned to KRW 22 trillion (USD 20 billion).[4] The project was hugely controversial within Korea and is discussed in Chapter 6.

United States

The US was the epicenter of the GFC and is also at the heart of the global environmental crisis, having the largest historical share of global greenhouse gas emissions. The GFC reached its peak immediately before the 2008 elections that brought Barack Obama to the White House. It was anticipated that the "hope and change" president would bring a drastically different approach to economic and environmental policy than that of his predecessor, George W. Bush. The cover

Table 1.3 Korea's Green New Deal budget and anticipated job numbers

Project		Total budget (KRW billion)	Anticipated jobs created
Core Projects	Four Major Rivers Restoration	14,478	199,960[5]
	Green Transportation	9,654	138,067
	Integrated Territory Management	372	3,120
	Water Resource Catchment	942	16,132
	Green Car and Clean Energy	2,053	14,348
	Water Resource Reuse	930	16,196
	Forest Protection	2,417	170,702
	Green Home Green School	8,050	133,630
	Eco-River	484	10,789
Related Projects	Disaster Risk Area Management	2,504	41,567
	Clean Korea	210	14,546
	Green Waterside Area	800	19,900
	Bio-Mass Energy	1,122	24,372
	Disaster Prevention, Forest Restoration	733	52,648
	Public Facility LED Replacement	1,336	10,030
	Green IT Technology	110	10,000
	Other	3,956	80,000
Total		50,151	956,007

Sources: Compiled by the author from data in Han (2010) and Kim, Han, and Park (2012).

of *Time* Magazine in November 2008 featured Obama's face photoshopped over a classic image of President Franklin Delano Roosevelt (FDR) with the caption "A New New Deal." This referenced a series of policies introduced by FDR to tackle the Great Depression that involved substantial government employment programs and the building of public works. Similarly, Paul Krugman, an unrepentant Keynesian, penned a piece in the *New York Times* entitled "Franklin Delano Obama?" in which he cautioned the new president to learn from both the successes and the failures of the New Deal (Krugman 2008).

However, these expectations were projected onto the president before he even took office. Obama was never an outspoken critic of neoliberalism and expressed his "love of the market" on more than one occasion (Klein 2008). Market mechanisms were clearly at the center of his plan to reduce carbon dioxide emissions by 80 percent by 2050, a campaign promise he reaffirmed after the election, despite the deterioration of the American economy (Broder 2008). A federal cap-and-trade scheme to place a price on carbon would ultimately never pass through Congress during Obama's tenure. As a result, his domestic legacy on clean energy is closely tied to his administration's stimulus package.

The first American stimulus response – the *Emergency Economic Stabilization Act* – was passed by the Bush administration in October 2008. It contained a USD 700 billion rescue package for the financial sector and USD 185 billion of tax cuts and credits, including USD 18.2 billion for clean energy (Robins et al. 2009a). It was immediately evident that this package was insufficient and, following the election, President Obama wasted no time preparing a larger stimulus plan. Green elements were discussed from the outset. A group of energy and environmental policy advisers met only days after the election and immediately began work on clean energy stimulus proposals. Joseph Aldy, a Harvard economist and energy adviser to the president, provides a fascinating insider account of how these proposals were developed (Aldy 2013).

The House of Representatives introduced the *American Recovery and Reinvestment Act of 2009* (ARRA) on January 26, 2009, and passed the bill two days later. Senate negotiations led to a slimmed-down bill, which was signed into law on February 17. ARRA provided USD 787 billion in stimulus. Almost 40 percent of the ARRA stimulus was in the form of tax cuts, which Krugman (2012, 121) argues "were probably only half or less as effective in stimulating demand as actual increases in government spending." The rest was primarily directed to the unemployment benefit scheme, Medicaid, and state and local government coffers, with only "a fairly small piece … for the kind of spending – building and fixing roads and so on – that we normally think of when we talk of stimulus" (Krugman 2012, 121). To Keynesians like Krugman, the size of the stimulus was "grossly inadequate" given the magnitude of the crisis and the size of the US economy.

ARRA included more than USD 90 billion in clean energy funding (Council of Economic Advisors 2010). Aldy (2013) notes that the clean energy investments in ARRA included many proposed by Obama's energy and environment team. However, he also asserts that some proposals were excluded from the package because they did not meet the "timeliness" criteria.

In addition to clean energy investments, other areas of spending could be considered green, such as nuclear site clean-up efforts. According to Feindt and Cowell (2010), Obama proposed USD 151 billion in green investments; however, Congress only approved USD 94.1 billion of the ARRA stimulus classified by HSBC as green (Robins et al. 2009b). Included in the HSBC team's calculation of US green stimulus was USD 4.9 billion of the 2009 Budget, which was allocated to waste and water, and rail (Robins et al. 2009b). Additional stimulus programs, such as "Cash for Clunkers" (see Chapter 5) were developed after the HSBC team reported on the stimulus. Total estimates for allocated funding and actual spending are provided in Table 1.4.

Aldy (2013, 2) argues that ARRA "represented an unprecedented investment in clean energy in the United States." Responses to the stimulus from environmental groups were also largely positive. For example, Greenpeace USA concluded that the clean energy provisions of the package would have a net positive effect on climate change, reducing greenhouse gas emissions by at least 61.5 million metric tons of carbon dioxide equivalent per year (MMT CO_2-e/yr) (Greenpeace USA 2009). However, the group also cautioned that the USD 27.5 billion of stimulus directed to road construction could negate many of the benefits of the clean energy investments.

The US stimulus dwarfs that of the other case study countries in both size and scope. Consequently, specific programs are covered in every empirical chapter in this book (see Table 1.4).

Table 1.4 Major green programs funded in the United States in 2009

Investment area	Initial allocation (USD billion)	Specific programs	Actual spend (USD billion)	Estimated environmental benefits
Renewable energy generation	26.6	1603 cash grant	25.7	See Chapter 7
		Clean renewable energy bonds	1.6	
	6	1705 Loan Guarantee	2.5	See Chapter 7
Energy efficiency	19.9	Weatherization Assistance Program	5.0	See Chapter 4
		State energy programs	3.1	688 trillion British thermal units (Btu) in energy savings and 2080 trillion Btu in renewable energy generation
		Energy Efficiency Conservation Block Grant Program	3.2	409 trillion Btu in energy savings to 2050
		Residential Energy & Energy Efficiency Property tax credit	10.0	
Transit	18.1	High-speed rail	8.0 (5.3 by 2016)	See Chapter 6
		Formula transit grants	8.78	
Grid modernization	10.5		10.4	
Advanced vehicles	6.1	Tax credit for plug-in hybrid and electric vehicles	2.2	
		Battery and component manufacturing	2.4	
		Biofuels	0.6	
		Alternative fuel vehicles	0.3	

(*Continued*)

Table 1.4 (Continued)

Investment area	Initial allocation (USD billion)	Specific programs	Actual spend (USD billion)	Estimated environmental benefits
		Diesel retrofits	0.3	30,900 old diesel engines being retrofitted, replaced, or retired, which has reduced lifetime emissions of carbon dioxide by 840,300 tons and particulate matter by 3,900 tons
		Federal fleet procurement	0.3	
Green innovation and job training	3.5	ARPA-e	0.4	See Chapter 7
		Training in energy efficiency and clean energy	0.5	
		Training in utility and electrical manufacturing	0.1	
CCS	3.4		2.1	See Chapter 7
Clean energy equipment manufacturing	1.6		2.3	
Cash for Clunkers	1.0		2.85	See Chapter 5
Other energy-related programs	0.4		0.4	
Environmental clean-up and preservation	28.0	Clean drinking water	6.0	
		Superfund site clean-ups	0.6	
		Leaking underground storage tanks	0.2	
		Brownfields clean-up	0.1	1,566 acres cleaned
		Parks	0.75	
		Army corps of engineers	4.6	
		Nuclear site clean-up	6	Reduced nuclear waste footprint by 69%, or 641 square miles
Total	125.1		111.28	

Sources: Compiled by the author from data in DOE (2012a), Environmental Protection Agency (n.d.), Council of Economic Advisors (2014), Government Accountability Office (2015), and Army Corps of Engineers (n.d.).

Outline of the book

The book comprises three parts. The first part, Chapters 1–3, introduces the literature on Green Keynesianism and provides further context for the cases. The second part, Chapters 4–7, covers the discussion of the empirical cases of green stimulus in action. The final part, Chapter 8, provides conclusions and future research directions.

Chapter 2 provides a conceptual framework for differentiating between Green Keynesianism and the rival concepts of a "green economy" and "green growth." It is argued that the state has a more prominent role to play in Green Keynesianism than it does in either of the other green discourses, a fact that has been overlooked by many critics. Further, the approach to economic growth also differentiates Green Keynesian proposals from green growth and green economy discussions. Although some of the critiques of Green Keynesianism are acknowledged to be fair, the approach advocated in Chapter 2 is to develop the concept as a progressive transitional project, rather than abandon it wholesale.

While the focus of the book is on national-level initiatives, it is impossible to ignore the global context in which government decisions took place in 2008–2009. Chapter 3 focuses on five global institutions that could have helped or hindered Green Keynesian efforts: the UNEP, G20, IMF, OECD, and World Trade Organization (WTO). Overall, the global institutional environment was not conducive to facilitating Green Keynesianism in 2008–2009. UNEP is a weak and ineffectual body that has largely accepted neoliberal ideology. Although it initially pushed for a Green New Deal, it quickly adopted a less progressive green economy approach. The G20 discussed a "green recovery" from the GFC, but there is no evidence that these discussions had any effect on government initiatives. The IMF, while supporting Keynesian stimulus efforts, took little interest in their environmental impact. The OECD has become a leading proponent of green growth, which, as indicated in Chapter 2, should be considered a rival model to Green Keynesianism. Finally, the WTO presented a potential obstacle to government efforts to create green jobs through stimulus measures because it prohibits the use of local content requirements, which could otherwise be used to ensure that manufacturing jobs (e.g., for solar panels) remain local.

Chapter 4, the first of the empirical chapters, covers cases in which stimulus was directed to home retrofit programs aimed at improving energy efficiency. The programs in the three countries (Australia, Canada, and the US) are discussed. Chapter 5 also examines stimulus measures aimed at increasing energy efficiency. It explores subsidies for durable products, namely cars and home appliances. The "Cash for Clunkers" program in the US is compared with Japan's "Eco-Car" program. Similarly, the "Cash for Appliances" program in the US is compared with the "Eco-Point" program in Japan. Chapter 6 examines stimulus funds directed to green infrastructure projects in Canada, Korea, and the US. These projects are the Northwest Transmission Line in Canada, the Four Major Rivers Project in Korea, and Obama's efforts to fund high-speed rail (HSR) projects in several parts of the US. Chapter 7 examines how the fiscal stimulus was used in 2008–2009 to encourage green technological innovation and increase the deployment and commercialization of existing technologies. The chapter focuses on two areas: CCS and renewable energy technology. Programs in Australia, Canada, and the US are compared.

Finally, Chapter 8 explores potential reasons for why stimulus packages were not greener and the lack of paradigmatic change in the prevailing economic model. It is suggested that neoliberalism is far more resilient than proponents of Green Keynesianism had anticipated. The chapter also addresses the need to better define green stimulus and offers a framework of modified "3Ts" (timely, targeted, and transitional) to this end. The chapter argues for the expansion of the scope of Green Keynesianism beyond stimulating aggregate demand and addresses the need for no growth or degrowth in advanced economies.

In addition to contributing to academic discussions on Green Keynesianism, this book also endeavors to inform policy. While governments lost interest in deficit spending very quickly once the economic recovery began, there are strong indications that the world will face another economic shock in the near future. It is highly likely in such circumstances that interest in Keynesian policy will again be revived. Even in the absence of an economic shock, some governments, such as Canada, are already considering Keynesian measures. While it is certainly too soon to proclaim the "Return of the Master" (Skidelsky 2009), Keynesianism is far from dead.

Notes

1 Winston Churchill is often credited with the coining the phrase, "never let a good crisis go to waste," although there does not seem to be any evidence linking him to this statement.
2 Interviews were conducted in accordance with the Australian National Statement on Ethical Conduct in Human Research. All interviewees cited in the text provided their consent; a small number chose to remain anonymous.
3 When exchange rates were not provided in the source material, an estimated value in USD is provided based on the following average exchange rates for 2009: AUD 0.79, CAD 0.88, JPY 0.01, and KRW 0.00078. These exchange rates are different than those used by HSBC, so spending amounts in USD may not match the data in Figure 1.1.
4 Using an average KRW–USD exchange rate for 2011 of 0.0009.
5 Other sources put this number at 340,000.

2 Green Keynesianism and its discontents[1]

> I do not believe that supporting a Green New Deal is a good opportunity for the left, because this project is fundamentally about restarting capitalist growth – and it is this growth that is the problem in the first place.
>
> Tadzio Mueller (in Mueller and Wolf 2009)

In the 1920s, England experienced a period of high unemployment, which prompted economist John Maynard Keynes to question some of the ideas at the core of classical economics. His work on an alternative economic model influenced government policy in England and the US during the Great Depression, although he did not publish his full treatise on the topic – *The General Theory of Employment, Interest and Money* – until 1936. In that book, which is considered his magnum opus, he outlined what he viewed as the major problems with free-market economics and policy options to manage them (Keynes 1997).

Although most scholars agree that government spending brought on by World War II ("military Keynesianism") finally ended the Great Depression, substantial credit is generally given to the New Deal for mitigating its worst effects (Milkis and Mileur 2002; Rauchway 2008). The New Deal was a series of economic programs introduced by US President FDR that focused heavily on fiscal stimulus to help the economy escape what is now known as the "paradox of thrift." Keynes explained the paradox in *The General Theory*, noting that individuals are prone to save when economic conditions are uncertain. However, this is the worst action they can take because the reduction in spending creates a self-reinforcing cycle of economic contraction (Cooper 2008).

Keynes and modern-day Keynesians argue that to reverse this cycle, the government has to intervene and "sustain aggregate demand in the economy by replacing lost private-sector demand with public expenditure" (Jacobs 2012, 9). Theoretically, government expenditure has a multiplier effect because people employed through government investment will, in turn, spend money in other parts of the economy (Gnos and Rochon 2008). In summary, one of Keynes's key contributions to economic theory was the argument that during severe recession or depression, governments should inject money into the economy through spending to increase demand for goods and services to achieve full employment.

Keynesianism, in a broad sense, was embraced for several decades after the end of World War II. However, the specific brand of Keynesianism to which most mainstream economists and governments subscribe is referred to as the "neoclassical synthesis" (Blanchard 2008). Followers of this accept the need for occasional government market intervention to boost aggregate demand, but many of Keynes's other insights (including the need for economic restraint during a boom) are jettisoned. As Eskelinen (2015, 105) argues, "the meaning of Keynesianism is reduced to a matter of counter-cyclical fiscal stimulus." Those in the post-Keynesian school, which arose in the 1950s and 1960s, argue that neoclassical synthesis has misrepresented Keynes's ideas. Post-Keynesians aim to both recover Keynes's theories and extend them into new areas. Importantly, post-Keynesians are interested in the state's role in the economy even when it is not experiencing a downturn. They argue that capitalism will normally not achieve or sustain full employment without government intervention (King 2008).

In the early 1970s, a crisis brought on by a spike in the oil price led to extremely high rates of inflation. When a supposedly Keynesian solution[2] was used to address the problem, a period of stagflation, with both rising unemployment and inflation, ensued. Keynesianism was widely viewed as having failed, providing an opening for free-market, laissez-faire ideology to reemerge as the dominant paradigm (Backhouse and Bateman 2008).

Thus, for more than three decades prior to the Great Recession, Keynesianism was out of favor with governments and the economics profession, at least in OECD countries. As Davidson (2009, 3) argues, the pervading view was that government regulation of markets and large government spending policies were the cause of all economic problems; ending "big government" was the only viable solution. The GFC and ensuing Great Recession disrupted this narrative and marked a return of Keynesianism, albeit in a limited and somewhat fleeting fashion. Many advocates of the free market were forced to admit that classical economic theory had failed to predict the crisis or offer any realistic ways to address it. Even Robert Lucas, who won a Nobel Prize for developing a theory that became a foundation of free-market economics, reportedly stated in 2008, "I guess everyone is a Keynesian in a foxhole" (quoted in Fox 2008). Nevertheless, once the most pressing phase of the crisis was over, and the major economies of the world had climbed out of the foxhole, the standard critiques of Keynesianism swiftly returned.

The classic complaint about Keynesian spending programs (other than claims that they do not work) is that they increase a country's national debt, which creates a burden for future generations (Chaddock 2009; Foster 2009). It is also commonly argued that governments will print money to spend on stimulus programs, leading to uncontrollable inflation (Melloan 2009). These arguments have been refuted elsewhere (e.g., Davidson 2009).

While Goldstein and Tyfield (2017) correctly point out that the Keynesian era was "petro-fueled" and had ecologically devastating effects, it is also the case that stronger welfare states generally have better environmental policies (Wurzel 2012). Further, Green Keynesianism is distinct from classical Keynesianism. As noted in Chapter 1, Green Keynesianism can be most simply defined as government intervention in the economy through public policies that aim to achieve full employment and environmental sustainability.

Critiques of Green Keynesianism

Green Keynesianism first emerged as a concept in Germany in the 1990s (Mueller and Wolf 2009). However, economic stimulus programs have historically included programs that would likely fit the definition, even if they were not explicitly framed this way. Aspects of FDR's New Deal, like the Civilian Conservation Corps (CCC), would likely be deemed "green" if established today. The CCC was a response to two grave problems facing the US at the time: unemployment, brought on by the Great Depression, and a substantially degraded natural environment (Leighninger 2007, 11). Between 1933 and 1942, the program employed more than three million young men who, among other things, planted approximately two billion trees and developed eight hundred new state parks (Maher 2008, 3–4). Although the program had widespread approval, some ecologists were highly critical of it. Among the detractors were the eminent ecologist and philosopher Aldo Leopold and the Audubon Society, a well-respected nonprofit association. Edward Farrington, the editor of *Horticulture* magazine, stated in 1938 that "unless the work of the CCC is done under intelligent supervision, what has been described as a project in the interest of conservation, may become instead a serious menace" (quoted in Maher 2008, 169). Critics argued that CCC projects involving the construction of campgrounds, trails, and other recreational facilities threatened wildlife habitat; that CCC reforestation efforts typically produced monocultures; and that CCC work to control pest and predator populations threatened to upset finely balanced ecosystems (Maher 2008, 167).

This book addresses similar concerns surrounding the stimulus packages of 2008 and 2009, and questions whether green projects were well considered and conducted under "intelligent supervision." However, most discussion of Green Keynesianism in existing academic literature has focused on theory, rather than practice. Scholars in the critical camp of IPEE have questioned whether Keynesian macroeconomic policy and environmental sustainability are compatible. Ecosocialists, in particular, appear to oppose Green Keynesianism in principle. This section reviews literature critiquing Green Keynesianism in theory. Later chapters will examine how green stimulus measures operated in practice.

There are three main categories of criticism of Green Keynesianism. The first comes from economists and US pundits, who argue that green sectors are not competitive with more traditional industries; many green jobs created through stimulus are likely to be temporary; and any addition of green jobs may correspond with employment losses in more polluting and resource-intensive sectors (Morriss et al. 2009; Michaels and Murphy 2009; Sharan 2010; Hughes 2011). Failed projects have provided fodder for these critics. Solyndra – a solar panel manufacturing company in California that received stimulus under ARRA and went bankrupt in 2011 – is frequently cited as a prime example of the folly of green stimulus (Chapter 7 discusses how Solyndra's failure has been exaggerated).

This set of critiques is not directly addressed in this chapter. However, subsequent chapters outline the evidence for job creation through green stimulus in each case study. Further, this subject is revisited in the concluding chapter.

The second set of critiques comes from critical environmental scholars and is aimed broadly at green capitalism. Much of this literature conflates Green Keynesian discourses with the concepts of green economy or green growth. The next section attempts to clearly distinguish Green Keynesianism from these concepts based on its approach to the role of the state, finance, and technology in addressing environmental and economic issues. It is suggested that many of the most contentious elements of the green economy and green growth discourses, which fit quite neatly with a market liberal worldview, are not present in Green Keynesianism.

The third set of critiques, made primarily by ecosocialists, addresses the fundamental sustainability of economic growth on a finite planet. Many posit Green Keynesianism's goal of fostering economic growth renders it "globalisation lite" (Salleh 2010), "oxymoronic" (Brand 2012), a "wolf in sheep's clothing" (Lander 2011), and as aimed principally at saving capitalism, rather than the environment (Gill 2011; Solty 2011). While critics are right to point out some of the underlying contradictions of Green Keynesianism, this chapter argues that rather than abandoning it, a more constructive response is to, as Wolf (in Mueller and Wolf 2009) puts it, "hijack" the idea and utilize the momentum around it to initiate a global transition away from fossil fuel-based and growth-oriented capitalism.

Varieties of green capitalism

This section attempts to make some sense of the conceptual soup of green discourses related to the economy. It differentiates the concepts of a Green New Deal and green stimulus, which can be considered part of a broader theory of Green Keynesianism, from the notions of green growth and a green economy.

Green New Deal

New York Times columnist Thomas Friedman used the term Green New Deal in two articles in early 2007; however, he did not use the expression in the sense that it has come to be understood over time. Importantly, his proposals were not made directly in response to the GFC, which was in its infancy when he was writing. Further, at the time, Friedman specifically rejected the notion that direct public investment in green projects should underpin a Green New Deal, citing that this was how his scheme differed from the original New Deal (Friedman 2007a, 2007b). In contrast, public investment became a key pillar of Green New Deal plans that emerged in 2008 and 2009.

The first comprehensive proposal was made by the Green New Deal Group (GNDG) – a collaboration between economists, journalists, and environmental advocates and driven by London-based think tank the New Economics Foundation – in July 2008. Although the influence of the GNDG's recommendations is debatable, the report undoubtedly helped to popularize the term. Further, while the GNDG targeted a British audience, many of its policy prescriptions could be applied across the developed world (Tienhaara 2014).

The GNDG identified and highlighted the link between the root causes of the financial and environmental crises, identifying that unsustainable levels of consumer debt contributed to the GFC and fueled unsustainable consumption of energy and other resources:

> The triple crunch of financial meltdown, climate change and "peak oil" has its origins firmly rooted in the current model of globalisation. Financial deregulation has facilitated the creation of almost limitless credit. With this credit boom have come irresponsible and often fraudulent patterns of lending, creating inflated bubbles in assets such as property, and powering environmentally unsustainable consumption.
>
> (GNDG 2008, 2)

The GNDG (2008, 2) report contained proposals for the "structural transformation of the regulation of national and international financial systems, and major changes to taxation systems" as well as specific suggestions on how to tackle climate change.

With respect to the short-term reform of the finance sector, the GNDG argued that the British government should take three actions: tighten controls on lending and the generation of credit; force the demerger of large banking and finance groups, splitting retail sections from corporate finance and securities dealing; and subject all derivative products and other exotic financial instruments to official inspection (2008, 24). The aim of all three policy recommendations is "an orderly downsizing of the financial sector" (2008, 25). In the longer term, the GNDG (2008) also proposed the reintroduction of capital controls, efforts to shut down tax havens, and a global jubilee of debt cancelation (across developed and developing countries) (24–27).

The more targeted green elements of the GNDG plan included a program of public- and private-sector investment in energy conservation (with a focus on the buildings sector) and renewable energy, backed by price signals created through carbon taxes and a high price for traded carbon (2008, 36). It was argued that these latter measures would help the British government fund the Green New Deal. Another source of funding discussed was a windfall tax on oil and gas companies (2008, 37).

Green New Deal proposals proliferated in 2008 and 2009. Most presented a significant departure from the GNDG report (e.g., Pollin et al. 2008; Edenhofer and Stern 2009; French, Renner, and Gardner 2009; Sustainable Prosperity 2009; UNEP 2009c). One exception was the Green New Deal platform of the European Greens (n.d.), which mentioned concerns and recommendations similar to those in the GNDG (2008) report. The key difference between the GNDG and European Greens proposals, and all others, was that the latter focused solely on the recovery (and not reform) pillar of a Green New Deal: in other words, on green stimulus.

Green stimulus

Fiscal stimulus is a well-understood concept in the field of economics. It can be defined simply as "government measures, normally involving increased public spending and lower taxation, aimed at giving a positive jolt to economic activity" (*Financial Times* n.d.). There are debates about what kinds of projects will have the biggest impact in terms of job creation and economic multipliers; there is a substantial amount of research related to these debates. However, the question of what makes green stimulus green has received significantly less scholarly attention. Most green stimulus proposals contained a laundry list of sectors, in which government investment is targeted. However, there has been little to no discussion of the specific attributes a stimulus measure must have to qualify as green. Many proposals shifted attention away from the exclusive focus given to renewable energy and energy-efficiency investments in the GNDG (2008) report and defined green stimulus measures very broadly, including everything from the expansion of marine-protected areas to funding research on CCS. Strand and Toman (2010, 2) suggested that green stimulus became "a somewhat imprecise catch phrase for various proposals to undertake economic stimulus activities that at the same time are seen to have advantageous environmental and economic growth effects."

As discussed in Chapter 1, a report on government spending commitments produced by a research team at HSBC Bank (Robins et al. 2009a) has been quite influential in establishing what measures are now broadly accepted as green. The report evaluated the stimulus packages of 11 countries and the European Union according to how they aligned with the bank's Climate Change Index. The Index groups investments into three categories: low-carbon energy production; energy efficiency; and water, waste, and pollution control. Essentially, a straightforward (even crude) approach is used to draw a boundary between environmentally beneficial and environmentally neutral or harmful stimulus measures. With this approach, measures that fall within a sector covered by one of the above categories are labeled green, regardless of the specific context of the investment, which could have significant implications for its environmental impact (Bowen and Stern 2010).

The HSBC report provides a useful overview of the stimulus. However, as will be illustrated in this book, a follow-up assessment is necessary to reflect on the tangible outcomes of the programs. As shown in Chapter 1, substantial funds allocated in 2009 were never actually spent on green investments. Further, as will be outlined in subsequent chapters, the HSBC data do not reflect each program's efficacy (a dollar spent on HSR does not equal a dollar subsidizing fuel-efficient cars). A key contention of this book is that the HSBC data do not accurately depict what happened on the ground with respect to the 2009 stimulus. As such, the many reports that have relied on HSBC data should also be viewed with caution. For example, the HSBC report was the key source for the *Financial Times* article "The greenest bailout?" (Bernard et al. 2009). The data informed the Wuppertal Institute's report on green stimulus for the European

Greens (Schepelmann et al. 2009) and were heavily utilized in the work of prominent environmental economist Edward Barbier (2010).

Green Keynesianism

The literature generally treats green stimulus, a Green New Deal, and Green Keynesianism as interchangeable terms, but they are not. As evident above, green stimulus describes a single type of policy and Green New Deal is a collection of policies (encompassing green stimulus and policies aimed at placing a price on carbon, reforming the financial system, etc.). Green Keynesianism should be viewed as the economic philosophy that underpinned the development of these policies. The last chapter of this book will chart a path for the further development of Green Keynesianism as a holistic philosophy of ecological political economy. However, for the purposes of the discussion in this chapter, the definition provided in Chapter 1 is sufficient. It characterizes Green Keynesianism broadly as government intervention in the economy through public policies that aim to achieve full employment and environmental sustainability. The critical element of Green Keynesianism, which distinguishes it from green economy and green growth discourses, is a "more economically active state" that reasserts itself in "fostering industrial, social and technological advance for the public good" (Goldstein and Tyfield 2017, 2).

Green economy

Once the initial phases of the GFC had passed and governments began to phase out stimulus plans and, in some cases, impose austerity measures, discussions of green stimulus, a Green New Deal, and Green Keynesianism waned. The next wave of policy proposals focused on the creation of a green economy. Although, as Huberty, Gao, and Mandell (2011, 6) note, discussions about the need for a green economy today "cover a spectrum from narrow concerns about climate change on the one hand, to larger critiques of the environmental sustainability of modern capitalism on the other," the conversation has largely been dominated and shaped by UNEP. This was especially apparent in the lead up to the UN Conference on Sustainable Development (UNCSD, popularly referred to as Rio+20) in 2012.

UNEP launched a Green Economy Initiative in late 2008. Although one of the first reports to emerge from the Initiative was its Global Green New Deal proposal, (UNEP 2009c), which was predominantly a green stimulus proposal, the organization soon jettisoned the New Deal symbolism and embraced a much larger platform. The new platform addressed a broad spectrum of environmental problems and paid greater attention to issues and initiatives in developing countries. The Initiative's main output – the 2011 report "Towards a Green Economy" – opened with a brief discussion of the GFC, but the remainder of the text is largely divorced from the overarching context.

UNEP (2010a, 5) defined a green economy as one that results in "improved human well-being and social equity, while significantly reducing environmental risks and ecological scarcities." This definition closely resembles the one commonly given for sustainable development. In fact, many observers have questioned whether there is any difference between sustainable development and a green economy (Brand 2012). For some, the discursive shift represents a sidelining of the social pillar of sustainable development in favor of greater emphasis on the environmental and economic pillars (Cook and Smith 2012). UNEP (2011a, 16) rejected this, arguing that sustainable development should remain the ultimate goal of governments and the new focus on the green economy merely reflects the "growing recognition that achieving sustainability rests almost entirely on getting the economy right."

In terms of policy prescriptions, there is a wide range presented by UNEP (2011a). Some echo Green New Deal and green stimulus discussions (e.g., calls for investment in renewables and energy efficiency). However, the most prominent set of proposals, which has become a focal point of scholarship surrounding the green economy, involves pricing ecosystem services. Ecosystem services are, in essence, the benefits for mankind (e.g., recreation, water regulation, carbon storage, pollination, chemicals with medicinal properties) produced by ecosystems, individual species, and genes. The maintenance of biodiversity ensures the continued production of such services. Therefore, it can be considered economically valuable.

As noted above, the green economy rose to prominence in the lead up to Rio+20. It was one of the conference's two major themes. While it was embraced by corporate actors – who "were actively positioning themselves as responsible agents for green economy transition" (Utting 2012) – there was considerable opposition to the theme from environmental activists. According to Utting (2012), "delegates arriving at RioCentro on the penultimate day of [the conference] were handed a copy of the Rio+20 newspaper, *Terraviva* (published by Inter Press Service/IPS), which carried the banner headline 'Green Economy, the New Enemy'" (see also Docena 2012). Developing countries were also wary of green economy discussions in Rio, with concerns ranging from fears of a new form of trade protectionism, a new version of structural adjustment, or more generally, a means of imposing greater responsibility for environmental issues on the global south (the home of the greatest stores of biodiversity to be priced) (Cariboni 2012; Docena 2012).

The outcome document from UNSCD (2012) – *The Future We Want* – defined the green economy in line with the UNEP position (i.e., as a tool for achieving sustainable development). However, the lack of consensus among states led to a watered-down text. Greenpeace International (2012) argued that the section on the green economy is "devoid of meaning," and suggested "countries are free to define for themselves what is green and what is not, and are free to simply do nothing."

It is worth noting that a business declaration, spearheaded by the UNEP Finance Initiative, was also launched at UNCSD. The Natural Capital Declaration, open to signature by financial institutions, "calls upon the private and public sectors to work together to create the conditions necessary to maintain and enhance Natural

Capital as a critical economic, ecological and social asset" (Natural Capital Finance Alliance 2012). BankTrack – a global coalition of civil society organizations – has strongly criticized the Natural Capital Declaration, arguing that in addition to being a "vaguely worded voluntary initiative with no immediate discernible impact on everyday investment decisions," it "is based upon a fatally flawed understanding of the root causes of [ecological] crises (imperfect valuation of 'Natural Capital and Ecosystem Services') and proposes an equally flawed solution to them (proper pricing)" (BankTrack 2012).

Finally, the parallel People's Summit in Rio also produced a position paper – *Another Future is Possible* – which rejected the UNEP vision for a green economy and its emphasis on commodifying ecosystem services (Thematic Groups 2012). Interestingly, many proposals in the position paper (e.g., separating commercial and retail banking, cracking down on tax havens, reregulation of the finance sector, creation of climate jobs) are strikingly similar to those made in the GNDG report.

Green growth

While UNEP has been the main champion of the green economy discourse, the OECD has dominated discussions of green growth. The OECD's (n.d.b) definition of green growth is "fostering economic growth and development while ensuring that natural assets continue to provide the resources and environmental services on which our well-being relies." This definition clearly overlaps with UNEP's definition of green economy (and hence, the definition of sustainable development). The difference is primarily one of emphasis – the OECD's definition of green growth is more anthropocentric (the environment is important only in terms of how it serves humanity). Further, the centrality of growth is afforded more prominent recognition, while equity is given less attention. These facts indicate that green growth discourse is firmly rooted in the dominant neoliberal order, despite some slight improvements in policy from an environmental perspective (e.g., the acknowledgment that natural assets are not infinitely substitutable) (OECD n.d.b).

The key policy prescriptions for green growth are largely the standard market mechanisms that have been proposed by environmental economists for the past several decades. These include a price on pollution through taxes or tradable permit schemes, and the removal of perverse subsidies that encourage pollution or overextraction of resources (OECD 2011). Technological innovation is viewed as primarily driven by the protection of intellectual property rights, and private-sector investment is perceived as critical to building green infrastructure (OECD 2011).

As noted in Chapter 1, Korea has been a major player in green growth discussions. The OECD (n.d.b) referred to the centerpiece of President Lee Myung-bak's Green New Deal (the Four Major Rivers Project – see Chapter 6) as a prime example of "green growth in action." In 2011, the OECD secretary-general dubbed Lee "the father of green growth" (Shin 2011). Some have hypothesized that Lee embraced green growth to gain international recognition for Korea and himself as a green leader (Shim 2010; Yun, Cho, and von Hippe 2011). As such, it is hardly surprising that he also actively pushed green growth onto the G20 agenda when, in 2010, the country became the first non-G8 member to host a summit (Cho et al. 2014, see chapter 3).

In addition to promoting green growth in the G20, Korea also launched the Global Green Growth Institute (GGGI) in 2010. Initially, GGGI was a non-profit foundation, but at Rio+20 it was converted into an international organization. GGGI focuses on knowledge sharing and the development of domestic green growth platforms around the world (predominantly in developing countries) (GGGI n.d.). Although the controversy surrounding the Four Major Rivers Project caused most of the Korean population to sour on the concept of green growth, and the development paradigm under Lee's successor shifted to the "creative economy" (Mundy 2015), GGGI continues to work from its base in Seoul.

Distinguishing between varieties of green capitalism

Green Keynesianism, the green economy, and green growth clearly have several elements in common. First, none presents a direct challenge to capitalism and, therefore, cannot be defined as revolutionary. Second, each relies upon the argument that investing in green sectors can boost employment (GNDG 2008; Pollin et al. 2008; UNEP 2011b). Proponents of all three models would argue that sectors such as renewable energy are more labor-intensive than traditional fossil-fuel industries (Pollin et al. 2008; Robins et al. 2009a). Although an emphasis on employment generation is shared among these forms of green capitalism, some, such as Nugent (2011), differentiate between "ecoliberalism" (green economy and green growth) and "Green New Dealism" (Green Keynesianism) by the fact that only the latter paradigm is concerned with job quality (i.e., with whether green jobs are well-paid, secure unionized roles).

The role of the state

The most significant distinction between Green Keynesianism and the green economy and green growth is with respect to the envisaged level of state intervention in the market. Green Keynesianism is fundamentally state-led. Stimulus funds may flow to either private entities or public works, but the government determines the amount and direction of investment. This is not the case with green growth and green economy proposals, which are typically either agnostic about whether initiatives are steered by states or private actors or emphatically pro-market in approach. Governments are largely restricted to creating the conditions required for green markets to operate (e.g., protection of intellectual property rights, creation of permit trading schemes). The three varieties of green capitalism can also be differentiated based on the views expressed about the financial sector and whether it should be harnessed or restrained in the pursuit of sustainability, and the role of technology in an economic transition.

The role of finance

As argued above, a defining feature of the Green New Deal is the identification of a connection between the root causes of the financial crisis (unsustainable debt) and environmental crisis (unsustainable consumption). This position (not found in green economy or green growth proposals) is accompanied by policy prescriptions aimed at reining in the financial sector. Proponents of the Green New Deal, such as Jenkins and Simms (2012, 6), emphasized the importance of this distinction:

> Attempts merely to overlay "green growth" onto the finance driven model of economic globalisation, will be like setting freshly spawned fish to swim against a flood tide. The proposers of the Green New Deal dwelt on finance so much, precisely because it is the rock upon which sustainability repeatedly flounders.

Many of the actors developing and promoting green economy and green growth proposals have connections with the financial sector. Prior to leading the UNEP Green Economy Initiative and the Economics of Ecosystems and Biodiversity study (on pricing natural capital), Pavan Sukhdev worked for Deutsche Bank for 14 years. The Natural Capital Declaration was developed and signed by private financial institutions and the International Finance Corporation. As such, it is perhaps unsurprising that rather than attempting to reregulate and reform the financial system, proponents of the green economy and green growth are eager to make environmental policy compatible with financial speculation (Jenkins and Simms 2012). The authors of *Another Future is Possible* (Thematic Groups 2012, 16) suggested that "the Green Economy is an attempt to extend the reach of financial capitalism and to integrate all that remains in nature into the market."

The role of technology

Salleh (2010, 15) argued that Green Keynesianism depends on "an overly optimistic 1990s ecological modernisation strategy – calling for a kind of green welfare state based on profitable technological innovations." It is true that Green Keynesians share with green economy and green growth proponents a view that technology will be important in creating a more sustainable economy. However, broadly speaking, there are few environmentalists that would not advocate for investments in some forms of technology, particularly renewable energy. However, the models differ on more specific issues such as the types of technologies deemed necessary and acceptable, and whether efficiencies created through technology need to be complemented by reductions in overall consumption of energy and resources.

Some Green Keynesian proposals in the wake of the GFC, such as that of the GNDG, focused exclusively on renewable energy and energy efficiency. Other proposals broadened the spectrum considerably and included controversial technologies such as CCS and nuclear power (Pollin et al. 2008; Edenhofer and Stern 2009; Robins et al. 2009a). It is argued that if progressives hijack Green Keynesianism, this all-encompassing approach should be jettisoned. As noted in Chapter 1, environmentalists were widely critical of efforts to portray investments in nuclear power and CCS as green. A limited approach focused on renewable energy and energy efficiency would help to further differentiate Green Keynesianism from green economy and green growth discourses. It would also align more closely with Keynesian thought. A strong understanding and concern with uncertainty underpinned all of Keynes's work. According to Berr (2015), an acceptance of Keynes's analysis logically leads to the adoption of the precautionary principle.

In terms of the extent to which technology can be relied upon to mitigate environmental damage, the degree of optimism varies among proposals. Many proponents of Green Keynesianism accept a core foundation of ecological modernization theory, often referred to as "decoupling." Decoupling is the notion that technological innovation creates efficiencies that allow growth to continue despite declining material throughput (OECD 2002). This premise has been extensively critiqued. For example, Jackson (2009, 67) highlights that it is important to distinguish between relative and absolute decoupling. With relative decoupling, resource use and environmental impact decline relative to GDP. If GDP rises, so too do these impacts, but not as quickly. Absolute decoupling would require that environmental impacts decline with rising GDP.

Some argue that a focus on relative decoupling ignores evidence that technological innovation and improvements in efficiency are continuously outstripped by increases in the scale of economic activity (a phenomenon known as Jevon's Paradox – see Chapter 5). UNEP (2011a) explicitly notes that absolute decoupling is required in a green economy. Despite acknowledging the lack of evidence that absolute decoupling occurs in any country, let alone at a global level (considering the shift of resource-intensive manufacturing industries to the global south), UNEP appears optimistic that it can occur in a green economy. Some economists would agree. Hepburn and Bowen (2012, 20) argued that the kind of massive technological shift to renewable energy required to combat climate change is not unprecedented in human history and that it is "too early to rule out absolute decoupling." Proponents of green growth have to believe that absolute decoupling is possible, as it is the foundation of that paradigm.

Some proponents of a Green New Deal are less optimistic about the prospects for absolute decoupling and argue that broader societal changes in addition to technological advancements are required. For example, the European Greens (2010, 9) suggested:

A partial "decoupling" of economic growth from material throughput might get us greater efficiency, though it will not be enough. The question of sustainability will not be solved by technology alone. One, because a realistic assessment of progresses made so far sheds serious doubts on the possibility to reach solutions on time. Two, because the problem is not only a technical one, it is a broader societal one.

The GNDG (2008) places a strong emphasis on the need to reduce consumption in addition to increasing efficiency, drawing on the experiences of war-time England and recent research that suggests that a society that consumes less can be happier and healthier than one that consumes more. This position would have to be adopted in a progressive version of Green Keynesianism.

Economic growth on a finite planet

Closely connected to decoupling and consumption is the larger issue of the sustainability of perpetual economic growth. Although discussions of this topic date back at least as far as the Club of Rome-commissioned study – *The Limits to Growth* (Meadows et al. 1972) – the Great Recession appears to have injected new life into the debate and brought it, if not into the mainstream, then at least back from the brink of obscurity (Unmüßig, Sachs, and Fatheuer 2012). For example, in a piece that appeared in the *New York Times* in March 2009, columnist Thomas Friedman (2009) asked:

> What if the crisis of 2008 represents something much more fundamental than a deep recession? What if it's telling us that the whole growth model we created over the last 50 years is simply unsustainable economically and ecologically and that 2008 was when we hit the wall – when Mother Nature and the market both said: "No more."

While Friedman failed to follow up on this question and instead quickly shifted to a discussion of green growth in subsequent paragraphs, the fact that he – a moderate commentator – even asked it in a major newspaper is notable.

Further evidence of the growing interest in alternatives to growth can be found in the slew of popular books published on the topic following the GFC. Examples of recent titles include *Prosperity Without Growth* (Jackson 2009), *What's the Economy for, Anyway?, Why it's Time to Stop Chasing Growth and Start Pursuing Happiness* (De Graaf and Batker 2011), and *The End of Growth* (Heinberg 2011).

How Green Keynesianism fits within this milieu depends on the proposal in question. UNEP (2009c) argued that its Global Green New Deal would contribute to "sustained economic growth" (UNEP 2009c, 3). The Center for American Progress also remains steadfast in its support for growth in its proposal for a green recovery (Pollin et al. 2008), as do Edenhoffer and Stern (2009) (adding modifiers such as "sustainable" or "low-carbon" when they discuss growth in their position paper). Whether these actors legitimately believe in the compatibility of growth and environmental sustainability, or instead simply fear that questioning the growth imperative would derail a policy proposal in good economic times, let alone during a major economic crisis, is debatable (Blackwater 2012). However, the political sensitivity of the issue does not dissuade the GNDG (2008, 32) from arguing that:

> The conflation of a growing economy with rising well-being in wealthy countries such as Britain has become a "given" in conventional economic theory

and the minds of policy-makers. To question it remains an economic heresy, punishable by excommunication from the company of the professional commentariat. But times have changed, and the theory is wrong.

Similarly, the proposal from the British Sustainable Development Commission (2009, 8) notes that while:

> Most analyses assume that the ultimate aim is to re-stimulate the kind of consumption-driven growth that has dominated the last few decades ... this goal is in the long-term entirely unsustainable without significant changes in both macro-economic structure and the social dynamics of consumerism.

Despite these statements, one could still question the commitment of these Green New Deal proponents to ending growth; they did, after all, argue for stimulus measures that would (in theory) help economies return to growth. However, if one conceptualizes green stimulus measures as part of a transitional project, it is possible to reconcile these seemingly contradictory positions. The authors of these proposals saw an opportunity to steer much-needed investment into renewable energy and energy efficiency projects and acknowledged that a serious recession or depression could have a horrific social impact. As such, they proposed plans that could potentially boost growth in the short term while also arguing for reforms that would more significantly reorient the British economy away from a financial-driven model of capitalism. Subsequent reports published by the New Economics Foundation and Sustainable Development Commission articulated in greater detail how such a transition could occur and reinforced the degrowth agenda of these organizations (Jackson 2009; Spratt et al. 2009; Simms, Johnson, and Chowla 2010).

Custers (2010) and Schwartzman (2011) recognize the transitional potential of a Green New Deal, suggest that it could eventually lead to a steady-state or eco-socialist economic model. Even Foster, York, and Clark (2011, 436), who argue for a comprehensive ecological revolution to usher in a new economic paradigm built on Marxist philosophy, accept that "both short-term and long-term strategies are necessary." Despite their strong critique of green capitalism, some of their recommendations for the short term (e.g., public investments in green infrastructure) are not substantially different from those found in Green Keynesian proposals.

Further, if we step back from modern proposals and return to Keynes's original work, there is a clear basis for the argument that any Keynesian project is transitional. Keynes felt there were moral reasons to curtail growth even though he did not have the benefit of scientific evidence of natural limits (Skidelsky 2009). In *Economic Possibilities for Our Grandchildren*, he predicted that the economy would eventually reach a point at which it would not need to grow further to meet basic human needs (Keynes 2016). Koch (2013, 8) argues that Keynes anticipated more recent critiques of economic growth, consumerism, and status competition, and:

did not regard quantitative economic growth as an historic and quasi eternal goal of economic action but as a temporary and historically specific necessity in order to reach a socio-economic development stage, in which basic needs are satisfied and where social actors devote more time to other than economic purposes.

Recently, there has been a concerted effort on the part of some post-Keynesian economists to more comprehensively address environmental issues and engage more substantively with ecological economics (Fontana and Sawyer 2016). Dealing with the paradox of achieving full employment without growth is a major focus in efforts to synthesize these two schools into a new ecological macroeconomics. Reduced working hours and increased income equality (for example, through the provision of universal basic income) are two key proposals frequently floated within this literature. These proposals are entirely in line with Keynes's moral philosophy and views about the purpose of economic growth (to achieve the "good life" and not as an end in itself) (Berr 2009).

In contrast, proponents of a green economy and green growth do not simply reject the notion that there are limits to growth. They argue that a green economy can grow faster than a normal one can. For example, UNEP (2011b, 22) predicted that its proposed green economy would, over a six-year period, produce higher GDP growth, "a classical measure of economic performance" (but notably one that is increasingly criticized by environmentalists for not properly accounting for environmental harm [see Talberth 2010]). The need for "(sustained) economic growth" was also mentioned 23 times in *The Future We Want*. In fact, as Goodman (2012) points out, the maintenance of economic growth was fundamental to discussions at Rio+20 – so much so, it was directly imbedded in the conference's logo. The logo consisted of a green leaf representing the environmental pillar of sustainable development and a red stick-man representing the social pillar, connected by blue steps representing economic growth – not development.

The continued emphasis on economic growth by UNEP could theoretically be attributed to the organization's global focus (as opposed to the GNDG's focus on the UK) and desire to appease developing countries' fears that green economy discourse is just another way for the global north to impose restrictions on growth in the global south. However, clear demarcation between the different approaches in these distinctive contexts could have alleviated such concerns (e.g., Alexander 2012).

Summary

Green Keynesianism had a very brief honeymoon period in 2008 and 2009, after which it was attacked vigorously by a wide variety of actors. Some critiques have addressed the issue of conceptual ambiguity (which opens space for greenwashing) and the numerous problems with green stimulus programs in practice. However, questions about the theoretical foundations of Green Keynesianism have also been raised. Some critiques are focused on "longstanding economic disputes about the effectiveness of Keynesian policy in general" (Jacobs 2012, 10). Others are specifically concerned with whether ecological sustainability is compatible with Keynesian macroeconomic policy.

This chapter has demonstrated that some problems IPEE scholars have with Green Keynesianism are misplaced. Further, conceptual clarity and differentiation from the rival concepts of a green economy and green growth could go a long way to addressing many concerns. As defined here, Green Keynesianism emphasizes the role of the state in addressing environmental problems, seeks to constrain the power of the financial sector, and takes a precautionary approach to the use of technology. In contrast, both the green economy and green growth paradigms are predominantly market based, see opportunities in expanding the reach of the financial sector by commodifying biodiversity, and support the deployment of risky and unproven technologies such as nuclear energy and CCS.

The approach to growth also differentiates Green Keynesian proposals from green growth and green economy discussions. However, here the water is rather muddied. There is no unified position on this issue across Green Keynesian literature. Even when an anti-growth position is adopted, it is unclear how this is to be squared with the inevitable reality that economic stimulation is fundamentally an effort to revive growth. Rather than throw the baby out with the bathwater, this book proposes that there is an opportunity to develop Green Keynesianism as a progressive transitional project. In doing so, it will be important to broaden Green Keynesianism from its focus on crisis-response mechanisms through a deeper engagement with the work of Keynes and post-Keynesian economists. The potential for the further development of Green Keynesian philosophy will be revisited in the concluding chapter of this book.

Notes

1 Parts of this chapter were previously published in Tienhaara (2014) and are reproduced here with permission.
2 Davidson (2009) argues that what was presented as Keynesian analysis of the situation bore little relation to Keynes's theories.

3 Global organizations

Helping or hindering Green Keynesianism?[1]

> Managing the global financial crisis requires massive global stimulus. A big part
> of that spending should be an investment – an investment in a green future. An
> investment that fights climate change, creates millions of green jobs and spurs
> green growth. We need a Green New Deal.
>
> Ban Ki-Moon (2008)

In December 2008, as the severity of the GFC began to sink in, government officials met in Poznan, Poland for the fourteenth Conference of the Parties (COP)
to the UNFCCC. It was hoped that a successful meeting in Poznan would pave
the way to a new agreement on post-2012 climate governance being adopted the
following year at COP-15 in Copenhagen. In his opening statement to the conference, UN Secretary-General Ban Ki-Moon argued that the economic and environmental crises facing the world presented "a great opportunity" and called for
a Green New Deal. Although this was a highly publicized moment, the COP was
never going to be a key forum in which Green Keynesianism would be discussed
and debated. Instead, the newly minted G20 leader's summits would prove to be
a critical arena, and relevant discussions would also take place in the traditional
headquarters of economic expertise – the OECD and IMF. UNEP, a peripheral
actor in global economic affairs, also attempted to influence the discussion with
its Global Green New Deal proposal. While not active in the deliberations around
Green Keynesianism in 2008, the WTO Dispute Settlement Body would, several
years later, decide the fate of a Canadian province's green recovery plan.

According to Newell (2015, 76), transforming the economy in a green direction
requires "regulation and steering at a time when many states have relinquished,
or been forced to relinquish, control" by global organizations. At the same time,
these organizations could use their structural power to drive a green transition.
This chapter examines how UNEP, the G20, the IMF, the OECD, and the WTO
influenced state responses to the GFC and assesses whether the organizations
facilitated or hindered efforts to implement green stimulus. These organizations
have different mechanisms through which they can constrain or enable the actions
of individual states. The IMF can place binding conditions on states that it provides loans to. Rulings by the WTO Dispute Settlement Body and Appellate Body

are enforceable through retaliatory tariffs. Conversely, the G20 and OECD do not have this kind of enforcement capacity and act more as ideational agents, helping ideas that have developed within a country to spread to other like-minded countries (Finnemore and Sikkink 1998; Marcussen 2001). UNEP also has the potential to act ideationally, although it has the least power of any of the organizations discussed. Therefore, it often tries to enlist other actors to assist in the pursuit of its objectives. All of the organizations have a role in the generation of norms that "identify what a modern state 'is'" and define the limits of appropriate conduct (Mahon and McBride 2008, 3). Finally, they play a crucial role in terms of surveillance – tracking what states are doing in a particular area (e.g., how much they are spending on stimulus packages) and making this information available to others.

This chapter argues that, although global organizations appeared to abandon neoliberalism and embrace Keynesianism in 2008, this shift in position was both incomplete and short lived. There was support at the global level for fiscal stimulus in 2008 and 2009 but, by early 2010, key organizations like the IMF, OECD, and G20 were calling for fiscal consolidation and even austerity measures just as economies began to recover. Most of the early calls for fiscal stimulus supported the notion that some investment should go to environmental programs and sectors; there was little opposition to the concept of green stimulus. However, green stimulus was broadly defined (e.g., to include nuclear power and CCS) and countries such as Korea were lauded as green champions, without any scrutiny of the actual environmental impacts of funded projects.

After the most severe stage of the GFC had passed, the global discussion shifted away from the role of the state to more traditional neoliberal market prescriptions. The G20, OECD, and IMF embraced green growth and UNEP shifted to a green economy frame (see Chapter 2). Meanwhile, the WTO made rulings that could potentially limit the scope and viability of Green Keynesian efforts in the future.

The sections that follow briefly introduce each global organization and explain their impact on Green Keynesianism. The chapter concludes with a discussion of whether there is a need for organizational reform at the global level to increase support and policy space for Green Keynesianism.

UNEP

UNEP is a subsidiary organ of the General Assembly. As it is a program, rather than an independent specialized agency, UNEP does not have operational functions. It does not implement projects on the ground but instead acts to "maintain an overview of the activities of national governments, global organizations, and nongovernmental bodies identifying needed environmental programs and catalyzing action toward their realization" (Ivanova 2007, 33). Since the birth of UNEP in 1972, global environmental governance has become increasingly fragmented with the emergence of numerous multilateral environmental agreements and their secretariats and the creation of additional entities such as the Commission on Sustainable Development (Inomata 2008). UNEP has been a catalyst for many of these initiatives, but the resulting patchwork is complex.

Many believe that UNEP lacks the resources to manage and coordinate efforts effectively (Andresen 2007).

Over the last two decades, there have been numerous calls for UNEP to be upgraded, reformed, or replaced by a World Environment Organization (WEO) or UN Environment Organization (UNEO) (Lodefalk and Whalley 2002; Biermann and Bauer 2005). At Rio+20, countries finally decided to strengthen UNEP, although they did not agree to upgrade it to a specialized agency. UNEP now has universal membership, which some suggest will increase its authority and weight, while others remain skeptical (Charnovitz 2012).

As noted in Chapter 2, UNEP released a Global Green New Deal proposal in 2009, which included the recommendation that USD 750 billion in fiscal stimulus (or one percent of global GDP) be devoted to green measures (UNEP 2009c). A policy summary was also produced, aimed at "informing the debate" at the London G20 Summit (see below) (IISD 2009). Aside from this initial push, and the strong praise it gave Korea for its stimulus package (despite vocal opposition from local environmentalists – see Chapter 6), UNEP's advocacy for Green Keynesianism was relatively weak. As noted in Chapter 2, UNEP shifted to a green economy frame when the immediate crisis abated, which focused less on state investment in green sectors and more on market-based solutions.

UNEP has largely accepted the neoliberal model of global capitalism and has not rejected the primacy of economic growth in policymaking (White, Rudy, and Gareau 2016). Some argue that UNEP's green economy agenda gained traction in the wake of the GFC because it could be seen a means to reinvent capitalism through the creation of new markets (e.g., in carbon and ecosystem services) (Kenis and Lievens 2015). UNEP's work toward a green economy model has not necessarily hindered Green Keynesianism, but there is little evidence that its advocacy has been effective at promoting it.

G20

The roots of the G20 can be traced back to the creation of the G7 in the 1970s. In 1999, in the aftermath of the Asian Financial Crisis, the G20 finance ministers group formed. Within a few years, suggestions for a G20 leaders' forum began to surface and were especially promoted by Paul Martin from Canada. However, it took another major crisis, this time a global one, for this to happen. The first leader's summit was held in Washington, D.C. in November 2008.

The G20 is composed of 19 countries (Argentina, Australia, Brazil, Canada, China, France, Germany, India, Indonesia, Italy, Japan, Mexico, Russia, Saudi Arabia, South Africa, South Korea, Turkey, the UK, and the US) and the EU. The limited membership of the G20 has attracted substantial criticism. The G20 defends its membership as representative of 90 percent of global GDP and two-thirds of the world's population. However, "these claims to legitimacy have not been wholly accepted by states external to the G20" (Slaughter 2013, 46). As Vestergaard and Wade (2012, 258) point out, the G20 is not a grouping of the 20 biggest economies or the 20 most populous countries. Rather, it is an ad hoc club that "reinforces a trend towards 'multilateralism-of-the-big' ... in which the clear majority of nations lose voice on matters that may affect them." Hampson and Heinbeker (2011) also note that there is no place at the table for the least developed countries and no one carrying their proxy. Moreover, there is no seat for smaller but often diplomatically constructive and innovative countries like Norway, Switzerland, New Zealand, and Singapore.

The G20 also has some significant organizational limitations. The body does not have a permanent secretariat, staff, or budget and relies entirely on the summit host to set the agenda for meetings and circulate preparatory documents. Although, in practice, the G20's "effectiveness as an enduring facilitating framework for global cooperation has proved mixed at best" (Kharas and Lombardi 2012, 1), it is an important source of political will (Carin and Shorr 2013) and allows for "much-needed and relatively functional dialogue" (Cooper and Pouliot 2015, 9).

The G20 does not have an official mandate, although the Pittsburgh Summit Declaration proclaimed it as the world's "premier economic forum." Originally conceived of as a "crisis committee," the G20 is increasingly expected to act as a "steering committee" on several social issues, including the environment (Cooper 2010; Van de Graaf and Westphal 2011). The expanded agenda of the G20 has been the subject of considerable scholarly and political debate (Luckhurst 2016). Those like Daniel Price (a representative or "sherpa" for the US at the G20 in 2008) argue that the G20 "is not a committee to save the world" and should stick to the "global economic issues squarely within its remit" (Price 2011). Alternatively, there is the argument that the G20 "is not only an economic policy forum but also the multilateral system's new venue for rising and established powers to sit together as peer equals" (Carin and Shorr 2013, 6).

The London Summit

In the lead up to the second G20 leaders' summit in April 2009 in London, there were numerous calls for G20 countries to aim for a green recovery. As noted above, UNEP produced a summary of its Green New Deal proposal with the aim of "informing the debate" at the London Summit (IISD 2009). According to Kirton (2013, 274), a letter was also drafted to G20 leaders supporting the push for a Green New Deal. Kirton (2013, 274) claims that this was strongly opposed by some within the UN (particularly the UN Development Programme), but the proposal received high-level support from Ban Ki-Moon and the UN sherpa in the G20 negotiations.

Other actors also tried to influence the outcome of the summit. Anders Fogh Rasmussen, prime minister of non-member country Denmark, called on G20 member states to include the environment in the discussions at London, arguing that sending a signal that the financial crisis and global warming can be tackled simultaneously could help pave the way for a climate change deal at the Copenhagen COP (Croft 2009). The Copenhagen Climate Council (2009) (a non-profit collaboration between business actors and scientists) agreed, sending an open letter to the G20 governments prior to the summit. Even a group of CEOs sent an open letter to the G20 leaders asking them to put to put low-carbon growth at the heart of economic stimulus measures (Business-Expert Task Force on Low-Carbon Economic Prosperity 2009). A report, prepared on behalf of the German Foreign Office by Ottmar Edenhofer (co-chair of the Intergovernmental Panel on Climate Change) and Nicholas Stern (chair of the Grantham Research Institute on Climate Change and the Environment), recommended that the G20 adopt a target of 20 percent green stimulus (Edenhofer and Stern 2009).

British Prime Minister Gordon Brown and US President Barack Obama appeared to have pushed for a strong green message to come out of London (Borger and Carus 2009; Lean 2009a; Williams 2009). In the lead up to the summit, the British government urged G20 leaders to consider the environmental implications of the fiscal measures taken. Brown also called for at least ten percent of a proposed USD 100 billion World Bank stimulus package for the developing world to be dedicated to climate change (Robins et al. 2009a). *The Guardian* reported that anonymous senior British officials were convinced that ensuring the G20 stimulus package had "a large green element" would be "as decisive in the battle against climate change as the outcome of the UN talks on climate change in Copenhagen" (Wintour, Adam, and Carrington 2009).

However, the British hosts faced many difficulties. First, it was thought that some countries might view discussions about green stimulus and green jobs as a potentially covert form of protectionism on the part of the developed country members (Wintour et al. 2009). During the summit, China was particularly prone to blocking anything substantial on the topic of green stimulus (Borger and Carus 2009; Lean 2009b). Mark Malloch Brown, the foreign office minister for Africa, Asia, and the UN, identified an additional problem: the negotiating officials were reluctant to work outside of their narrow areas of expertise and wanted to "hold the line against what they see as mission creep" (quoted in Borger and Carus 2009). A more practical problem was that it was simply too late to discuss a green recovery in London; most countries had already released stimulus packages and were reluctant to act further (Kirton 2013).

The outcome of the London Summit was a pledge by the leaders "to do whatever is necessary to ... build an inclusive, green, and sustainable recovery" (G20 2009a, para 4). G20 members further agreed "to make the best possible use of investment funded by fiscal stimulus programmes towards the goal of building a resilient, sustainable, and green recovery" (G20 2009a, para 27).

According to Kirton (2013, 271–272), G20 commentators were in near-universal agreement about the success of the London Summit. However, environmentalists were generally dismayed with the outcome, viewing it as an unfortunate missed opportunity (Gilbert 2009). Greenpeace UK Executive Director John Sauven stated:

> Tacking climate change on to the end of the communiqué as an after thought does not demonstrate anything like the seriousness we needed to see. Hundreds of billions were found for the IMF and World Bank, but for making

the transition to a green economy there is no money on the table, just vague aspirations, talks about talks and agreements to agree.

(quoted in Borger and Carus 2009)

Similarly, the *Guardian* environmentalist and columnist George Monbiot (2009a) wrote:

> The G20's strategy for solving the financial and economic crisis, in other words, is detailed, innovative, fully costed and of vast scale and ambition. Its plans for solving the environmental crisis are brief, vague and uncosted. The environmental clauses – which contradict almost everything that goes before – have been tacked onto the end of the communiqué as an afterthought. No new money has been set aside. No new ideas are proposed; just the usual wishful thinking: let's call the whole package green and hope for the best.

Some were more optimistic. Britain's environment secretary at the time, Ed Miliband, noted that the mere presence of the environment and climate change in G20 discussions was "a sign of that much-needed commodity, momentum" (quoted in Borger and Carus 2009). However, in retrospect, that momentum does not appear to have galvanized action, either at the Copenhagen COP (which failed to produce a new agreement on climate change) or in further green stimulus. Most green stimulus spending, as tracked by HSBC, has come from the G20 and adds up to about 0.7 percent of the combined GDP of members. (Barbier 2010, 2). However, most of this was committed before the London Summit (see Figure 3.1).

Based on available data on the green components of stimulus packages released before and immediately following the London Summit, one could conclude, like Robins et al. (2009b) do, that the London Summit "paved the way" for further green stimulus in three countries: Japan, Australia, and the UK. However, on closer inspection, this claim is unconvincing. Japan's Green New Deal had been planned prior to London (Robins et al. 2009a) and was announced only a week after the summit concluded. Therefore, it is unlikely that the discussions in London exerted much influence on the content of the package.

In Australia, the May 2009 Budget did contain additional spending on solar and CCS demonstration projects (discussed further in Chapter 7). However, the projects funded were related to the government's plans for an emissions trading scheme, and were not implemented in response to the G20 meeting (Tienhaara 2015). Further, the May 2009 Budget contained a stimulus that was decidedly nongreen: AUD 4.8 billion (USD 3.8 billion) allocated to road projects, touted as part of "the biggest road investment program in the nation's history" (Commonwealth of Australia 2009, 14).

As summit host, the UK had been reportedly pushing for a strong commitment on green stimulus. It seems unlikely that the weak outcome from the London Summit would have had much of an impact on the government's plans. However, a stronger commitment from the G20 might have enabled Brown to secure a larger green stimulus package, given that his efforts in that area had been repeatedly blocked by Chancellor Alistair Darling (Lean 2009a).

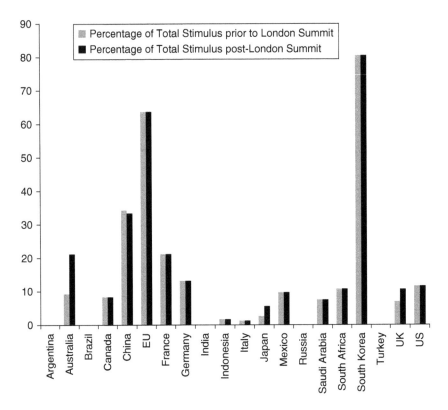

Figure 3.1 Green stimulus committed to before and after London G20 Summit
Source: Tienhaara (2016).

Thus, while it is possible that global coordination through the G20 encouraged policymakers to implement stimulus packages in the first place (IMF 2013), there is little evidence that it influenced the greenness of those packages. After London, there was never another big push for green stimulus at the G20. At the Pittsburgh Summit in September 2009, it was simply noted in the communiqué that "as leaders of the world's major economies, we are working for a resilient, sustainable, and green recovery" (G20 2009b, para 32). In Toronto, the "commitment to a green recovery" was reiterated (G20 2010a). After that, there was no further mention of a "green recovery." Stimulus packages started to be wound down and austerity policies were implemented in many countries. Paul Krugman (2010a) remarked in the lead up to the Toronto Summit that the "deficit hawks" had "taken over the G20." As noted in Chapter 2, when Korea hosted the summit for the first time in November 2010, President Lee Myung-bak successfully shifted the focus of environmental discussions from green stimulus to green growth. The final Seoul Summit document included a statement that the G20 was "committed to support country-led green growth policies that promote environmentally sustainable global growth along with employment creation while ensuring energy access for the poor" (G20 2010b, para 68). Kirton and Kokotsis (2015, 251) argue, "despite Korea's ambitious domestic actions on green growth, Seoul's final communiqué did not deliver much in meaningful plans for its implementation." The G20 has not made significant progress on green growth since Seoul (Tienhaara 2016).

The IMF

John Maynard Keynes was involved in the development of the IMF as the lead British negotiator for the Bretton Woods conference in 1944. However, Keynes's original proposal – for a Global Clearing Union that would manage global trade flows and minimize surpluses and deficits – was rejected. The design of the IMF drew more heavily from the US plan, put forward at the conference by Harry Dexter White (Boughton 2002; Woods 2006).

The IMF has played an important but also contentious role in the formulation of the domestic economic policy of many countries since its inception. Broome (2010, 37) suggests that the IMF is "one of the most controversial global organizations in history." Through conditional lending, the IMF has shaped economic policy, particularly in developing countries and in response to crises (Woods 2006; Ban and Gallagher 2015). However, this is not the only method through which the IMF exerts power. Especially in recent times, surveillance has become the organization's *raison d'etre* (Dreher, Marchesi, and Vreeland 2008; Hinterleitner, Sager, and Thomann 2016). Through surveillance and reporting, the IMF sends signals to global investors about sovereign risk.

Prior to the GFC, the IMF was viewed as increasingly irrelevant and facing an uncertain future (Babb 2013; Broome 2015). At the London Summit, G20 countries decided to triple the IMF's funds to USD 750 billion. In addition to reviving the Fund, according to Lütz (2015, 85), the crisis also marked an "ideological break with the past." For the period between the demise of the Bretton Woods system in the 1970s and the outbreak of the GFC in 2008, the IMF was a key proponent of the "Washington Consensus." The Washington Consensus is a neoliberal economic doctrine with three pillars: fiscal austerity, privatization, and market liberalization (Stiglitz 2003; Woods 2006; Babb 2013). 2008 saw a marked departure from this position, when the IMF became an "influential spokesman for coordinated macroeconomic stimulus following the collapse of Lehman Brothers" (Dhar 2014, vii).

Nevertheless, many scholars are skeptical that this was more than simply a change in rhetoric, as it does not appear to have translated into a consistent shift in the type of advice provided by the IMF to governments (Broome 2010; Grabel 2011; Güven 2012; Babb 2013;). It also appears to have been a short-lived change in position, as, by early 2010, the IMF was beginning to advocate for fiscal consolidation. The failure of austerity policies has since prompted the IMF to reassess its approach to fiscal policy once again (Dhar 2014).

Ban and Gallagher (2015) argue that while the IMF has generally softened its stance on fiscal policy since the GFC, it has never fully embraced a Keynesian approach. Fund advice remains that fiscal stimulus only makes sense in certain contexts, such as when the country in crisis has fiscal space and very low interest rates, rendering monetary policy useless. A policy paper from the Fund (IMF 2013, 1) outlined this position:

> The crisis has provided evidence that fiscal policy is an appropriate counter-cyclical policy tool when monetary policy is constrained by the zero lower bound, the financial sector is weak, or the output gap is particularly large. Nevertheless, a number of reservations regarding the use of discretionary fiscal policy tools remain valid, particularly when facing "normal" cyclical fluctuations.

Since Ban and Gallagher's (2015) article was published, there have been some indications that the IMF has become more critical of austerity policy. For example, in 2016, IMF Deputy Director Jonathan Ostry, Division Chief Prakash Loungani, and economist Davide Furceri published a paper entitled, "Neoliberalism: Oversold?" in which they argue that fiscal consolidation hurts demand, thereby exacerbating unemployment (Ostry, Loungani, and Furceri 2016).

In terms of green stimulus more specifically, the IMF did not issue press releases or add significantly to the public discourse on the subject during the GFC. However, a staff position paper written by two members of the Fund's Fiscal Affairs Department provides insight into how those within the organization viewed the subject. The paper suggests that green stimulus measures adopted in 2008 and 2009 helped sustain aggregate demand and employment in the short term, and there was evidence that such measures might confer stronger growth effects than conventional stimulus did (e.g., consumption or income support measures) (Jones and Keen 2009). The authors have also noted elsewhere that "hasty investment decisions" could have a negative impact on climate change mitigation efforts by "making reducing future emissions even harder" (Jones and Keen 2009b, 7). The green stimulus measures that the authors favor are energy efficiency measures in buildings, low-carbon infrastructure, investments in adaptation, and research and development. The authors also feel that some public investment in renewable energy technology may be warranted, although they suggest that public financial support was already high ("perhaps too high") in many countries before the crisis (Jones and Keen 2009, 13). The authors are mostly positive in their appraisal of green stimulus. However, they argue that some green stimulus measures, such as vehicle retirement schemes, were not particularly effective in increasing efficiency or environmental performance (see Chapter 5). More broadly, they caution that green spending could not be a substitute for putting a price on carbon, as this would result in "an inefficient policy mix" in which polluters would be undercharged for the cost of climate change and the fiscal position of countries would be further weakened (Jones and Keen 2009, 12).

In a subsequent publication, other Fund staffers proposed a definition of "green investment" as "investment necessary to reduce greenhouse gas and air pollutant emissions, without significantly reducing the production and consumption of non-energy goods" (Eyraud et al. 2011, 5). In this view, green investment (which can originate from the public or private sector) covers low-carbon energy production (including nuclear power, hydroelectric power, and biofuels); energy efficiency measures (including transitioning to "super-critical" coal-fired power generation); and carbon sequestration (including CCS, crop and soil management, and reforestation/avoided deforestation).

In summary, the IMF was increasingly supportive of Keynesian fiscal stimulus after the GFC, but only in certain circumstances. Due to changes in the IMF's approach, countries may now have "more policy space to reclaim the role of the state as a critical actor in economic development" (Ban and Gallagher 2015, 135), but the extent of this remains unclear. In terms of Green Keynesianism, the IMF does not appear to have strongly influenced the environmental content of stimulus packages. However, by promoting austerity, the Fund may have affected the amount of green stimulus measures developed after 2010 and even encouraged cutbacks to programs funded in 2008 and 2009. The position outlined in staff papers suggests that the IMF has a fairly mainstream, neoliberal approach to defining green stimulus and green investment and views market mechanisms (carbon pricing) as a superior policy tool to address climate change.

OECD

In 1948, the Organisation for European Economic Cooperation (OEEC) was established to manage the US-financed Marshall Plan intended to assist Europe with reconstruction following World War II. Canada and the US joined 18 existing European OEEC members in the establishment of the OECD in 1960. The membership of the OECD has since grown to 35. Member countries are primarily advanced economies, although some emerging economies (e.g., Mexico, Chile, and Turkey) are also included. All countries studied in this book are members and, in any case, the organization's influence extends beyond its membership.

Historically one of the least researched global organizations, the OECD has received greater attention from scholars in recent years (Mahon and McBride 2008; Schmelzer 2016). Described variously as a "think tank" or "rich man's club," the OECD is a key forum for economic expertise. Schmelzer (2016, 16) suggests that the OECD's key task is "authoritatively defining good economics and the ruling norms of adequate government behavior." Mahon and McBride (2008, 10) argue that the OECD's research capabilities enable it to "highlight certain trends, to identify common problems, and to map out a range of appropriate solutions." Crucially, for the purposes of this book, the OECD is, according to Schmelzer (2016), the global organization most closely associated with economic growth. Economic growth is, in fact, the first objective listed in the OECD Convention.

The OECD has sometimes been referred to as "the house that Keynes built." However, Schmelzer (2016, 191) suggests that although in the early days, the OECD (and its predecessor the OEEC) "was a stronghold of interventionist

Keynesian policies," the Keynesian influence on the organization has been over-emphasized. According to Schmelzer (2016), the OECD has generally expressed a preference for Keynes within its own countries (through demand management and economic planning) and Adam Smith at the international level (global competition and free-market policies). This has changed over time as Keynesianism has gone in and out of fashion. Some scholars mark the beginning of the period of neoliberal dominance in the OECD with an influential report in 1977, *Towards Full Employment and Price Stability*, sometimes referred to as the McCracken Report, after its main author (McBride and Merolli 2013).

While many would agree with Paul Krugman's (2010b) assessment that the OECD is "a deeply cautious organization; what it says at any given time virtually defines that moment's conventional wisdom," there are sections of the organization that, at times, appear to be moving in somewhat different directions. According to Mahon (2008), the Economics Department is the most firmly committed to neoliberalism, while the Directorate for Employment, Labour and Social Affairs has tended toward a more inclusive liberalism.

The GFC created an opportunity for internal debate within the OECD on the organization's commitment to neoliberalism, but it was the Economics Department that led the response to the crisis (McBride and Merolli 2013). The Interim Economic Outlook, produced by the Economics Department and published by the OECD in March 2009, assessed the impact of fiscal stimulus measures adopted by member states on short-term growth (OECD 2009b). The tone was generally supportive of fiscal stimulus but, as McBride and Merolli (2013, 305) assert, "even at this early point, limits to spending and a clear plan to scale back spending as the economy recovered were central to the OECD's advice to member states." As early as June 2009, the OECD advocated for fiscal consolidation, including terminating stimulus and introducing spending cuts (OECD 2009e). By the end of 2010, austerity was the OECD's order of the day.

When the OECD was still in favor of stimulus, it produced statements advocating for it to be green and "not lock-in inefficient or polluting energy technologies or dirty modes of production and consumption" (OECD 2009c, 29). The OECD has a long history of involvement in environmental issues, although its focus has predominantly been on "the use of economic instruments and the reliance of market mechanisms to solve environmental problems" (Schmelzer 2016, 332). The OECD secretary-general praised both China and Korea for the greenness of their stimulus packages (OECD 2009d). The types of green stimulus that the OECD promoted included investments in public transport, renewable energy production and distribution systems, CCS facilities, and energy efficiency retrofits in buildings (OECD 2009c).

In June 2009, the OECD Meeting of Council at Ministerial Level brought together ministers of economy and finance from OECD countries and the major emerging economies. A focus of discussions was how best to foster a green recovery. The prime minister of Korea chaired the meeting. The delegates agreed "to do all that is necessary to overcome the crisis and go beyond to build a stronger, cleaner, and fairer world economy" (OECD 2009d, 2). The main output of the meeting was a Green Growth Declaration, endorsed by the OECD members, as well as Chile, Estonia, Israel, and Slovenia. The declaration states:

> A number of well-targeted policy instruments can be used to encourage green investment in order to simultaneously contribute to economic recovery in the short-term, and help to build the environmentally friendly infrastructure required for a green economy in the long-term, noting that public investment should be consistent with a long-term framework for generating sustainable growth.
>
> (OECD 2009f, para 1)

This declaration, combined with the OECD's more general retreat from fiscal stimulus, positioned the OECD to take a lead advocacy role for green growth (see Chapter 2), but not to provide much further commentary on green stimulus. However, one document shed further light on how the OECD viewed the performance of green stimulus in hindsight. A 2012 report emphasized that while "the potential for green stimulus measures should be exploited fully when the macroeconomic conditions justify fiscal stimulus, governments should bear in mind that there are limits to the contribution that macro-stabilisation measures can make to fostering greener growth" (OECD 2012a, 95). The report emphasizes that the three Ts criteria should dictate where green stimulus money flowed and suggests that "the very different time horizons involved in the short-run stimulus measures and the long-run environmental policy means that it is not always possible for policies to serve both objectives well" (OECD 2012a, 95). The OECD (2012a, 95) concludes that "green stimulus during recessions is unlikely to make a major contribution to a long-term transition towards a low carbon economy." It further cautions that "policy packages that are intended to further both environmental and employment objectives need to be considered over a longer time horizon."

While it is hard to argue against the notion that green investment is needed on a longer timescale (see further Chapter 8), the OECD's position on green stimulus fits with McBride and Merolli's (2013) assessment that the organization advocated for Keynesian measures only as an extraordinary response to the unique situation presented by the GFC. In their view, the OECD was determined to return to orthodoxy as quickly as possible. As such, the OECD helped reconstitute the neoliberal paradigm, rather than develop an alternative economic paradigm. However, the tide may be turning once again. As with the IMF, the OECD has been forced to confront the failure of austerity policies and is once again supporting Keynesian fiscal stimulus in some countries (Chu 2016). According to Paul Krugman (2014), the selection of Catherine Mann (one of his former students) as chief economist for the OECD in 2014 was a strong signal of change within the organization.

WTO

An International Trade Organization was created in 1948, but never received the support of the US. Instead, the General Agreement of Tariffs and Trade (GATT) became the focus of trade discussions for most of the latter half of the twentieth century. In 1995, the WTO was created as the "legal and organizational foundation of the world trading system" (O'Brien and Williams 2013, 121). Dispute settlement was a key area in which the WTO was considerably stronger than the GATT. Disputes are adjudicated first by a Panel and, if necessary, by the Appellate Body. Since 1995, over 500 disputes have been brought to the WTO and over 350 rulings have been issued (WTO n.d.).

Although sustainable development is one of the objectives outlined in the Marrakesh Agreement – the document that established the WTO – the organization has a complex and contentious relationship with environmental governance. This is encapsulated in the "trade and environment debate," which has focused on several trade disputes over government measures taken to protect wildlife (e.g., turtles and dolphins) and, more recently, environmental subsidies (Charnovitz 1993; Esty 1994; Cosbey 2011). The WTO has not engaged actively in discussions about Green Keynesianism or a green economy, although the secretariat did prepare a document for Rio+20 in which it argues that WTO mechanisms were useful in the surveillance of green economy measures "so as to enhance understanding and dialogue and avoid risk of trade tensions" (WTO 2011, 9). The key area in which such tensions have arisen is government support for renewable energy projects.

Renewable energy programs have fallen afoul of two WTO Agreements: the Agreement on Trade-Related Investment Measures (TRIMs) and the Agreement on Subsidies and Countervailing Measures (SCM). The WTO disputes brought by the European Union and Japan against Canada demonstrate the relevance of these agreements to Green Keynesianism.

EU and Japan versus Canada

Ontario is Canada's most populous province. The province's economy, which accounts for 40 percent of Canada's total economic output, has traditionally been based primarily on manufacturing. The election of a Liberal (centrist) government led by Premier Dalton McGuinty in 2003 "marked a distinct shift in the direction of Ontario politics" (Winfield 2012, 152). The environment figured prominently in the election and the Liberals had committed, among other things, to closing all Ontario coal-fired power plants by 2007. The government restructured the electricity sector in 2004 and created the Ontario Power Authority. In 2006, a feed-in-tariff (FIT) for small renewable-energy projects was launched. FITs reduce financial and regulatory risk by guaranteeing renewable energy producers a set price for their energy over a fixed period. Despite these efforts, it was clear that the deadline to phase out coal generation would be difficult to meet. Prior to the 2007 election, the government renewed its commitment but extended the deadline to 2014 (Winfield 2012).

The manufacturing sector had already been hurting from the rise in the value of the Canadian dollar when the GFC hit. The auto industry was one of the worst affected, with 250,000 jobs lost between the fall of 2008 and spring of 2009

(Winfield 2012). In response, the government of Ontario decided to link environmental sustainability to the province's economic recovery. *The Green Energy and Green Economy Act of 2009* was designed to replace coal with renewable energy sources (predominantly wind and solar) while turning Ontario into a hub of green energy manufacturing. A key component of the Act was a large-scale FIT program, the first of its kind in North America.

The Ontario FIT program had two streams: regular and micro FIT (for projects not exceeding 10 kW of capacity). In addition to solar and wind, hydroelectric and bioenergy projects were also eligible for the program. FIT contracts for solar and wind projects were generally for 20-year terms. Importantly, the program included local content requirements to help create manufacturing jobs.

Local content requirements are widely used policy measures that require investors (foreign or domestic) to utilize a certain percentage of goods manufactured domestically or locally (i.e., in a specific country or region) (Cosbey 2011; Kuntze and Moerenhout 2013). For example, in the renewables sector, this could be a requirement that to access a FIT or a public tender for projects, components (e.g., wind turbines) must be manufactured locally or that labor and consulting services be secured from domestic sources (OECD 2015). In Ontario, the requirement was that by 2012, large wind installations have 50 percent local content and solar photovoltaic projects have 60 percent local content (Charnovitz and Fischer 2014). As Charnovitz and Fischer (2014, 4) suggest, "Ontario's goals were not only to increase the role of wind and solar in the supply-mix of electricity, but also to 'enable new green industries' and to provide incentives for investment in the manufacturing of renewable energy technology."

The OECD (2015, 48) concludes that the economic benefits of local content requirements are contested, but concedes that "creating local content can help broaden the base of support for renewable energy incentive programmes." Others have also made this point. Cosbey (2011, 1) suggests that "in many cases the green jobs argument is the deciding factor that convinces governments to dole out support." Kuntze and Moerenhout (2013, 5) note "incentive schemes alone are difficult for policy makers to sell, especially in times of fiscal restraint, without at least some arguments that the environmental benefits will also be accompanied by economic benefits."

While the merits of local content requirements are debated, it is clear that they are forbidden under the WTO, as the Ontario government discovered. Parallel WTO cases were initiated by Japan and the EU in 2010, arguing that the local content requirements in the Ontario FIT program prohibited subsidies within the meaning of SCM Articles 3.1(b) and 3.2 (which forbid subsidies contingent on the use of domestic over imported goods). It was further claimed that the requirements in the FIT constituted a violation of Article 2.1 of the Agreement on TRIMs and the national treatment obligation found in GATT Article III:4 (Charnovitz and Fischer 2014). The Panel and Appellate Body (ruling in December 2012 and May 2013, respectively) found that the local content requirements under Ontario's FIT breached GATT Article III:4 and Article 2.1 of TRIMs. Neither the Panel nor the Appellate Body gave a definitive conclusion on whether the FIT qualified as a subsidy under the SCM Agreement. This is because they could not determine the price at which electricity generated by renewable energy should be bought. Therefore, they were unable to conclude definitively that the recipient of the "subsidy" had received a "benefit" as required under the SCM definition (Cosbey et al. 2014; Charnovitz and Fischer 2014; OECD 2015). The Ontario government subsequently removed the local content requirement for the regular FIT and lowered the requirement for the micro FIT.

This case, while the first renewable energy dispute to be resolved in the WTO, would not be the last. The US brought a claim against China over wind power subsidies that required domestic content in 2011. That case was settled (with China terminating the program) (Cosbey 2011). China has also been on the other side of disputes, having requested consultations with the EU over Italian and Greek FITs with local content rules. The US and India have engaged in a tit-for-tat battle, challenging each other's schemes to support solar power (Beattie and Chaffin 2012; ICTSD 2016).

The implications for Green Keynesianism of these various disputes chiefly concern the claims that governments can legitimately make about supporting green jobs through stimulus measures. While some green jobs are inherently local (e.g., solar panel installation), jobs in the renewable energy manufacturing sector (which are more likely to be considered "good" green jobs, especially by unions – see Hess 2012) are much harder for governments to create. Whether local content rules are the best tool for governments to support green manufacturing jobs, and whether their use will slow the spread of renewable energy in certain countries, remain topics for debate. However, it is evident that the policy space available to governments considering their options in a Green Keynesian framework is restricted by WTO rules.

Summary and key policy recommendations

There is no champion for Green Keynesianism at the global level. All organizations reviewed in this chapter (except for the WTO, which does not generally voice opinions on matters of policy outside its purview) agreed that the GFC should not be used by states as an excuse to postpone action on the environment, and climate change mitigation in particular. Further, they saw the crisis as an opportunity for a green recovery. However, these organizations only accepted state intervention in the market begrudgingly and temporarily. The form of Green Keynesianism that was promoted was weak and always accompanied with the caveat that it was inferior to a market-based approach (e.g., putting a price on carbon). The primacy of economic growth was never questioned by these organizations and, very quickly, green growth discourse overtook any discussions of green stimulus or a Green New Deal. In essence, each organization briefly flirted with Keynesianism and then swiftly returned to the comforting arms of neoliberalism. However, there is evidence that neoliberalism's ideological grip on some of these organizations again shows signs of weakening, with the election of Mann at the OECD and IMF Staff Papers openly questioning the doctrine.

Scholars would make different recommendations for institutional reform, depending on their IPEE approach (see Chapter 1). From a market liberal perspective, global governance is operating largely as it should. The UNEP, G20, IMF, and OECD are right to promote market-based solutions to environmental problems, and the WTO rules maintain an open global market in renewable energy technology. A brief foray into Keynesian territory was justified by the extraordinary circumstances presented by the GFC, but these organizations are correct to have returned to a market focus. However, market liberals should be concerned that the G20 has not progressed substantially in eliminating fossil-fuel subsidies (as it committed to in 2009), which are market-distorting.

From a critical IPEE perspective, these organizations are deeply flawed and require radical reform, if not abolition. While there are many different problems with each organization, the one that unites them all is an obsession with growth. As Slaughter (2015) highlights, the primary function of the G20 is to legitimate global capitalism, particularly in its neoliberal form. A similar analysis would likely show as much for the OECD and the IMF. Critical IPEE scholars believe that neoliberal global capitalism is inherently unsustainable, and only radical shifts in the global economic order will allow for a sustainable future (e.g., Foster 2002).

This book adopts a more critical approach than many advocates of Green Keynesianism. However, at the global level, there do appear to be some opportunities for moderate reform. Taking a cue from an institutionalist approach, environmentalists can advocate for a champion for Green Keynesianism at the global level. While there have been volumes written on how to reform or upgrade UNEP, the G20 might be a more promising candidate to promote Green Keynesianism. In the event of another crisis, the G20 will likely resume its role as the key "crisis committee." In this case, clearer goals for a green recovery (to avoid greenwashing) and the integration of state commitments into the G20 accountability assessment process could improve outcomes. This could be facilitated by the introduction of a G20 environmental ministers meeting, following the model used by finance ministers and, more recently, energy ministers. It would also make sense to have UNEP at the table, despite the organization's limitations.

If another financial crisis brought an appetite for more substantial organizational reform or a new organization to replace the G20, greater scope for green leadership may emerge. For example, Vestergaard and Wade (2012) proposed a Global Economic Council (GEC), comprising 25 seats, nine of which would be allocated based on GDP and 16 allocated among four regions (Africa, Americas, Asia, and Europe). In addition to exercising "strategic oversight" over the Bretton Woods organizations, Vestergaard and Wade suggest that the GEC could reach further to oversee other economic and social UN bodies. While the proposal is mainly targeted at dealing with critiques of the G20's membership, increased representation would also likely increase support for Green Keynesianism (especially the inclusion of Nordic countries and African states). With some fine-tuning, the proposal could also provide additional green dividends. For example, giving UNEP a formal position within the GEC (as the World Bank and IMF hold in the

G20) could go some way to increasing consideration of environmental issues. A similar opportunity for a UNEO/WEO to emerge seems unlikely in the near term. As such, proponents of a UNEO/WEO might want to consider directing their attention to G20 reform and ensuring that any body that might replace it will drive a sustainable environmental agenda, as well as an economic one.

The other most obvious candidate for reform is the WTO. Kuntze and Moerenhout (2013) claim that it is in the best interest of the WTO and its members to make rules on local content requirements more specific and coherent. In part, this is because it would help prevent a flood of claims reaching dispute settlement. They highlight, as exemplified by the US–India cases, that the countries that challenge local content requirements imposed by others often employ them themselves. Further, while the WTO did not find Ontario's FIT to be a prohibited subsidy, there have been calls to redraft the SCM Agreement to "account for the rationale of subsidies" (Cosbey and Mavroidis 2014, 2). Cosbey (2011) points out that the predecessor to the SCM (the Tokyo Round Subsidies Code) focused on trade-distorting subsidies and did not prohibit local content requirements. The SCM and the TRIMs are very much a product of the Washington Consensus view that governments should not engage in industrial policy (Cosbey 2011).

As Ashmelash (2015) points out, renewable energy investments receive much less public funding than fossil fuels, and yet no disputes over fossil-fuel subsidies have been launched within the WTO. Ashmelash (2015, 278) reasoned that this was because "the existing multilateral subsidy rules tend to be better suited for challenging renewable energy subsidies." Ashmelash (2015) suggests that if the WTO is going to support action on climate change, there will need to be explicit exemptions for environmental subsidies written into the agreements as well as new means to discipline states that maintain fossil-fuel subsidies.

In summary, the current global governance architecture is not conducive to the promotion of Green Keynesianism. This may be changing, albeit slowly, as Keynesianism more broadly shows some signs of returning to favor. Reform of key organizations could improve the current global environment, although a more radical ideological shift will be required before organizations are willing to embrace a deep-green version of Keynesianism that rejects the primacy of economic growth. Future research should examine organizations not covered in this study, such as the ILO, to consider whether they would be more amenable to championing Green Keynesianism at the global level.

Note

1 Parts of this chapter were previously published in Tienhaara (2016) and are reproduced here with permission.

Part II
Case studies

4   The low-hanging fruit

Home retrofits[1]

> When it comes to saving money and growing our economy, energy efficiency isn't just low hanging fruit; it's fruit laying on the ground.
>
> Steven Chu (quoted in White House 2009)

When proposals for green stimulus measures were circulated in 2008 and 2009, a common theme emerged. There appeared to be one point of agreement between proposal authors: increasing the energy efficiency of buildings was a "low-hanging fruit" that was ripe and ready to be picked (GNDG 2008; UNEP 2009c). US Energy Secretary Steven Chu went so far as to suggest that it "isn't just low hanging fruit; it's fruit laying on the ground" (quoted in White House 2009). Renovating existing buildings can be a relatively cheap way to create significant energy savings and emission reductions. Examples of energy-efficiency measures in buildings include sealing gaps, installing insulation, and upgrading windows with double- or triple-glazed panes. Investments in these areas can offer an ongoing stream of cost savings that are generally far greater than the value of the initial investment (Brownlee 2013; Hoicka, Parker, and Andrey 2014). As discussed in the cases below, some have questioned the cost effectiveness of energy-efficiency measures. Nevertheless, there is little dispute that improving energy conservation is cheaper than increasing energy production capacity (Brownlee 2013; Hoicka et al. 2014).

Another benefit of energy-efficiency retrofits is that they can change the longer-term disposable income of households (especially low-income households). Thus, they can achieve a greater stimulative effect than one-time grants or other temporary measures (Ladislaw and Goldberger 2010). In addition to savings for households, there is significant potential for job creation with such programs, given the low barriers to entry into the retrofit industry. According to Wei, Patadia, and Kammen (2010, 928), energy-efficiency investment "offers a high payoff in induced jobs." A study in British Columbia estimated that 13–17 jobs are created for every CAD 1 million (USD 880,000) additional output from the building retrofit sector (Lee and Carlaw 2010).

Three home retrofit programs are discussed in this chapter: Australia's HIP, the ecoENERGY Retrofit – Homes program in Canada, and the Weatherization

Assistance Program (WAP) in the US. Energy usage by homes is a prominent issue in these three countries. About 40 percent of household energy in Australia is devoted to heating and cooling, and homes account for about a quarter of the country's total energy consumption (Crawford and Stephan 2012). In 2008, the Canadian residential sector was responsible for 17 percent of total energy consumed and 15 percent of the country's greenhouse gas emissions (NRCAN 2011). Residential energy use in Canada increased by 14 percent between 1990 and 2008, in part because the average household became larger and the use of air conditioning increased (NRCAN 2011). Space and water heating constituted 80 percent of residential energy use in 2008, which is unsurprising given the country's climate. Although space heating was not as significant in the US, it was still the largest single source of residential energy use in 2009 (42 percent) (US Energy Information Administration 2013). Unlike Canada, the general trend in the US up to 2009 had been a decline in residential energy consumption, despite increases in the number and the average size of homes (Energy Information Administration 2012).

Given the substantial capacity to increase the energy efficiency of homes in these countries and the cost effectiveness of improvements, why had this "fruit" not been picked by 2007? There are several barriers to the voluntary take up of energy-efficiency measures – things that keep many people away from the "tree" entirely. The first, and most significant, is up-front costs and access to cheap finance. While many home improvements can pay for themselves over time (e.g., through reduced space heating and cooling costs), the initial outlay of funds can be a substantial obstacle for many homeowners, particularly in the absence of favorable loans. Second, there are information barriers; many homeowners are simply unaware of how much a retrofit like insulation can reduce their energy consumption and costs. Third, for many homeowners, there is uncertainty about whether they will live in a home long enough to collect a return on the investment (Brownlee 2013). Fourth, in the rental market, there is a conflict of interest between the owner who would have to make the investment and the occupier who would reap the reward through lower energy costs. Finally, fluctuations in the cost of energy can affect the cost-benefit analysis of home improvements (David Suzuki Foundation 2011).

To overcome these barriers, governments have utilized several policy tools in recent years. The most popular in the case study countries in the wake of the GFC was to directly subsidize retrofits. While subsidies have the benefit of overcoming the barrier of up-front costs, they introduce a separate problem that economists refer to as the "free-rider effect" (Blok et al. 2004). This is the concern that the government will provide subsidies to individuals who would have undertaken energy-efficiency measures in the absence of incentives. For free riders, no behavior change is induced by the incentive and taxpayer money is effectively wasted (although, arguably, in the context of an economic crisis, if the free rider spends the money that he or she has saved elsewhere in the economy, the goal of economic stimulation is still achieved).

Another major issue that arises whenever governments offer payments is fraud. Due to the specific nature of home retrofits, and the haste with which stimulus programs were rolled out, some health and safety issues also arose, most notably in Australia.

Cases

Australia: The Home Insulation Program

Various parts of the Australian government worked on a variety of policy options to promote household energy efficiency throughout 2008. A whole-of-government taskforce was established in the Department of the Prime Minister and Cabinet (PM&C) to examine options to minimize the impact of the proposed emissions trading system (known as the Carbon Pollution Reduction Scheme) (Royal Commission into the HIP 2014l) on households. The program under consideration at the time was "technology-neutral" and involved energy audits to determine the most suitable efficiency measures for a given household (Royal Commission into the HIP 2014l, 1). This was in line with the recommendations of the 2008 Strategic Review of Australian Government Climate Change Programs (Wilkins 2008).

Ultimately, this program was never adopted. Instead, an insulation-only program became the centerpiece of the government's green stimulus. Two members of the Department of the Environment, Water, Heritage and the Arts (referred to hereafter as the Department of the Environment) were asked by the PM&C to develop a proposal for a two-year program to insulate ceilings in 2.7 million homes at no cost to homeowners (Royal Commission into the HIP 2014l). Department of the Environment staff members costed a two-year program and a five-year option, and recommended the latter because it would allow the insulation industry more time to adjust to a significant short-term uptake in activity and an inevitable long-term contraction (a boom and bust scenario) (Royal Commission into the HIP 2014l). The recommended level of rebate was AUD 1,200 (USD 948) per household and the model of delivery involved the outsourcing of the implementation of the program to numerous organizations (Royal Commission into the HIP 2014b, 2014f). The Department of Finance requested a recosting at a rate of AUD 1,600 (USD 1,264) per household, which was the level of rebate eventually adopted (Royal Commission into the HIP 2014b, 5).

On January 28, 2009, the Strategic Priorities and Budget Committee, made up of the prime minister and three senior ministers, considered the proposals from PM&C and decided to establish the Energy Efficient Homes Package. This was officially announced along with the rest of the Nation Building and Jobs Plan on February 3, 2009 (Royal Commission into the HIP 2014a). The HIP was the largest part of the Energy Efficient Homes Package, with AUD 2.8 billion (USD 2.2 billion) in funding over two years. It is worth noting that the Minister for the Environment at the time, Peter Garrett, was not consulted on the development of the program, nor was he included in the meeting of the Strategic Priorities and Budget Committee that approved it (Royal Commission into the HIP 2014e).

From the outset, the government sold the HIP as a measure with twin goals: job creation and energy efficiency. Energy efficiency was linked to both climate change and reducing household energy bills. A press release from PM&C (2009) described the HIP as supporting jobs and setting Australia up "for a low carbon future." A joint press release from the prime minister and treasurer specifically claimed that the HIP would cut household energy costs by AUD 200 (USD 158) per year and "reduce greenhouse gas emissions by around 49.4 million tonnes by 2020, the equivalent of taking more than 1 million cars off the road" (Swan and Rudd 2009).

The announcement of the program prompted a somewhat tepid reaction from nongovernment organizations (NGOs) and other political parties. The Australian Conservation Foundation called it a "good step," but argued that the stimulus package could have done more to create green jobs (quoted in Webb, Kompo-Harms, and Styles 2009). The Greens welcomed the program, but sought amendments to the stimulus package, including assurances that high-energy-efficiency standards would also be achieved in buildings funded through the school infrastructure and social housing programs (Milne 2009). Malcolm Turnbull, then leader of the Liberal-National Coalition, supported the idea of an insulation rebate, but felt it should be much lower and means-tested (Hartcher 2009). Others were less impressed. Greenpeace Australia Pacific called the program "tinkering around the edges," while Friends of the Earth Australia went so far as to refer to it as "tokenistic" and an attempt to "greenwash" the stimulus package (Webb et al. 2009; *ABC News* 2009).

To oversee the implementation of the stimulus package, Rudd established the Office of Commonwealth Coordinator General and appointed Senator Mark Arbib to the newly created position of Parliamentary Secretary for Government Service Delivery (a role upgraded to a ministerial portfolio in June 2009) (Royal Commission into the HIP 2014a). The Department of the Environment had purview over energy-efficiency measures and, therefore, was responsible for the HIP. However, according to Department of the Environment staff, the work was closely monitored by the Office of Commonwealth Coordinator General and there was "very centralised control of the stimulus measures at the time in response to the global financial crisis" (Royal Commission into the HIP 2014c, 7).

The HIP proceeded in two phases. During the first phase, from the first announcement of the program until the end of June 2009, the Department of the Environment administered all aspects of the scheme, including approving and distributing payments directly to householders that applied for the rebate. In this phase, 73,005 rebates were paid to households at a cost of AUD 103.1 million (USD 81 million) (Office of the Auditor General 2010, 21). Phase 2 began on July 1, 2009, when Medicare Australia took over the payments, which were, from that point, made directly to installers rather than to householders.

The model in Phase 2 was not what had been proposed by the Department of the Environment, which argued for the direct delivery of the program through a series of regional head contractors. The installer-rebate model was developed by the Office of the Coordinator General, much to the consternation of Department of the Environment staff (Royal Commission into the HIP 2014c, 2014f). The Office of the Coordinator General preferred this model for two reasons. First, there was time pressure associated with the July 1 deadline for the Phase 2 rollout. Department of the Environment staff believed this deadline was dictated by the Prime Minister to ensure a swift response to the GFC (Royal Commission into the HIP 2014c). The Office of the Coordinator General thought that payment processing in Phase 1 had been too slow (Royal Commission into the HIP 2014i). Second, the Office of the Coordinator General viewed the installer-rebate model as more efficient because it was a "light touch" regulatory model that would "let the market operate with few restrictions" (Hanger 2014, 131). Parker (2013, 228) argues that the installer-rebate-model "relied on pro-market ideologies that depict government provision as necessarily slow, centralised, and less efficient than market provision."

The decision to directly pay installers significantly affected the outcome of the program. Providing a direct financial incentive, in a largely unregulated sector, led to a substantial increase in inexperienced installers. Although a training program accompanied the HIP, it was not mandatory (Australian National Audit Office 2010). Due to inexperienced contractors and inadequate training, numerous individuals were injured in workplace accidents. The use of improper materials and poor installation practices also led to an estimated 100 house fires (Taylor and Uren 2010). In total, four people lost their lives in activities related to the program. In response to these tragedies, the government terminated the program on February 19, 2010. Environment Minister Peter Garrett was shortly thereafter demoted and responsibility for energy-efficiency policy was transferred to another minister and a revamped Department for Climate Change and Energy Efficiency (Hall 2010).

Initially, it was expected that the government would renew funding for home insulation under the newly developed Renewable Energy Bonus Scheme. Despite lobbying from the insulation industry, which was under considerable financial pressure following the early termination of the HIP, the newly responsible minister, Greg Combet, recommended against the inclusion of insulation in the new program because he did not have confidence that it "could be implemented with satisfactory mitigation of safety and non-compliance risk" (Royal Commission into the HIP 2014d, 7). To manage the fallout from the program's demise, Combet developed an industry assistance package and safety programs involving house inspections and the removal of improperly installed insulation. The government also endeavored to investigate claims of fraud.

The HIP was responsible for insulation installation in 1.1 million houses at a cost of AUD 1.45 billion (USD 1.1 billion) (not including compensation paid to families and industries and the price of implementing safety programs, which was at least AUD 425 million [USD 336 million]), and is estimated to have created between 6,000 and 10,000 jobs (Australian National Audit Office 2010, 26). While the issue of the free-rider effect was not notable in public discourse, it can be assumed to have been quite low given that prior to the HIP, the annual rate of home insulation retrofits was only about 70,000 per year (Hanger 2014), or even less (Energy Efficient Strategies 2011). If we assume that 70,000 of the 1.1 million households that benefited from the HIP scheme were free riders, the rate of free riding was only 6.4 percent.

Between 0.5 and 1.65 metric tons (MT) of carbon dioxide equivalent (CO_2-e) are estimated to be saved each year for every insulated Australian house (Hawke 2010; Daley and Edis 2011). This means that the program should produce annual savings of 0.55–1.8 million MT (MMT) CO_2-e or 5.5–18 MMT CO_2-e from 2010 to 2020. The Department of Climate Change and Energy Efficiency (2011) estimated that the HIP would result in 14 MMT CO_2-e reductions by 2020. Energy Efficient Strategies (2011) (in a report commissioned by the Insulation Council of Australia and New Zealand) projected a slightly lower 10 MMT CO_2-e reduction by 2020. This reduction would be associated with a cumulative savings in space heating and cooling energy costs of AUD 3.88 billion (USD 3.1 billion) by 2020 (Energy Efficient Strategies 2011). Daley and Edis (2011) have estimated between 6 and 11 MMT CO_2-e reductions by 2020. None of these estimates considers the energy requirements and greenhouse gas emissions associated with the manufacturing of insulation for the HIP. Crawford and Stephan (2012) suggest that, even when these factors are considered, insulation will still result in significant energy savings and greenhouse gas emissions reductions, but only in the long term. For the HIP, they estimate that the environmental benefits will not begin to accrue until after 2030.

When compared with past Australian rebate schemes for solar photovoltaic (PV), the HIP provides a better return on investment in terms of emission reductions per dollar spent (Daley and Edis 2011). The most cost-effective policy initiatives do not rely on direct subsidies, like the Renewable Energy Target (Daley and Edis 2011). However, the HIP had a dual purpose – it was also intended to create large numbers of jobs. In fact, the available evidence suggests that economic goals were given priority by the government in the implementation of the program. Civil servants in the Department of the Environment suggest that, from their perspective, the PM&C had chosen to target a stimulus toward insulation because it was an industry with low entry requirements for new employees (Royal Commission into the HIP 2014c, 2014f). In other words, jobs could be created very quickly. Government materials produced following the termination of the HIP appeared to scale back the emphasis on the green aspects of the program. In a factsheet produced by the Department of Climate Change and Energy Efficiency (2011), the HIP was described as "designed primarily to promote employment and stimulate the Australian economy in response to the global financial crisis." Energy efficiency and the lowering of household energy bills were referred to as "additional benefits of the program."

Many would argue that a technology-neutral assistance program for energy efficiency would have been more suitable to meet the objective of emissions reductions. This would have involved household energy audits in conjunction with rebates for technologies that would maximize energy-efficiency yields. Such an approach was proposed in the Wilkins Review (2008, 142) and was the focus for discussion in the Department of the Environment prior to the introduction of the HIP (Royal Commission into the HIP 2014b, 2014h). According to a policy adviser to Minister Garrett, there was a feeling at the Department of the Environment that, in comparison, the HIP "wouldn't necessarily be providing the energy-efficiency investment that was best suited to that household. You would be just giving everyone insulation" (Royal Commission into the HIP 2014h, 6).

Although Department of the Environment staff and Minister Garrett were keen to bolster the energy-efficiency aspects of the program, they were under pressure from the Office of the Coordinator General to deliver the program quickly. Ross Carter, first assistant secretary responsible for the Renewables and Energy Efficiency Division in the Department of the Environment, notes:

> My recollection is that it was impressed on us by the [the Office of the Coordinator General] that any delay was not in the government's mind, in terms of the stimulus effect, and the need to get stimulus out at a household level and to get employment opportunities out at a dispersed level. Energy efficiency outcomes were not, in my observation, equally important. The primary objective was about creating economic stimulus and providing for jobs.
>
> (Royal Commission into the HIP 2014c, 8)

The dominance of the program's job creation goal is reflected in the fact that the program was rolled out over a shorter period than recommended by the Department of the Environment staff (two rather than five years). The head of the Royal Commission that investigated the HIP argues:

> There was an inevitable and predictable conflict or tension between the two aims of the HIP. One aim was to insulate 2.2 million homes and the other was to stimulate the economy. Both were doubtless admirable aims but there was an inherent conflict between them: the first required detailed and careful planning over time, and the other required speed. In the case of the HIP, planning was sacrificed to speed.
>
> (Hanger 2014, 5)

Of course, while the shorter time frame did result in the creation of many jobs in a brief period, it also resulted in a boom and bust scenario for the industry. Established insulation businesses would have preferred a more measured rollout of the program over a longer time frame, as originally proposed by Department of the Environment staff (Hanger 2014).

Whether due to haste or poor design, other issues minimized the environmental benefits of the program. Concerns were raised over the course of a Senate inquiry about the failure of program designers to consider the appropriateness of different types of insulation in Australia's various climatic zones. In the hotter areas of the country, bulk insulation (e.g., pink batts) may prevent heat from escaping from houses at night (Environment, Communications and the Arts References Committee 2010, 65), which could lead to increased use of air conditioning, with associated increases in CO_2 emissions. The Senate Committee was unable to determine the seriousness of this problem, due to the conflicting submissions of bulk and foil insulation representatives. However, it concluded that the Department of the Environment should have ensured that homeowners were given proper advice about the type of insulation that was most suitable for their region. The inquiry also revealed broader problems associated with the privatization of the standard-setting agency meant to deal with such issues (Parker 2013, 232).

Others have pointed out that the mode of delivery of the HIP permitted insulation to be installed in very old houses that might be demolished shortly thereafter (Royal Commission into the HIP 2014k, 555). As there is an energy cost involved in making insulation, such a result is counterproductive from an energy-efficiency perspective. Minister Garrett also disagreed with the PM&C's plans to extend the program to holiday homes because he wanted the focus to be where the greatest energy-efficiency gains could be made (Royal Commission into the HIP 2014a, 8).

Some insulation was also imported, particularly from the US and China. In addition to the carbon cost associated with shipping, some materials were reportedly substandard. However, the government was not able to restrict imports because of its free trade agreement obligations (Environment, Communications and the Arts References Committee 2010, 62).

Perhaps the HIP would have been more successful if Minister Garrett had been successful in launching an educational campaign on energy efficiency. According to his policy adviser, Garrett wanted a campaign that "would actually drive behaviour change in energy efficiency" rather than one that simply advocated that people "go out and get insulation" (Royal Commission into the HIP 2014h, 12). Independent research has indicated the importance of governments acting to induce behavioral change to increase energy efficiency in addition to helping develop and disperse new technologies (Allcott and Mullainathan 2010). However, the coordinator general and Minister Arbib wanted to focus on the economic benefits of the stimulus and jobs creation. Apparently, the eventual approach favored their view rather than Garrett's (Royal Commission into the HIP 2014h).

Canada: ecoENERGY Retrofit – Homes

The Canadian home retrofit program was precisely what some of the critics of Australia's HIP would have preferred to see – a technology-neutral, energy audit-based scheme. Unlike its Australian counterpart, the Canadian program did not originate as a response to the GFC. The EnerGuide for Houses program, developed by the Office of Energy Efficiency of Natural Resources Canada (NRCAN) in cooperation with the Canada Mortgage and Housing Corporation, was piloted in April 1998 and officially launched in 2003. The program involved providing homeowners with information on how they could improve the energy efficiency of their homes. Rebates under EnerGuide for Houses averaged about CAD 750 (USD 660) per home, with several provinces providing top-up grants. By the end of 2005, the federal government had allocated CAD 452 million (USD 398 million) to the program and participating homeowners had reduced their energy use by an average estimated 27 percent (Bramley and Partington 2009). The program was terminated in 2006 when the conservative government led by Stephen Harper came to power. However, in an unexpected about-face, the government launched a very similar scheme, re-branded as ecoENERGY Retrofit – Homes (part of a suite of ecoACTION initiatives) in 2007.

There are some crucial differences between EnerGuide and ecoENERGY, and experts debated which program was better designed. A key change introduced with ecoENERGY was that instead of basing the subsidy on a home's energy-efficiency improvement rate, a set rebate value was introduced for each type of retrofit undertaken, capped at CAD 5,000 (USD 4,400). Hamilton (2010, 41) explained that the incentive structure for the ecoENERGY program was "piece-meal or 'à la carte' – allowing consumers to pick and choose which measures to pursue" and did "not provide any inducement for being comprehensive." Another difference was that energy audit costs were subsidized under the EnerGuide pro-gram but not under ecoENERGY. This meant that the initial cost of participation rose from approximately CAD 200 (USD 176) to something more in the range of CAD 500 (USD 440). Some argue that this created a barrier to participation, although it may also have contributed to the increased rate at which participants followed through with retrofits after the initial audit under ecoENERGY com-pared with the rate under EnerGuide (Boyle 2007; Hamilton 2010). While the nuances of each program's specific design features were discussed among policy experts, they did not enter the broader public discourse, in which the verdict on the ecoENERGY Retrofit – Homes program was overwhelmingly positive.

After an initial budget allocation of CAD 160 million (USD 141 million) in 2007 to be spent over four years, the program received a substantial boost (CAD 300 million [USD 264 million]) through the 2009 stimulus package. This was generally well received by environmental organizations, although a Pembina Institute report rated the program as "neutral" for its climate change impacts, suggesting that while it was "generally good" it did not involve "a plan to under-take home energy-efficiency retrofits on the scale needed" to create a substantial reduction in greenhouse gas emissions (Bramley and Partington 2009, 9).

In addition to the retrofit program, the federal government also offered a Home Renovation Tax Credit in 2009. The value of this credit varied depending on the level of taxable income and the amount of total renovation expenditures of the household. The program was criticized for its lack of requirements that renova-tions lead to improved energy efficiency (CCPA 2009). In fact, the credit could be used for renovations that would decrease the energy efficiency of a home (e.g., the installation of a hot tub).

The provinces and one of the territories also had retrofit programs operating to supplement the federal subsidies. For example, homeowners in Ontario received a 50 percent discount on the cost of the energy audit and a matching of the federal rebate on retrofits (Hoicka et al. 2014). The City of Toronto and other local gov-ernments added their own incentives as well (Hamilton 2010).

Under the ecoENERGY Retrofit – Homes program, a homeowner (of a single-occupancy residence of fewer than three storeys) would first contact an NRCAN-certified energy auditor to book a home energy evaluation. The audit included a diagnostic test ("blower door" test) to measure the home's air tightness and locate leaks. The homeowner would also be provided with an EnerGuide rating that would rank the home's energy efficiency from 0 to 100 (CELA 2011). The homeowner had to cover the cost for this pre-retrofit audit (unless it was subsidized by a provincial scheme). Then, the homeowner would decide, based on the evaluation, what recommended retrofits he or she wished to undertake. Retrofits would have to be completed within 18 months or before March 31, 2011 (whichever came first) (NRCAN 2009). Eligible upgrades included heating and cooling systems; heat-recovery ventilators; insulation; draft-proofing; windows, doors, and skylights; hot water systems; and water conservation systems (CELA 2011). Once retrofits were completed, auditors would return to the home to evaluate the upgrades, conduct a second air tightness test, and provide a new energy rating. Auditors would process the paperwork for the homeowner to receive the rebates from the federal and provincial/territorial governments. The subsidies were fairly substantial, up to 50 percent of the cost of many major measures such as efficient furnaces, attic insulation, and wall insulation (Hamilton 2010). Costs could be further reduced by the supplemental grants provided by the provinces.

One survey suggested that about 58 percent of homeowners who had received ecoENERGY Retrofit – Homes grants did not implement all measures recommended by auditors because of the prohibitive cost of implementation. However, a majority implemented more retrofits than they had planned prior to the audit (NRCAN 2010). Of those surveyed, 78 percent had planned to do an average of 1.6 retrofits, the energy adviser recommended an average of 5.8 retrofits, and they ended up implementing an average of 3.7 retrofits (NRCAN 2010). The recommendations of energy auditors may have also directed homeowners to retrofits they had not considered. For example, of the grant recipients surveyed, only five percent indicated that they were considering implementing air sealing or caulking retrofits before the energy assessment. After the recommendation, 42 percent implemented this retrofit. There is also evidence of spillover effects from the program. One study showed that people who booked an energy audit implemented unplanned retrofits without applying for a rebate and others implemented retrofits in non-eligible properties without receiving a financial incentive (NRCAN 2010).

The popularity of the program resulted in an early exhaustion of funds. The government provided a CAD 285 million (USD 251 million) funding top-up in 2010 (the majority of this was diverted from the Clean Energy Fund discussed in Chapter 7) but, by March 2010, no further applications were accepted. A year later, the conservative government, to secure opposition support for its budget, reluctantly agreed to renew the program for one more year, with an injection of CAD 400 million (USD 352 million) (Ivison 2011). It maintained this commitment following the subsequent 2011 election, but terminated the program two months early in January 2012, ostensibly due to concerns that it would go over budget. However, the early termination of the program resulted in CAD 188.57 million (USD 166 million) remaining unspent (NRCAN 2013). In the termination announcement, Natural Resources Minister Joe Oliver argued, "the decision to provide time-limited funding demonstrates prudent management by our government to ensure that we can return to balanced budgets during this time of fiscal restraint" (Tapper 2012).

The sudden termination of the program was highly controversial and heavily criticized by opposition parties and representatives of the energy audit and retrofit industries (McCarthy 2012). Critics pointed out that a boom and bust environment had resulted from the continued uncertainty over the program's future (Belluz 2011; Blackwell 2011). A heavily censored NRCAN briefing note obtained by CBC News through the *Access to Information Act* concluded that the program should have been better planned and longer lived (McKie 2013). New Democratic Party natural resources critic Peter Julian suggested that the government "just didn't seem to want the program to succeed." Tim Weis, an energy specialist with the non-profit Pembina Institute, argued that the program's demise was indicative of a lack of a longer-term federal strategy to deal with energy conservation (McKie 2013).

In total, over 640,000 homes received audits between 2007 and 2012 and retrofits under the ecoENERGY Retrofit – Homes program. It is estimated that energy consumption in homes included in the program was reduced on average by 20 percent, for ongoing annual savings of more than CAD 400 million (USD 352 million) (International Energy Agency 2013).

No specific estimates have been made regarding the creation of jobs by eco-ENERGY Retrofit – Homes. NRCAN (n.d.) estimates "thousands" were created or protected but provides no basis for this figure. NRCAN notes that 2,000 energy auditors were trained over the course of the program, so this could be the basis for the claim. An independent evaluation of the program in 2010 suggests that the program "fostered observable job creation in the energy consultant sector" (NRCAN 2010). However, questions have been raised about the longevity of these jobs in the boom and bust scenario that played out.

The requirements for energy audit costs to be paid by homeowners and for retrofits to be funded up front meant that the program was largely restricted to middle- and upper-income earners. There was a separate program (the Homeowner Residential Rehabilitation Assistance Program) that specifically targeted low-income households for energy efficiency, as well as major repairs to heating, electrical, plumbing, and fire safety (CELA 2011). Nevertheless, Lee and Card (2012) argue that low-income earners should be the target of future programs like ecoENERGY.

In terms of free riding, while it appears that a significant deciding factor for participants was pre-existing renovation plans, most homeowners doubled the number of retrofits carried out as a result of their participation. An internal audit suggested that 23–29 percent of surveyed homeowners that received a grant would have undertaken the retrofit even without a financial incentive, though potentially not to the same level of energy efficiency. This level of free ridership is equal or lower to that found in similar programs in other jurisdictions, and was deemed "acceptable" by NRCAN (2010).

In terms of environmental impacts, NRCAN (n.d.) indicates that participants in ecoENERGY Retrofit – Homes reduced their greenhouse gas emissions by approximately 3 MT CO_2-e per house, per year. Over 2008–2012, the entire retrofit program (including subsidies for commercial buildings, which made up a smaller component) was anticipated to produce reductions of 4.78 MMT CO_2-e. This was equivalent to 18 percent of all emissions reductions attributable to federal government policies at the time. In comparison, the ecoENERGY for Renewable Power program (which received no additional funding through the stimulus package and had exhausted its entire budget by 2011) continued to provide nearly 70 percent of emissions reductions in the same period (Environment Canada 2011). The National Roundtable on the Economy and the Environment criticized the government's initial estimates for the greenhouse gas emissions reductions for the program, arguing that they did not appropriately consider free ridership or a potential rebound effect. However, NRCAN considered these critiques and the audit findings, and lowered its estimates in 2011. The Roundtable (2011, 21) "considers the updated forecast" (cited above) "to be a reliable estimate of the program impacts." Canada withdrew from the Kyoto Protocol to the UNFCCC in 2012, and the federal government stopped reporting emissions reduction data, as had been required under the *Kyoto Protocol Implementation Act*. Consequently, there are no data available to attribute actual emissions reductions to the ecoENERGY Retrofit – Homes program.

There were also less tangible effects. In a survey of 442 grant recipients, 70 percent indicated that participating in the ecoENERGY Retrofit – Homes increased their understanding of energy efficiency and greenhouse gas emissions (NRCAN 2010). Further, 60 percent reported that their experience with the program encouraged them to apply further energy savings measures (NRCAN 2010).

The ecoENERGY Retrofit – Homes program did not experience any reports of significant fraud or health and safety issues on the scale of the Australian HIP. There was one issue with an insulation product recommended by energy auditors under the program – it contained urea-formaldehyde (UFFI), which has been banned in Canada since 1980 under the *Hazardous Products Act* (Sutts, Strosberg LLP 2009). However, this issue arose prior to the stimulus phase of ecoENERGY Retrofits – Homes, and was not related to the hasty rollout of the program, as was the case with Australia's HIP.

United States: Weatherization Assistance Program

Energy efficiency and weatherization was at the core of Obama's green stimulus plan. Van Jones, Obama's special adviser on green jobs, was a particularly strong advocate for retrofitting programs. In an op-ed in the *Seattle Times* in July 2009, he argued:

> While the enthusiasm for tomorrow's technologies sometimes overlooks the practical solutions being deployed today, the recovery package is also making sure that humbler technologies – like caulking guns, insulation, high-performance boilers and windows – are also being deployed all across America. These hardworking solutions create jobs and save money for Americans every day.

As was the case in Canada, the US opted to provide stimulus funding to an existing home retrofit program. Similarly, the program took a "whole-of-home" approach to efficiency measures, rather than focusing on one technology such as insulation. The main difference between the Canadian and US programs was that the US

WAP focused exclusively on low-income families. Middle- and upper-income homeowners could only apply for a tax credit – the Residential Energy Property Credit (section 1121 of ARRA).

Congress created WAP in 1976 under Title IV of the *Energy Conservation and Production Act* (Tonn et al. 2015). It is funded through federal appropriations that have averaged between USD 100 million and USD 450 million annually. In 2009, it received a massive influx of USD 4.7 billion under ARRA. The dramatic increase in funding was premised on the assumption that weatherization was a "shovel-ready" program, capable of being quickly ramped up and employing significant numbers of individuals.

Each of the 50 states, the District of Columbia, territories, and several Native American tribes are designated as grantees under WAP and receive funding from the Department of Energy (DOE). The grantees oversee a network of more than 900 local weatherization agencies (subgrantees): community action agencies, nonprofit organizations, and local government agencies. Subgrantees qualify eligible households and oversee home energy assessments and installation energy-saving measures. They also inspect the completed work. There is no cost to the homeowners.

Under ARRA, the income eligibility threshold for the program was raised from 150 percent of the federal poverty level to 200 percent. The average allowable funding spent per home was raised from USD 2,500 to USD 6,500. It is important to note that under ARRA, WAP grantees and subgrantees must adhere to the provisions of the *Davis-Bacon Act*. This Act stipulates that the prevailing wage for the sector must be paid through any federal government programs. In 2009, there was no established prevailing wage for the retrofit sector, and consequently, a new job classification had to be created. This slowed the initial dispersal of the WAP stimulus, with only 30,252 homes retrofitted in 2009 (Grunwald 2012). However, the program eventually picked up speed and by the end of the ARRA period (2011), over 650,000 homes had been retrofitted, exceeding the original target of 600,000 (DOE 2012a).

As the operation of the WAP during the ARRA period was expected to be unlike that of previous years, the government commissioned two evaluations to track its administration before (in 2008) and under ARRA (in 2010). Researchers at the Oak Ridge National Laboratory carried out the evaluations. The researchers found that 340,158 units were retrofitted under the program in 2010 at a cost of USD 2.3 billion (USD 2 billion of which came from WAP). The average cost to weatherize a DOE unit was USD 6,812 (Tonn et al. 2015).

During the ARRA period, the WAP supported approximately 28,000 jobs (directly and indirectly) and increased national economic output by USD 4 billion. However, many of these jobs were temporary, with 25 percent of auditors, 27 percent of crew chiefs, and 40 percent of crew members leaving the field of low-income weatherization only two years after their initial involvement in the WAP (Tonn et al. 2015). In terms of environmental impacts, carbon emissions declined by an estimated 7.3 MMT CO_2-e (Tonn et al. 2015). There were also health and social benefits of the program. The Oak Ridge laboratory study valued these at USD 3.8 billion in 2010, or USD 14,148 per household (Tonn et al. 2015).

Some of the ARRA period challenges identified in the Oak Ridge study included increased oversight for subgrantees, which drove up administrative costs; increased media and political attention; and pressure on subgrantees to rapidly increase and train the new workforce. In part, because of these challenges and increased costs, the estimated cost effectiveness of the program during the ARRA period was lower than that for 2008. Other commentators agreed with this assessment, suggesting that the tremendous pressure to push money out to the field, and the considerable number of new and inexperienced employees, drove up the average cost per home (Kushler 2015).

Although the Oak Ridge study reached largely positive conclusions about WAP, Fowlie, Greenstone, and Wolfram (2015) have been more critical. In a controversial working paper, the authors studied the WAP's operation in Michigan and found, to their apparent surprise, that although there was no cost to participants, there was very little voluntary uptake by low-income households (Fowlie et al. 2015). They also argue that the retrofits provided were not cost effective because the amount spent under WAP would not be recovered in energy bill savings for the homeowner over a 10-year period. They suggest that the cost of emissions reductions under the program was very high (USD 329 per MT CO_2-e). One of the authors, Catherine Wolfram, a professor at the University of California, noted that the findings of the study did not align with the conventional wisdom because "the perception is that energy efficiency is not just the low-hanging fruit, but the fruit already fallen on the ground, waiting to be picked up. The free lunch you're paid to eat" (quoted in Detrow 2015).

The study generated significant media attention and strong rebuttals from many quarters. Steven Nadel, executive director of the American Council for an Energy-Efficient Economy (ACEEE), was not surprised that low-income families were not eager to participate in the WAP because they are often extremely busy (working multiple jobs) and may also be generally distrustful of government programs based on past experiences (quoted in Detrow 2015). He, and others, have argued that programs like WAP are the least likely efficiency programs to be cost effective because they involve outreach efforts and numerous non-energy retrofits, like the removal of asbestos and mold (Detrow 2015; Plumer 2015). These retrofits are also done to improve the comfort of low-income households, for example by allowing people to heat their homes more in the winter without increasing their energy bills. Programs like WAP are done "for equity reasons and social service reasons as much as savings" (Nadel quoted in Detrow 2015). Similarly, Kushler (2015) argues that the greenhouse gas emissions reduction benefits "are just a bit of frosting on the benefits cake. No one would suggest WAP should be considered as entirely, or even primarily, a mechanism to fight climate change."

It is also worth noting that the Fowlie et al.'s (2015) study inadvertently suggests something positive about the WAP. If it was difficult to convince people to participate in the program even though there was no cost, it is highly unlikely that there was a substantial amount of free riding. In fact, free riding would be unlikely in a program focused on low-income households, regardless of participation rates, as low-income households are less likely to have the means to invest in significant home upgrades.

Summary and key policy recommendations

The US, Canadian, and Australian case studies discussed in this chapter demonstrate the significant government interest in the wake of the GFC in funding home retrofit measures to support economic and energy-efficiency goals. Overall, all programs reviewed in this chapter did achieve economic benefits, including (temporary) job creation and reductions in greenhouse gas emissions. Nevertheless, many see the latter as a drop in the ocean. Notably, despite the ecoENERGY Retrofit – Homes program, emissions from residential buildings in Canada are predicted to rise to 2 MMT CO_2-e over 2005 levels by 2020 (Environment Canada 2014). Residential electricity consumption grew by 1.5 percent between 2008 and 2011 in Australia, despite the HIP, although this has been attributed to population growth rather than an increase in per capita use (Vivid Economics 2013).

The retrofit programs discussed were distinct and presented their own advantages, disadvantages, and lessons for future initiatives. The Australian program was successful in generating numerous jobs and insulating a significant number of homes in a very short time. However, it was also poorly designed and inflicted long-term damage on the public's trust in the federal government to effectively engage in this space. It was also criticized for not adopting a "whole-of-home" approach, which is generally considered superior to simply providing every household a single technology such as home insulation. According to proponents of this view, the house should be viewed as a complex system of interrelated components: "Air leakage, insulation, moisture, heating systems, combustion safety, moisture problems, air quality, etc., are all inter-related and need to be considered comprehensively" (Hamilton 2010, 19). Making residential improvements simultaneously, rather than one at a time across a lengthy period, is more efficient and avoids excessive transaction costs (Hamilton 2010). Energy audits can also have multiple benefits, including increasing the awareness of the homeowner about ways to reduce energy consumption. However, audits also substantially add to retrofit program costs and can reduce participation in energy-efficiency programs if they are not at least partially subsidized (Hamilton 2010).

Canada and the US both took a whole-of-home approach and benefited from the existence of established programs. Australia could have potentially avoided some of the pitfalls of the HIP if it had simply allocated the stimulus to existing state-run retrofit programs. Canada's ecoENERGY Retrofit – Homes program was reasonably cost effective. However, the audit and retrofit industries suffered the consequences of the on-again, off-again funding model, inflicted by a federal government that seemed reluctant to support the scheme despite its popularity with the electorate.

The US scheme was the largest studied and came at the highest cost. However, Harris (2013) argues that a major nationwide program for building energy-efficiency retrofits could easily absorb ten times the funding that the WAP received under ARRA. Arguably, the WAP had the greatest public benefit of the three programs studied. Although the program experienced delays at the outset of the ARRA period, it was ultimately successful in achieving its goals. It differed from the Australian and Canadian schemes in its focus on low-income households. Rather than "nudge" homeowners who could afford to do retrofits but did not prioritize them for whatever reason, the WAP delivered energy savings and other social and health benefits to those who needed them the most.

According to Gamtessa (2013), increasing the amount of the incentives paid to low-income homeowners rather than stretching the budget across all income groups is likely to enhance the performance of federally funded efficiency programs. A focus on low-income households also provides other benefits. Hernández and Bird (2010) point out that poor households tend to be the least efficient, these are the lowest-hanging fruit. As noted above, targeting low-income households also greatly reduces, if not eliminates, the problem of free riding because low-income earners simply cannot afford to undertake retrofits.

The problem of free riding should not be overstated; it tends to be of great concern to economists and individuals who dislike governments "distorting the market" through subsidies. However, from an environmental perspective, it presents an opportunity cost. Every dollar spent on free-riding consumers is a dollar that cannot be spent on another environmental initiative. In Canada, the government argued that setting hurdle rates for program participants and requiring significant investment on the part of the individual reduced the potential for free ridership (NRCAN quoted in National Roundtable on Environment and Economy 2008). However, the National Roundtable on the Environment and Economy (2008, appendix A) points out that requiring a substantial investment from grant-receivers "does not, in and of itself, indicate that the receiver was less likely to have made the change absent the grant-in fact, it might be that the opposite is true." The group cited the example of a homeowner that has to undertake a $15,000 renovation to obtain a $1,000 grant; in such a scenario, it seems unlikely that all renovations are the direct result of the grant program.

Targeting low-income households tackles free riding without abandoning the idea of subsidized energy efficiency. Further, from a stimulus point of view, it is widely acknowledged that the multiplier effect is greater when low-income earners are targeted. Furthermore, as indicated in Chapter 2, addressing income equality aligns with Keynes's moral philosophy and could help contribute to a society less focused on growth for growth's sake.

The focus on low-income households appears to be something that more actors are now embracing. For example, the Green Budget Coalition (2016) in Canada has recommended a revival of the ecoENERGY Retrofit – Homes program, but with grants targeted at low-income families. Households that do not qualify for grants would be able to access government loans to fund retrofits in a "pay as you save" scheme.

Note

1 Parts of this chapter were previously published in Tienhaara (2015) and are reproduced here with permission.

5 Product subsidies and the paradox of green consumption

> It is wholly a confusion of ideas to suppose that the economical use of fuel is
> equivalent to a diminished consumption. The very contrary is the truth.
>
> William Stanley Jevons (1865)

The previous chapter discussed government subsidies to encourage homeowners to increase the energy efficiency of their homes through retrofits. This chapter also examines subsidies directed at individuals, but in this case, the focus is rebates for durable products, namely home appliances and cars.

Programs of this nature were found in stimulus plans across the G20. Vehicle retirement schemes were particularly popular, rolled out in many European countries, China, the US, and Japan. This is perhaps unsurprising, given that the automotive sector was particularly hard hit by the GFC. There are several arguments that these schemes provide environmental benefits along with an economic boost. First, there is the decommissioning of old, high greenhouse gas-emitting automobiles (commonly referred to as "clunkers" or "gas guzzlers"), which often account for a small percentage of vehicles on the road but are responsible for a disproportionately large share of automotive emissions (Posada et al. 2015). In addition to cutting greenhouse gas emissions, removing these vehicles from circulation can also achieve reductions in other air pollutants (Posada et al. 2015). Second, vehicle trade-in schemes can aid in the modernization of the fleet, including potentially increasing the market penetration of new technologies, such as hybrid and electric vehicles. Consequently, many organizations, such as the World Resources Institute (WRI), were in favor of the inclusion of vehicle retirement schemes in stimulus programs (Houser et al. 2009).

These arguments have not convinced everyone about the merit of these schemes. Many economists deplore product subsidies because they distort the market and allow free riding (see Chapter 4). Paying consumers to buy something they would have purchased without a subsidy is perceived as a waste of taxpayer money. While typically this is used as an economic argument against subsidies, it also has relevance for the environment because of opportunity costs; every dollar wasted on free-riding consumers is a dollar that cannot be spent on other environmental initiatives. Unfortunately, free riding appears to be a difficult problem to avoid with product subsidies and it arises as an issue in the cases discussed in this chapter.

However, market distortion and free riding are not the primary concerns of environmentalists, who tend to be skeptical of, or downright hostile to, product subsidy programs for other reasons (e.g., Monbiot 2009b). "Eco" subsidies are often aimed at improving energy efficiency, but paradoxically, this often has the effect of increasing energy consumption. This type of relationship was first identified in 1865 when British economist William Stanley Jevons published *The Coal Question: An Inquiry Concerning the Progress of the Nation, and the Probable Exhaustion of our Coal-Mines*. In it, Jevons postulated that technological efficiency gains – specifically the more economical use of coal in engines doing mechanical work – counterintuitively increased the overall consumption of coal, iron, and other resources, rather than saving them. This is now known as Jevons Paradox.

In modern studies of ecological economics, scholars have identified a similar phenomenon, which they call the "rebound effect" (Berkhout, Muskens, and Velthuijsen 2000; Binswanger 2001). The rebound effect occurs when potential energy savings from energy efficiency measures are reduced. A rebound effect of greater than 100 percent of energy efficiency savings (i.e., when energy use actually increases as a result of the introduction of energy efficiency measures) is referred to as the "backfire effect" (Sorrell 2007). The classic example of the rebound effect, which is directly relevant to this chapter, is a driver who replaces a car with a fuel-efficient model to save on fuel and reduce his carbon footprint, but then proceeds to drive much more frequently, reducing or negating the beneficial effects of increased efficiency. This is described as a "direct" rebound effect (Sorrell 2009). Notably, direct rebound effects do not appear to be significant for "dedicated" energy-efficiency technologies such as home insulation (discussed in the previous chapter) (Sorrell 2009). In addition to direct rebound effects, there are "indirect" rebound effects (Sorrell 2009). For example, even if a driver does not use his or her new fuel-efficient car more than the old one, he or she may take the money saved on fuel and use it to purchase other energy-intensive goods. In the case of the rebate programs discussed in this chapter, the opportunity for indirect rebound effects is magnified because the consumer saves not only on fuel or other energy costs but also through the government subsidy.

In addition to free riding and rebound effects, a further concern for environmentalists is the environmental cost of retiring a product before the end of its useful life. Life-cycle analysis is a technique used to assess environmental impacts associated with every stage of a product's life, from cradle to grave. The analysis enables the estimation of the cumulative environmental impact of the product, from the gathering of raw materials to their final disposal. It provides a more complete picture of the "greenness" of a product than a mere focus on energy efficiency, for example (US EPA 2006).

Life-cycle analysis is relevant to the programs discussed in this chapter because they involved scrapping products before the end of their useful life and bringing forward the manufacture of new products to replace them. When governments estimate the environmental impacts of these programs, they generally focus on a strict efficiency gain assessment. However, as noted below, several scholars have used life-cycle analysis in independent evaluations of the programs to provide a more realistic indication of their environmental impacts.

This chapter focuses on programs in the US and Japan, where subsidies for durable products were major aspects of the green stimulus packages introduced by governments in the wake of the GFC. Although Korea provided tax incentives in 2009 for individuals to replace their old cars, this program is not discussed because it did not include a substantial environmental component; old cars were not necessarily scrapped (they could be kept or sold) and there were no restrictions (e.g., fuel economy) on new vehicle purchases (Min 2015).

Cars

Japan: Eco-Car scheme

The Japanese car market, in which about three million passenger cars are sold annually, is the third-largest market in the world (after the US and China). Toyota is the largest Japanese car manufacturer, holding around 43 percent of the market, and Nissan and Honda are the second and third largest, with 17 percent and 15 percent, respectively. More than 90 percent of cars sold in Japan are Japanese-made (Taiju 2013).

The GFC hit automobile sales particularly hard. Japan's automobile production in May 2009 was a record 41 percent lower than in the previous year, reflecting a drop of more than 50 percent in exports and 19 percent in domestic sales, the sharpest decline in production the country had experienced since data started to be collected in 1967 (OECD 2009g).

In the second GFC stimulus package announced by the Japanese government in April 2009, JYP 357.2 billion (USD 3.5 billion) was allocated to a program that can be roughly translated as "Green Vehicle Purchasing Promotion Program," but was often denoted as simply the "Eco-Car" program. A further JYP 230.4 billion (USD 2.3 billion) was added to the program's budget later in 2009, bringing the total to close to JYP 588 billion (USD 5.8 billion) (Sekiguchi 2015). The Eco-Car program originally applied to all new vehicles sold before March 31, 2010 that met the program requirements; it was later extended to September 2010 (METI and MLITT 2010). Under the Eco-Car program, consumers had the option of replacing an old car (over 13 years old) with a new car that met Japan's 2010 fuel-efficiency standards. Alternatively, consumers could purchase a new car without a trade-in, in which case the new car had to have a fuel efficiency at least 15 percent higher than the 2010 fuel-efficiency standard and a "four-star" emissions performance rating (meaning emissions levels 75 percent below Japanese standards set in 2005) (Canis et al. 2010; METI and MLITT 2010).

Under the replacement program, a consumer purchasing a standard or small car was eligible for a subsidy of JYP 250,000 (USD 2,500). If the replacement vehicle was a mini "kei" car, the subsidy was JYP 125,000 (USD 1,250). Under the non-replacement program, a consumer purchasing a standard car or small car was eligible for a JYP 100,000 (USD 1,000) subsidy. If the vehicle purchased was a kei car, the subsidy was JYP 50,000 (USD 500) (Canis et al. 2010; METI and MLITT 2010). In the first 17 months of the Eco-Car program, 3.6 million vehicles were sold. For 2.5 million of those sales (69 percent), consumers opted not to trade in a vehicle (Canis et al. 2010).

In addition to the rebate under the Eco-Car program, Japan introduced tax incentives in 2009 to further stimulate car sales. Both the automobile acquisition tax and automobile weight tax were reduced under this scheme. For hybrid vehicles, the weight tax was reduced to zero and the standard acquisition tax was halved (Xu et al. 2015). Eligibility was based on fuel efficiency and incentives were not restricted to hybrid, electric, or alternative fuel vehicles. In fact, 70 percent of all cars sold in Japan in 2009 were eligible (Shiraishi 2010; METI 2010). Shiraishi (2010) points out that consumers would receive tax breaks regardless of whether he or she purchased a Prius or a Corolla Mion, despite the substantial difference in fuel efficiency (38 km/l versus 16.6 km/l). In fact, as Matsumoto (2015b) asserted, the tax benefits were greater when purchasing a larger and more expensive "eco-car."

Alhulail and Takeuchi (2014) analyzed monthly sales data for ten representative car models from April 2006 to March 2013 and found that the Eco-Car subsidy increased car sales by 21.5 percent. Shiraishi (2010) attributed a two percent GDP boost and an eight to nine percent increase in industrial production in 2010 to the program. In contrast, Miyazaki (2015) found that while Eco-Car did achieve a stimulus effect, this was small and insignificant four months after the policy was introduced.

With respect to environmental impact, Shiraishi (2010) calculated a reduction in greenhouse gas emissions from the program of only 0.1 percent. Matsumoto (2015b) examined the average fuel economy of vehicles in Japan from 1995 to 2012 and discovered an improvement of 71.5 percent. Despite this, total consumption increased by 9.3 percent. These findings suggest that the rebound effect significantly affected the environmental outcomes of the Eco-Car program.

As pointed out by Japanese scholars, the Japanese government essentially induced a strong rebound effect by incentivizing driving. The government introduced a discounted highway fee as part of the stimulus package, which encouraged people to drive more and consequently increased vehicle emissions (Arimura and Iwata 2015). While lawmakers lowered the fee to stimulate tourism, Komine (2010) argues that it simply changed the method by which people traveled (driving instead of taking the train) rather than the frequency with which they did so.

The United States: Cash for Clunkers

In the US (the world's biggest auto market at the time; it was overtaken by China in 2010), car sales declined sharply from the beginning of 2008 and bottomed out in the first half of 2009. During the lows reached in early 2009, both Chrysler and General Motors filed for protection under Chapter 11 of the *United States*

Bankruptcy Code, through which the US government purchased majority interests in each company.

The idea for a national vehicle retirement or "car scrapping" scheme in the US was first proposed in a *New York Times* opinion piece by economist Alan Blinder in July 2008. His proposal was for a straightforward cash payment for "clunker" trade-ins, with no restrictions on what that payment could be put toward (i.e., it did not have to be spent on a new car). Blinder (2008) argues that such a program would benefit the environment, provide economic stimulus, and serve the objective of more equal income distribution (he proposed the program to be means-tested). Further support for the idea arose from a joint paper by the Center for American Progress and SmartTransportation.org (2008) that was distributed to members of Congress. Another proposal from the ACEEE (2009) called for a government rebate of between USD 1,500 and USD 4,500 for drivers who scrapped a vehicle with a fuel economy of less than 18 miles per gallon (mpg) and purchased a new or used vehicle with a fuel economy that was at least 25 percent above Corporate Average Fuel Economy (CAFE) standards. Notably, in this proposal, the voucher received when the vehicle was scrapped could also be used for public transportation (Houser et al. 2009).

The Consumer Assistance to Recycle and Save Act (CARS) was passed by the House of Representatives on June 9, 2009 and by the Senate nine days later. Signed into law by the president on June 24, CARS established what was popularly known as "Cash for Clunkers." The program provided subsidies to car owners who traded in their older vehicles to purchase a new and more efficient vehicle. Trade-in vehicles had to be registered, insured, and in drivable condition. They also had to have lower than a specified combined fuel economy (18 mpg for passenger cars, 16 mpg for small trucks, and 14 mpg for large trucks). Additionally, an age limit was introduced (trade-ins could not be pre-1984) to appease lobbyists for antique auto-parts suppliers and car collectors (Vartabedian and Bensinger 2009). New vehicles were required to have at least 0.42–1.7 km/l (1–4 mpg, depending on the vehicle type) better fuel economy than the trade-in to receive a USD 3,500 rebate, and at least 0.85–4.25 km/l (2–10 mpg, depending on the vehicle) for a USD 4,500 rebate. Trade-ins were crushed to ensure that they would not return to the road. The program was officially launched on July 27, 2009 and lasted less than a month. It was overwhelmingly popular and the initial allocation of USD 1 billion in stimulus quickly evaporated. Congress pulled USD 2 billion out of the DOE Loans Programs for clean energy (discussed in Chapter 7) to replenish the Cash for Clunkers program (Grabell 2012). In total, the program involved 678,359 transactions at a cost of USD 2.85 billion (Gayer and Parker 2013).

Although enormously popular with the public and probably the most widely known of all stimulus measures in the US (over 89 percent of people polled in July 2009 had heard of it), the program was not without its critics (Tyrrell and Dernbach 2011). On the economic side, the general complaint was the exorbitant cost of Cash for Clunkers. *The Wall Street Journal* Editorial Board (2009) called the program "one of Washington's all-time dumb ideas." There were also questions about how much the US economy would benefit from the program, especially given the high prevalence of foreign cars in the market. In the end, 49 percent of the cars sold under the program were manufactured in the US. The National Highway Traffic Safety Administration (NHTSA) (2009) estimated that the program boosted GDP by USD 4–7 billion and saved or created more than 60,000 jobs in automobile manufacturing, sales, and related industries.

Of course, these numbers are contested. Some commentators have suggested that sales were simply pulled forward from the future. For example, Li et al. (2013) used Canada (where there was no car rebate program) as a control group to estimate that 45 percent of those who benefited from the Cash for Clunkers program would have purchased a new vehicle in the absence of the program, suggesting significant free riding. However, they still found that it had a stimulating effect in the short term. Mian and Sufi (2010) found that almost all additional purchases under the program were pulled forward from the near future. Copeland and Kahn (2013) also discovered significant shifting of purchases from the future and calculated that by January 2010, the cumulative effect of the CARS program on auto sales was essentially zero. However, they believed that it was more important to examine the impact of the program on production rather than sales because increases in the former are more likely to positively affect GDP and employment. Overall, they determined that the program had a very modest and short-lived effect on production and a negligible direct effect on GDP (Copeland and Kahn 2013). Nevertheless, it could still be argued that the program buoyed the car industry when it was in dire need (Tyrrell and Dernbach 2011).

With respect to the green aspects of Cash for Clunkers, the White House and Obama frequently extolled the expected environmental benefits of the program. After its first week, Obama released a statement praising the program for delivering "environmental benefits well beyond what was originally anticipated" (quoted in Lenski, Keoleian, and Bolon 2010, 1–2). Environmentalists were skeptical that the program would benefit the environment and were critical of its design. For example, while the size of the rebate was linked to the difference in mpg between the trade-in vehicle and the new car, larger vehicles, such as sport utility vehicles, were not excluded from the program. The program could have required much tougher efficiency standards for replacement vehicles and more effectively linked greater fuel savings to bigger rebates. It is also fair to suggest that the program excluded people who wanted to give up their cars altogether and switch to other more sustainable forms of transport (e.g., public transport or cycling). Some also expressed concerns about whether the program was equitable because it only benefited people who could afford to purchase a new vehicle (Tyrrell and Dernbach 2011). Allowing rebates to be used to purchase used but efficient vehicles could have rectified this, but that would not have delivered the desired stimulus effect to the car industry.

Estimates of the greenhouse gas emissions reductions created by Cash for Clunkers diverge widely. The average fuel economy of the scrapped cars was 15.8 mpg, while the average fuel economy of the replacement vehicles was 24.9 mpg. NHTSA estimated in 2009 that over the next 25 years, 824 million gallons of fuel use and 9 MMT CO_2-e would be avoided. The monetized benefit of this is estimated to be USD 278 million (by 2008 currency values). NHTSA also estimated that the program resulted in a USD 3.8–6.8 billion increase in GDP (NHTSA, 2009). However, the Government Accountability Office (2010) criticized the NHTSA's methodology, in part because it relied on a poorly designed survey. Lenski et al. (2010) also point out that NHTSA's assessment ignored life-cycle impacts. Building a car produces about 7 MT CO_2-e on average (Niman 2009). In the assessment by Lenski et al. (2010), taking into account such impacts, Cash for Clunkers still had a moderately positive environmental outcome, causing a one-time reduction in greenhouse gas emissions of about 4.4 MMT CO_2-e, or just under 0.4 percent of total annual light-duty vehicle emissions in the US. This is reduced to 3.9 MMT CO_2-e if a ten percent rebound effect is factored in. Regardless of the figures deemed most accurate, it seems fair to conclude that the program was an "extremely expensive way to mitigate [greenhouse gases]" (Lenski et al. 2010, 7), with price estimates ranging from USD 92/MT CO_2-e to well over USD 600/MT CO_2-e (Lenski et al. 2010; Li et al. 2013). In comparison, 1 MT CO_2-e emissions would have cost USD 13 under the proposed (but never adopted) national cap-and-trade system in the US.

Others interested in the life-cycle impacts of the program have considered issues beyond greenhouse gas emissions reductions. For example, Niman (2009) highlights that the steel and aluminum used to make cars comes from materials like bauxite that are excavated through strip mining, resulting in deforestation in many countries. The interiors of cars are also full of PVC, a material whose production and disposal releases persistent carcinogenic environmental toxins such as dioxin (Niman 2009). Santisi (2013) points out that while almost all parts of a vehicle can be recycled, most cars traded in under Cash for Clunkers were simply shredded. This is because the scheme mandated that the engines of scrapped vehicles be destroyed (meaning many parts of the vehicles could not be reused for other purposes). Further, all cars had to be crushed or shredded within 180 days of trade in, regardless of whether all usable parts had been salvaged (for comparison, under normal circumstances, a vehicle could stay at a professional parts dealer for up to 36 months) (Santisi 2013). For each ton of metal recovered by a shredding facility, roughly 500 pounds of shredder residue (including polyurethane foams, polymers, metal oxides, glass, and dirt) are produced and sent to landfills (Santisi 2013). Thus, a direct consequence of the mandate to crush or shred the clunkers quickly was that much more waste was created than was necessary.

Appliances

Japan: Eco-Points

In 2007, Japan's Ministry of Environment (MOE) was conducting a review of the country's Kyoto Protocol Target Achievement Plan and developing ways in which the country could reduce its emissions (Aoshima and Shimizu 2012). It was during this process that the MOE first developed a scheme to incentivize consumers to purchase energy-efficient goods. This became the Home Appliance

Eco-Points program (hereafter Eco-Points), rolled out as a stimulus measure in April 2009.

Eco-Points was originally allocated a budget of JYP 294.6 billion (USD 2.9 billion) and was expected to run until the end of 2010, but was extended to March 2011 (with some modifications), with a total cost of JYP 692.9 billion (USD 6.9 billion) (Board of Audit 2012; MOE n.d.; Sekiguchi 2015). While it was first envisaged as a predominantly environmental program under the sole purview of MOE, its goals changed with the eruption of the GFC (Aoshima and Shimizu 2012). First, METI became involved in developing and implementing the program. According to Aoshima and Shimizu (2012), METI had long endeavored to tie Japan's energy conservation technologies to industry competitiveness and the GFC was the perfect opportunity to do so. Then the Ministry of Internal Affairs and Communications (MIAC) and another policy objective – spreading digital televisions in advance of a planned discontinuation of analog broadcasting in July 2011 – were added to the mix. This would substantially affect the implementation of the program and television purchases would dominate the scheme (over 72.4 percent of Eco-Points were created from television purchases) (Board of Audit 2012).

In addition to televisions, the program covered air conditioners and refrigerators. To qualify for the program, products had to have an energy efficiency ranking of four stars (this increased to five stars in January 2011) (Nakano and Washizu 2017). A consumer that purchased an appliance in one of these categories would receive Eco-Points (worth JYP 1 [USD 0.01] each) for between five and ten percent of the value of the purchase (Holroyd 2014). Eco-Points could be redeemed for other "green" goods or gift certificates and prepaid cards. Alternatively, consumers could opt to donate all of their points to an environmental NGO (total donations to environmental charities amounted to JYP 10.5 billion [USD 105 million]). Toward the end of the program, donations could also be made to the Tohoku triple disaster aid effort (totaling JYP 100 million [USD 1 million] at the conclusion of the program) (Kobayashi 2012; Board of Audit 2012). The most popular choice by far was the exchange of Eco-Points for prepaid cards (Nakano and Washizu 2017). In fact, Matsumoto (2015a) cited data from the MOE that indicate over 97 percent of Eco-Points were redeemed for cards and gift certificates.

Eco-points were based on product size, with bigger rebates offered for larger products (Aoshima 2010). As Yamaguchi, Matsumoto, and Tasaki (2015) point out, larger products are typically more energy intensive. In the case of televisions, customers could expect an effective rebate of JYP 7,000 (USD 70) for a television with a screen smaller than 26 inches and more than five times as much for a screen larger than 46 inches. Similarly, doubling the capacity of a refrigerator purchase (from 250 liters [L] to 500 L) would more than triple the Eco-Points that the customer received (Arimura and Morita 2015).

As is often the case with rebate programs, Japan's Eco-Points program proved to be very popular with the public. Over the course of the program, there were 45.84 million applications for Eco-Points: 33.2 million for televisions, 7.38 million for air conditioners, and 5.26 million for refrigerators (Board of Audit 2012).

Over JYP 649.9 billion (USD 6.5 billion) worth of Eco-Points were issued (Board of Audit 2012).

According to interviewees, corporations played a significant role in driving decisions about the Eco-Points program and strongly supported it when it was rolled out (Professor Toshi Arimura, Tokyo, March 28, 2016; Professor Yoshida Fumikazu, Nagoya, March 29, 2016). For example, Fumio Ohtsubo, president of Panasonic, said:

> Flat panel digital TVs, refrigerators and air conditioners are all flagship products for Panasonic, they all contribute to the global environment, and this new policy will be a stimulus not just for us, but for our supporting industries and [our] suppliers too.
>
> (quoted in Harding and Soble 2009)

By utilizing a scheme that did not allow for a direct cash rebate, the government aimed to ensure a Keynesian multiplier effect – consumers could not save the money, they had to spend it in the economy. However, Komine (2010) argues that this did not happen in practice because the popular prepaid cards could be used for everyday necessities, allowing individuals to save money that they would have had to spend in the program's absence. In terms of the impact on targeted industries, from May 2009 to April 2010, total sales of televisions, air conditioners, and refrigerators increased 30 percent from the same period in the previous year (Kojima 2010). Official estimates from the ministries implementing the program suggest a boost in GDP of JYP 5 trillion (USD 50 billion) and the creation or retention of 300,000 jobs for each year that the program ran (MOE, METI, and MIAC n.d.). However, these numbers have been questioned. Professor Yaichi Aoshima notes that the program did not differentiate between local and imported products and that, for example, sales of cheaper televisions from Taiwan increased (interview with the author, Tokyo, March 30, 2016). The government could not limit the program to domestic appliances because this is not permitted under the WTO and other trade agreements. This means the program could have had a negative impact on Japanese electronics companies (Aoshima and Shimizu 2012). Miyazaki (2015) found that the stimulus effect of the Eco-Points program on domestic appliance production was insignificant. Matsumoto (2015a) argues that the program was regressive because it provided higher subsidies for larger (more expensive) products, which benefited the rich more than the poor.

In terms of the environmental impacts of the program, the ministries responsible for the Eco-Points program attested that it resulted in reductions of 2.7 MMT CO_2-e (0.7 MMT CO_2-e million from televisions, 1.2 MMT CO_2-e from fridges, and 0.8 7 MMT CO_2-e from air conditioners) (MOE et al. 2011). However, the Board of Audit (2012) criticized the lack of transparency of the three ministries regarding their calculation of this figure and proposed its own estimate of only 210,000 MT CO_2-e.

Both of these estimates fail to provide a full accounting of the program's environmental impact. To do that, one would need to consider numerous factors.

First, did the appliances purchased under the program replace existing inefficient goods or were they additional (e.g., a second or third television for the household)? Additions would result in an increase, rather than a decrease, in greenhouse gas emissions and would be especially problematic if they were purchases that would not have been made in the absence of the program. One interviewee admitted (in confidence) that he made a purchase of two televisions under the program that he would not have made in its absence.

Second, even when the products purchased are legitimate replacements, there is the issue of the size of goods. Larger home appliances typically use more energy than smaller ones do (Yoshida et al. 2010). The Eco-Points program encouraged the purchase of larger goods by providing points relative to size. If most customers were replacing small appliances with larger ones, the energy savings from increased efficiency may have been negated.

Several studies have examined whether the program produced energy savings. Aoshima and Shimizu (2012) examined the impact of television purchases. They note that while a 50 percent reduction in annual power consumption from 250 kilowatt hours (kWh) to 125 kWh per television was projected by the government, the actual reduction was closer to 16 percent, from 130 kWh to 109 kWh. They explain this discrepancy by pointing out that the government had assumed that 1995 television models were the standard before replacement. However, research suggests that most consumers replace their television within ten years or less (meaning that in 2009, the standard before replacement would have been a television bought in 1999 or later). Further, they argue that replacement purchases were "accompanied by rapid advances in the enlargement of television size" (Aoshima and Shimizu 2012, 10). They conclude that the Eco-Points program was not an effective environmental policy and question its value in prolonging the life of Japan's television manufacturing industry. Yamaguchi, Matsumoto, and Tasaki (2015) also examined televisions and concluded that Eco-Points increased annual energy consumption from television usage by 23,975,135 kW.

Mizobuchi and Takeuchi (2015) examined the impacts of air conditioner purchases under the program. They found that households that replaced their air conditioners with more efficient models did not save more electricity than those that did not. They hypothesize that this result could stem from the fact that some new air conditioning units, while more energy efficient, have more features and consume more power overall. They also considered that the rebound effect might be to blame for the lack of energy savings (i.e., people used their new air conditioners more).

Nakano and Washizu (2017) discovered that energy-saving electrical appliances became more widespread after the introduction of the Eco-Points program, particularly in households with large electricity consumption. Nevertheless, electricity consumption expenditure remained largely unchanged for households of all attributes before and after implementation.

Going beyond questions of efficiency, one could also consider the energy and materials (including the increased demand for steel) required to make new appliances and the waste created by the disposal of replaced products before the end of their useful life (Capozza 2011). According to Holroyd (2014, 23), "the Eco-Points program could ... be said to encourage unnecessary replacement of usable products." Further, Professor Ken-ichi Akao argues that in some instances, delayed replacement is preferable from an environmental standpoint if technology is advancing quickly, because more savings can be made by waiting a brief period for the next model (interview with the author, Tokyo, March 28, 2016).

Finally, there is also the question of the energy costs and environmental impacts of the goods purchased with the Eco-Points. Theoretically, using a points system (as opposed to a cash rebate) could have allowed the government to steer consumer spending toward green sectors. There is evidence of some environmentally beneficial purchases – for example, Jessup (2011) argues that the program had a positive impact in terms of expanding the adoption of LED lighting in Japan. LEDs were introduced to the program in December 2009 and, beginning in April 2010, consumers could use Eco-Points to buy LED lamps at a two-to-one ratio (MIAC 2010). By March 2011, 420,000 applications had been submitted by customers wishing to exchange approximately JYP 3.52 billion (USD 35.2 million) worth of Eco-Points for LEDs (MOE et al. n.d.). However, most Eco-Points were used for travel, everyday products, and vouchers for local retailers (Yoshida et al. 2010). In other words, there was nothing particularly green about most of the products purchased with Eco-Points. In fact, Eco-Points could even be redeemed for domestic and international air travel.

The United States: Cash for Appliances

When the Cash for Clunkers program was in full swing in July 2009, US Energy Secretary Steven Chu announced what became popularly known as the "Cash for Appliances" scheme (DOE 2009). This was not a new program, but a new injection of funds (USD 296 million) into the existing State Energy Efficient Appliance Rebate Program, first established as part of the *Energy Policy Act of 2005*. Under the program, the DOE allocates funds (based on population) to state energy offices, which provide rebates to consumers for the purchase of appliances with ENERGY STAR labels (DOE 2009). ENERGY STAR is a joint program of the Environmental Protection Agency and the DOE.

The stated aims of the Cash for Appliances program were to increase household energy efficiency and stimulate economic recovery. Chu noted, "appliances consume a huge amount of our electricity, so there's enormous potential to both save energy and save families money every month." He stated that the "rebates will help families make the transition to more efficient appliances, making purchases that will directly stimulate the economy and create jobs" (DOE 2009).

The program deferred substantially to the discretion of state regulators, who decided what appliances would qualify for the programs, how much of a rebate to provide, and how consumers would receive the rebate. The only federally mandated requirement was that the appliances be ENERGY STAR rated. The DOE (2009) recommended that the focus of programs be on heating and cooling equipment, appliances, and water heaters (because these products offer the greatest energy savings potential), but other products were also eligible. ENERGY STAR-qualified appliance categories for rebates were central air conditioners, heat pumps (air source and geothermal), boilers, furnaces (oil and gas), room air conditioners, clothes washers, dishwashers, freezers, refrigerators, and water heaters. Most states allocated rebates for products that just met the ENERGY STAR certification, although for clothes washers and dishwashers, several states adopted efficiency criteria that were more stringent (Houde and Aldy 2014).

States were given only a few months to propose their plans to the DOE. The DOE aimed to have at least some states with operational programs before the start of the Christmas shopping period. Most programs were established by April 2010. Some programs exhausted their funds very quickly (Iowa, Illinois, Massachusetts, and Texas did so in only one day) but, on average, they lasted 26 weeks (Houde and Aldy 2014).

The Cash for Appliances program was not as substantial as the Cash for Clunkers program and has not received as much attention in the policy literature. However, there have been a few analyses of the program that are worth mentioning. Pon and Alberini (2012) discovered that income was the most significant factor in determining whether a household would purchase a new appliance. Households with higher incomes were more likely to purchase new appliances, while those with lower incomes were more likely to keep an appliance until the end of its life cycle. They suggested that their findings indicate that the Cash for Appliances scheme was not significant in convincing homeowners to replace their older appliances with new energy-efficient models. However, they believed the program was somewhat effective in encouraging homeowners who were already looking to replace an appliance to select a more energy-efficient model than they otherwise would have.

A study by Houde and Aldy (2014) focused on the three major appliance categories that attracted the most funds: refrigerators, clothes washers, and dishwashers. They determined that in these categories, the program did not have a meaningful impact on aggregate electricity consumption. For example, the average energy savings for refrigerator rebate programs was only 0.08 percent. They argue that there was a very high rate (72–93 percent) of free-riding behavior by individuals claiming the rebates. This is partly a result of the fact that ENERGY STAR products had a significant market share prior to the introduction of the program. Houde and Aldy (2014) also point out that by nominating ENERGY STAR as the key criterion for product eligibility, reductions in absolute energy consumption were not prioritized. This is because product attributes such as size and optional functions can have a greater impact on absolute energy consumption than efficiency. They provided the example of an ENERGY STAR-certified refrigerator with a bottom-mounted freezer and through-the-door ice-maker, which requires more electricity than a non-certified fridge with a top-mounted freezer and no through-the-door ice-maker. Houde and Aldy (2014) also found some evidence that when rebates were particularly generous, consumers were induced to purchase larger appliances than they otherwise would have, which again could negate any potential energy savings.

Summary and key policy recommendations

In summary, both Japan and the US devoted significant resources to subsidizing durable product purchases as part of their green stimulus programs. However, there is little evidence that this had significant long-term economic or environmental benefits in either country. This has also been the experience with similar schemes in other parts of the world (Aldred and Tepe 2011; Davis, Fuchs, and Gertler 2014; Jiménez, Perdiguero, and García 2016). Several lessons can be learned from the Japanese and US cases.

First, although both governments claimed that the programs were intended to benefit the economy and the environment, the principal goal of each program was economic, and environmental concerns were secondary. For example, as Copeland and Kahn (2013) argue, the timing and limited duration of Cash for Clunkers suggests that the primary purpose of the program was to stimulate the automotive industry and economic activity more generally. In Japan, in addition to economic objectives, the goal of phasing out analog broadcasting took precedence over reducing greenhouse gas emissions in the Eco-Points program.

Opportunities to achieve better environmental outcomes from the programs were missed, even when their likely impacts on the stimulus effect would have been negligible. For example, simply increasing the fuel economy requirements for new vehicles would have increased the environmental benefits from Cash for Clunkers (Li et al. 2013). Perhaps driven by a desire to spend stimulus money quickly (the timeliness criterion), governments also provided overly generous rebates. As such, opportunities to derive more environmental and economic "bang for the buck" were missed (Lenski et al. 2013).

Significantly, rebound effects and life-cycle impacts were substantial in all cases and not considered by governments in the design or assessment of the programs. The fact that subsidies aimed at energy efficiency can have substantial unintended effects does not mean that governments should never undertake such measures. However, policies must be designed with the aim of reducing such effects as much as possible. The opposite occurred in Japan, where the government actively encouraged individuals to drive more by providing a reduction in the highway toll. In both countries, consumers were encouraged to buy bigger, more expensive goods with more features than they might otherwise have done. Yamaguchi et al. (2015) assert, from an environmental perspective, that the size of a subsidy should never be based on product size or price, but on a criterion of absolute energy efficiency. However, this runs contrary to the stimulus objective and the interests of large manufacturing companies.

Indirect rebound effects were also ignored in policy design. While Japan's Eco-Points system theoretically could have reduced indirect rebound effects by directing points spending to green sectors, policymakers permitted points to be used for purchasing everyday goods and even flights, which are hardly defensible as an "eco" purchase.

In terms of the retirement side of these programs, life-cycle analysis is useful in determining the most appropriate policy in a given context. On the one hand, there was no trade-in requirement with the appliance subsidies; this means consumers might have continued to use inefficient items (e.g., purchasing a second or third television or putting a second refrigerator in the basement) and simply increased their overall consumption. On the other hand, the scrapping requirement in the Cash for Clunkers scheme prevented the reuse and recycling of many functional parts, which was viewed by many as wasteful.

In addition to sensible policy design, subsidies should also be coupled with other policies to reduce consumption, like taxes, quotas, and educational programs. As Daly (1991, 35) argues, "sustainable development is about sufficiency as well as efficiency." Governments have a role to play in ensuring that consumers understand that more efficient products still need to be used judiciously (Alcott 2005; Toshimitsu 2010). It is notable that, in recent years, Japan has been quite successful with educational programs that aim to reduce energy consumption. For example, in 2005, the MOE launched a national campaign called Team Minus 6 Percent, the goal of which was to raise awareness of the emissions target of a six percent reduction on 1990 levels. Recommendations included setting the air conditioner to 82.4 Fahrenheit (28 degrees Celsius) or higher in summer and 68 degrees Fahrenheit (20 degrees Celsius) or lower in winter. This was accompanied by another campaign called Cool Biz that attempted to change cultural norms around office attire so that employees would be comfortable enough in a warmer office in summer (Iwata, Katayama, and Arimura 2015). However, education was not prominent in the Eco-Points or Eco-Car programs.

It is also worth examining the type of behavior that these subsidy programs aimed to reward. On the consumer side, they did not reward individuals who had taken their own initiative to switch to more efficient appliances and vehicles before the programs were introduced. Green (2006) argues that subsidy programs may reduce the willingness of individuals to change their behavior voluntarily in the future. This is because paying people to do something may reduce the impact of externally or internally enforced norms or commitments. The programs discussed in this chapter also failed to reward those who opted for more sustainable lifestyles, like living more simply and relying on public transport, walking, or cycling. In other words, the programs encouraged what Fuchs and Lorek (2005) refer to as "green consumerism" instead of "sustainable consumption." While some have argued that consumer involvement in these programs shows that people want to adopt more environmentally friendly lifestyles, it is equally possible that being "deal prone" is the key factor for participation (Conner 2010). On the corporate side, the subsidies rewarded industries (particularly the automotive industries) renowned for their endeavors to resist and undermine government efforts to improve environmental standards (Tyrrell and Dernbach 2011). As Feindt and Cowell (2010, 205) put it, one could criticize schemes like Cash for Clunkers for "propping up industries that have been reluctant to respond to the environmental challenge."

Finally, even if these programs had a slight positive or neutral impact on the environment, there is still the issue of opportunity costs. Every dollar spent subsidizing purchases for individuals is a dollar that could have been spent on a stimulus program that might have had a greater environmental benefit, such as improved public transportation. Further, such programs could have provided a more equitable distribution of benefits. As such, there was a missed opportunity to work toward the objective of a more equal society.

While these lessons generally suggest that subsidy schemes for efficient products should be low on the list of green stimulus priorities, it seems probable that governments will continue to favor them because they are popular with the public and powerful vested-interest groups.

6   Green (washed) infrastructure

> An essential policy that developed and developing countries should pursue in overcoming the crisis is to build infrastructure suitable for the 21st century.
>
> Jeffrey Sachs (2009)

It was inevitable that some spending on infrastructure was going to be a part of the stimulus packages developed in 2009. Paul Krugman (2008), renowned economist and steadfast Keynesian, noted that it was "a good time to engage in some serious infrastructure spending," and an advisory note from Deutsche Bank called infrastructure spending "a well tried and understood response" to economic downturns (Deutsche Bank Advisers 2008, 8). Larry Summers, one of President Obama's key advisers on the US stimulus plan, was initially a "savage" critic of infrastructure spending (because it would take too long to have an impact) (Grunwald 2012, 63). However, even he eventually came to believe that it was important to include some infrastructure projects in ARRA.

It is generally accepted that public infrastructure has a positive productive effect on the economy, although the magnitude of that effect is debated (Stevens, Schieb, and Andrieu 2006). While infrastructure often only directly creates jobs in the short term, the temporary boost to employment can be significant. Further, in the long term, infrastructure can contribute indirectly to employment creation. Frischmann (2012, xii) argues that infrastructure resources are the "basic inputs into a wide variety of productive activities" and when people engage in those activities they often produce spillover benefits to the broader society.

Despite these benefits, many developed countries have neglected to make the necessary investments to maintain and upgrade infrastructure in recent decades. The GFC offered an opportunity to rectify what many considered an increasingly dire situation and to ward off a looming "infrastructure crisis" (Flynn 2009). For environmentalists, the key concern was how much stimulus was going to be channeled into traditional or "brown infrastructure" – the kind that would have a negative impact on the environment – and how much would go to environmentally friendly "green infrastructure."

It is important to note at the outset that the term "green infrastructure" has different meanings in different contexts. For some, it refers only to the use of vegetation within urban environments (e.g., green roofs). In the context of the 2008–2009 stimulus packages, green infrastructure encompassed such initiatives (e.g., Hewes 2008), but was generally thought of in much broader terms. Proposals for investing in green infrastructure ranged from making improvements to waste and water treatment facilities, to creating smart electrical grids, and building certain types of transportation infrastructure (e.g., rail lines but not roads). The International Union for the Conservation of Nature has suggested that systems of protected natural areas should also be considered green infrastructure, given that they provide ecosystem services such as clean water (Marghescu 2009). Some would also include enhanced energy efficiency of buildings and renewable energy generation in the definition; however, these topics are excluded here as they are discussed in other chapters of this book.

Environmentalists provided two rationales for favoring green infrastructure over brown infrastructure. First, investing in green infrastructure would provide direct environmental benefits. For example, investing in HSR would (theoretically) reduce dependence on air and road travel and, therefore, lead to greenhouse gas emissions reductions. Second, in addition to these direct benefits, there were the indirect benefits of investing in a green infrastructure project instead of a brown counterpart. If money was diverted from brown infrastructure, this would further contribute to environmental objectives. This diversionary effect can be particularly significant given the long life span of physical infrastructure. Choices made about infrastructure in 2009 would essentially lock in the carbon intensity of an activity for decades (Kennedy and Corfee-Morlot 2013). For example, highways have a life span of 20–50 years, in which they "all but guarantee emissions of carbon dioxide" (Brown 2011, 20).

In practice, it is unclear how much (if any) diversion occurred. What is evident is that the stimulus packages covered in this study did not contain substantial investments in green infrastructure. In contrast, governments poured considerable money into brown infrastructure, particularly roads. For example, Australia, which had no dedicated green infrastructure program (some investments were made in public transportation), allocated AUD 4.8 billion (USD 3.8 billion) to road projects, touted as part of "the biggest road investment program in the nation's history" (Commonwealth of Australia 2009, 14). Canada pumped four times the amount of money that it allocated to the dedicated Green Infrastructure Fund (CAD 1 billion [USD 880 million]) into its nongreen Infrastructure Stimulus Fund (CAD 4 billion [USD 3.5 billion]).

What obstacles prevented more funding flowing to green infrastructure projects? The timeliness criterion for stimulus may have been significant. As Brahmbhatt (2014) notes, the planning and permitting processes for large infrastructure projects often take far longer than actual construction does. This was the main reason Summers initially opposed infrastructure spending. However, most subnational/municipal governments have an existing wish list of close to shovel-ready if not shovel-ready brown infrastructure projects (many of them upgrades to existing infrastructure). On the contrary, innovative green infrastructure project plans, that previously had very little chance of being funded, are unlikely to remain on a project list, ready to be picked up and rolled out at the opportune moment.

In terms of permitting, EIAs are considered by many to be a "red tape" task that can delay the progress of an infrastructure project. As noted in Chapter 1, in one of the most ironic and cynical of policy decisions during the crisis, the Canadian government, under the leadership of Prime Minister Stephen Harper, exploited the GFC as an opportunity to water down EIA requirements for stimulus-funded infrastructure projects. Unfortunately, Canada is not the only country to have adjusted its environmental approvals process in the wake of the crisis. The WRI has monitored other countries that also rolled back EIA procedures for stimulus projects (Zomer 2009). In the US, an effort was launched by Republican Senator John Barrasso to suspend the *National Environmental Policy Act*. However, Democratic Senator Barbara Boxer blocked the move and passed an amendment to strengthen EIA procedures (Zomer 2009).

In short, it is likely that the shovel-ready mandate for the stimulus had a negative impact on the greenness of infrastructure spending in two respects. First, it led to the prioritization of brown projects that were nearly ready to be rolled out. Second, in some countries, it reduced oversight of those brown infrastructure projects, increasing the likelihood that they would be environmentally damaging. However, the timeliness criterion cannot be solely blamed for the meager attention given to green infrastructure in the wake of the GFC. As the cases below indicate, decisions about infrastructure are also heavily influenced by power politics.

Cases

Canada: The Northwest Transmission Line

According to Infrastructure Canada's website, eligible projects for funding under the CAD 1 billion (USD 880 million) Green Infrastructure Fund (launched in 2009 as part of Canada's Economic Action Plan to respond to the GFC) were "those that promote cleaner air, reduced greenhouse gas emissions, and cleaner water" and fall within any of the following categories: wastewater infrastructure, green energy generation and transmission infrastructure, solid waste infrastructure, and CCS infrastructure. Funding was to be allocated based on merit with a focus on "a few, large scale, strategic infrastructure projects" (Infrastructure Canada n.d.a). As noted in Chapter 1, the Green Infrastructure Fund lost CAD 170 million (USD 150 million) that was transferred to other departments (Infrastructure Canada 2016). Another CAD 105 million (USD 92 million) was unallocated and removed from Infrastructure Canada's budget. This left CAD 725 million (USD 638 million), which was spent on 20 projects (see Table 6.1).

Some interesting observations can be made from an examination of the portfolio of projects in Table 6.1. First, most projects are located in Ontario and Quebec. This is rather unsurprising as these are the two most populous and politically important provinces in Canada. However, it is remarkable that all the projects in Ontario concern wastewater treatment plants, while all the projects in Quebec

Table 6.1 Green Infrastructure Fund spending

Project name	Province	Project type	Key environmental claims	Total cost (M CAD)	GIF (M CAD)
Northwest Transmission Line	BC	Electrical transmission line	Transfer small communities from diesel generation to "clean" energy	404	130
Wastewater Treatment for the Capital Regional District	BC	New wastewater treatment plant	Reduce marine pollution by vastly improving the quality of municipal wastewater discharged into the Strait of Juan de Fuca	782.7	50
Protecting the Red River and Lake Winnipeg	MB	Wastewater treatment plant upgrade	Reduce the number of times raw sewage overflows into Red River and Lake Winnipeg	33	11
Building a Wastewater Treatment Plant for the Future	ON	New wastewater treatment plant	Preserve the environment around Murdock Creek and Blanche River in Northern Ontario and improve water quality in the Great Lakes Basin	35.5	16
Upgrades to Wastewater Treatment Help Rejuvenate Hamilton Harbour	ON	Wastewater treatment plant upgrade	Significantly improve the quality of effluent discharged into Hamilton Harbour	300	100
New Treatment Plant Helps Clean Up Great Lakes	ON	New wastewater treatment plant	Cleaner wastewater effluent discharges into Nipigon Bay	9	4.5
Cleaning Up Georgian Bay	ON	Wastewater treatment plant upgrade	Noticeable improvement in the quality of water in Georgian Bay and the availability of the Bay for recreational purposes	45	15
Cost-Saving Design for Upgraded Wastewater Treatment Plant	ON	Wastewater treatment plant upgrade	Noticeable improvement in the quality of water in the St. Lawrence River for the community of Iroquois and the surrounding area	18	9
Cleaning Up the Saint Lawrence River	ON	Wastewater treatment plant upgrade	A substantial reduction in the amount of contaminants, nutrients, and solids discharged into the Saint Lawrence River and a subsequent positive impact on the aquatic environment of the Great Lakes	55.5	18.5

(Continued)

Table 6.1 (Continued)

Project name	Province	Project type	Key environmental claims	Total cost (M CAD)	GIF (M CAD)
Meeting Rapidly Increasing Wastewater Treatment Demand	ON	Wastewater treatment plant upgrade	Maintenance or improvement in the levels of phosphorous discharged into Hamilton Harbour, which can have a negative effect on fish habitat	158	51.5
Upgrades to Wastewater Treatment in Timmins	ON	Wastewater treatment plant upgrade	Fewer contaminants will be discharged into the Mattagami River	59.5	19.8
Northumberland Strait Power Cable Project	PEI	Electrical transmission line	Reduced reliance on generators, access to cleaner energy	140	50
Landfill Gas to Power Municipal Trucks	QC	Organic waste treatment facility	The diversion of 60% of the region's biodegradable waste will eliminate the emission of the equivalent of 7,455 tons of CO_2 annually with additional reductions from the replacement of fossil-fuel-generated gas in municipal vehicles	14.7	4.1
Turning Landfill into Renewal Energy	QC	Organic waste treatment facility	Reduce greenhouse gas emissions by 16,000 tons of CO_2 equivalent annually	57	16.6
Diverting Organics from Landfills	QC	Waste sorting center, and organic waste treatment facility	Reduce the environmental impacts from landfill and from hauling garbage over long distances as well as producing biogas to meet various energy demands	215.5	67
Transforming Garbage into Renewable Energy	QC	Organic waste treatment facility	Reduced landfill requirements and significant reductions in annual CO_2 emissions	107.5	30.6
Producing Renewable Energy from Organic Waste	QC	Organic waste treatment facility	Estimated greenhouse gas reduction of 36,094 tons of CO_2 equivalent annually	85.7	21.5
Eliminating Organic Material in Landfills	QC	Organic waste treatment facility	Reduced pressure on landfills and generation of biogas	133	27.7
Organic waste processing using biomethanation in Saint-Hyacinthe	QC	Organic waste treatment facility	Reduced pressure on landfills and generation of biogas	31.4	11.4
Increasing Clean Energy Generation	YT	Upgrade to hydroelectric facility and connection of two existing grid systems	Reduce forecast dependence on diesel fuel for power generation by 40% and cut greenhouse gas emissions in the region by 50%	160	71
TOTAL				2845	725.2

Source: Compiled by the author from information provided on the NRCAN website.

concern organic waste and biogasification plants. The only project in Manitoba also involves a wastewater treatment plant upgrade. While there is no doubt that wastewater treatment has notable environmental benefits, the large portion of funds allocated to this (41 percent of total spending) makes the Green Infrastructure Fund closely resemble the Infrastructure Stimulus Fund, which received CAD 4 billion (USD 3.5 billion) in Canada's Economic Action Plan for investments in areas including water and wastewater infrastructure (Infrastructure Canada n.d.b).

The only project in Prince Edward Island (PEI) was not even announced until 2015 and, therefore, cannot be considered a part of the stimulus response to the GFC. The remaining two projects – in British Columbia (BC) and the Yukon – both concern electrical transmission and received far more than the average amount of funding (approximately CAD 36 million [USD 32 million]). The Northwest Transmission Line (NTL) in Northern BC, which received the largest grant (CAD 130 million [USD 114 million]), is the focus of this section.

The NTL, a 287-kV transmission line stretching nearly 217.5 miles (350 km) through forest, swampland, and mountains was first given the green light by the Provincial Government of BC in 2007 (*The Province* 2007). Two mining companies, Teck Cominco and NovaGold, which each had a stake in a project known as Galore Creek, were supposed to cover CAD 158 million (USD 139 million) of the cost of the NTL (originally estimated at CAD 404 million [USD 356 million]). However, less than two months after the provincial government announced that the NTL would go ahead, the companies dropped out and halted development of Galore Creek, claiming that escalating costs had made the mine economically unviable. Consequently, the provincial government chose to put the NTL on hold.

At this point, it is clear that the NTL was viewed as a straightforward infrastructure project aimed at fueling mining investment in the northern part of the province. When the Galore Creek project was shelved, the provincial minister for Energy, Mines and Petroleum Resources, Richard Neufeld, stated:

> Until we get some sense that there is maybe someone else out there who would maybe want to consume that kind of electricity and actually contribute substantially to the construction of it, I think it's prudent for government to say, "Well, why would we build a line up there that's not going anywhere?"
> (quoted in Simpson 2007)

Less than a year later, Premier Gordon Campbell announced that the government would invest CAD 10 million (USD 9 million) to restart the EIA process for the NTL. In his announcement, the premier cited a report by the Mining Association of British Columbia that claimed the NTL could attract at least CAD 15 billion (USD 13 billion) in new mining investments and power generation to the region (Office of the Premier 2008).

In May 2009, the Northwest Powerline Coalition (a lobby group composed of mining companies and local government representatives in the region and sponsored by the Mining Association of British Columbia) released an update of the

Mining Association's report on the NTL, with the new title "Delivering Green Power to Northern British Columbia" (Northwest Powerline Coalition 2009). In the preamble, the Coalition noted that it "committed time and resources" to update the previous report "to reflect the new global economic environment, the increasing concerns related to global warming, and to reflect the new information and data related to the projects planned and proposed along the corridor." In essence, the Coalition identified an opportunity to access stimulus funding under the Green Infrastructure Fund and tailored its document accordingly. The Mayor of Terrace (a small town in Northern BC) David Pernarowski, who sat on the Coalition's board of directors, described meetings with federal government ministers:

> We met a number of times with federal government ministers and we actually provided a document that talked specifically about the benefits of the power line relating to green aspects and that was really the focus – once we had some initial meetings with the federal government that's what they told us they were looking for, that's where the project would fit best if we could show them the plan that made sense around the green energy and the green stimulus projects or how that would fit.
>
> (interview with the author, Terrace, BC, December 15, 2010)

The Coalition's main claims about the NTL's environmental benefits concerned greenhouse gas emissions reductions. Specifically, the report focused on the connection of small communities in Northern BC (that were reliant on diesel power) to the "clean" (predominantly hydro) energy that would be supplied by the NTL. The Coalition's estimates in this respect were: Iskut, reduction of 2,819 MT CO_2-e/yr; Telegraph Creek, 2,094 MT CO_2-e/yr; and Dease Lake, 335 MT CO_2-e/yr. These estimates may be reasonable, but their inclusion in the document is misleading. As asserted by many environmental groups, the planned terminus of the NTL at the time was more than 62 miles (100 km) south of the most accessible community mentioned (Iskut). As such, none of these communities would have been connected to the grid under the original proposal.

Despite this glaring problem, a formal proposal for Green Infrastructure funding was made by the BC Transmission Corporation (BCTC 2009) (a crown corporation that later merged with BC Hydro) to Infrastructure Canada. In this proposal (which was not made public and was obtained by the author through an Access to Information request), the same claims were made about the greenhouse gas emissions reductions that can result from connecting small communities to the NTL:

> The [NTL] will extend BC's high voltage transmission grid into the Northwest portion of the province, enabling a new era of green electricity generation to this important region and the isolated communities within it. *In connecting this region and these small, remote communities to the provincial electric grid, NTL will help to eliminate these small communities' reliance on diesel generation.*
>
> (emphasis added, on file with author)

Only Iskut was specifically mentioned. A footnote clarified that the NTL was not actually planned to extend as far as Iskut and that a connection for the community would require an additional distribution line at a cost of CAD 8 million (USD 7 million).

In an email (obtained through Access to Information and on file with author) from a policy analyst at Infrastructure Canada to the director of market operations and development at BCTC on September 1, 2009 (15 days before Prime Minister Harper made his announcement that the NTL would receive stimulus funding through the Green Infrastructure Fund), it is evident that justifying the funding was a concern for the federal government:

> Just to recap our discussion this morning, one of our key issues concerns the actual versus potential environmental benefits arising from the project. As you know, we are bound by established program requirements and it would bolster our project rationale greatly to be able to confirm actual and direct benefits as a result of the NTL, i.e., linking remote communities to the energy grid.

Subsequently, Infrastructure Canada stipulated in its funding agreement with BCTC that an extra extension to Iskut had to be built, and no later than 12 months after the "Substantial Completion Date" of the NTL (Canada and British Columbia 2009). The details of this requirement were only made public when the funding agreement was obtained by a journalist and published online (Pollon 2011). In March 2013, it was finally announced that Imperial Metals would build a 57-mile (93 km) extension to the NTL to service its planned Red Chris Mine. BC Hydro would purchase this extension for CAD 52 million (USD 46 million) and build a smaller line to ultimately connect Iskut (Richards 2013). The extension was completed in 2014.

The NTL came online in July 2014. The final cost of the project was estimated at CAD 716 million (USD 630 million), which represented a CAD 312 million (USD 275 million) overspend on the original budget (BC Hydro, n.d.). AltaGas, which is connecting a hydro project to the NTL, contributed CAD 180 million (USD 158 million) to the cost of the NTL, while Canadian taxpayers contributed CAD 130 million (USD 114 million) through the stimulus (BC Hydro n.d.). BC Hydro ratepayers contributed the remaining CAD 406 million (USD 357 million). No official figures for the number of jobs directly created by the project have been released by BC Hydro or Infrastructure Canada.

Infrastructure Canada (n.d.a) estimated that getting Iskut off diesel would reduce emissions by 2,080 MT CO_2-e/yr. For context, Canada's total emissions in 2009 amounted to 541 MMT CO_2e (Energy Information Administration, n.d.). When compared with other projects in the Green Infrastructure portfolio, it does not appear that the federal government received a decent green return on its investment in the NTL; for a fraction of the funding (CAD 21.5 million [USD 19 million]), the Producing Renewable Energy from Organic Waste project in Quebec is expected to reduce greenhouse gases by 36,094 MT CO_2-e/yr (Infrastructure

Canada, n.d.b). The other transmission line funded in the Yukon also provided more emissions reductions (14,350 MT CO_2-e/yr) at a lower cost (CAD 71 million [USD 63 million]) (Infrastructure Canada 2016).

An even more crucial issue is that extending the electrical grid is not the most cost-effective or environmentally friendly method to shift remote communities away from diesel power generation. Bruce Hill from the Headwaters Initiative noted:

> It is so ironic. When we talked to BCTC when they had their initial meetings here [they] said it was not cost-effective to put in a sub-station at Iskut to reduce the power down from 287 to a voltage like 440 volts; it would take millions and millions of dollars of investment to get power off that grid to a village of 150 people.
>
> (interview with the author, Terrace, BC, December 16, 2010)

Nikki Skuce, an energy campaigner with nonprofit organization ForestEthics, suggests, "if the federal government was truly serious about developing renewable energy and getting remote communities off diesel, they would be looking at community-owned power linking the region to its own grid system" (ForestEthics 2009). Will Horter of the nonprofit Dogwood Initiative agrees, arguing that because the communities in the region are very small, they simply do not need a powerline the size of the NTL. They could easily become self-sufficient with a modest capital investment in retrofits, and small-scale renewable energy projects (wind, solar etc.) (interview with the author, Victoria, December 3, 2010). An example of such a project, funded through Canada's Clean Energy Fund, is discussed in Chapter 7.

Although Infrastructure Canada's website and BCTC's proposal suggest several other environmental advantages of the NTL, communications between these two parties reveal that these were considered "potential" rather than "actual" benefits:

> As page 15 confirms that link to [Iskut] would be done "under first phase of the project", and *as this connection would be the only actual benefit realized under this project*, note that it would be recommended as a condition for funding.
>
> (emphasis added, on file with author)

Nevertheless, it is worth briefly exploring the additional claim that the NTL would avoid emissions in the mining sector (Northwest Powerline Coalition 2009; BCTC 2009). Ben Chalmers of the Mining Association of British Columbia noted that "the way we sold [the NTL] as green was that it would allow a number of mines to be built with hydroelectric power rather than onsite diesel generation, so it's green from a greenhouse emissions point of view" (interview with the author, Vancouver, November 25, 2010). BCTC (2009) estimated that the avoided emissions would be more than 2 MMT CO_2e/yr, which they compare to "removing over 350,000 cars from the roads." However, the crux of the issue is how to determine whether emissions are really avoided; arguably, at least some mines would not be developed in the absence of a cheap and reliable power source. According to Andrew Gage, Staff Counsel at West Coast Environmental Law:

> There will be some industry that would have gone ahead anyhow that gets onto the grid and therefore gets off diesel but a much larger number of industries that probably wouldn't have gone ahead at least in the short term ... that are now much less costly to go ahead. Essentially [the NTL is] a subsidy – it's public dollars making those projects viable, it's a windfall for those companies.
>
> (interview with the author, Victoria, BC, December 3, 2010)

Evan van Dyk of the Terrace Development Authority pointed out that there are many mining sites in the region that have been staked for years. He suggested that mining companies "have been looking for a reason to start developing – [the NTL] is the reason" (interview with the author, Terrace, December 15, 2010).

Given the NTL's clear role in spurring mining development, it seems worth briefly exploring the environmental impacts associated with such development. An EIA for the NTL was conducted at the provincial level (BC Environmental Assessment Office n.d.). Typically, this type of project would also require a federal assessment but, as noted earlier, the Harper government streamlined the assessment process for stimulus projects. The provincial assessment only focused on the direct environmental impacts resulting from the construction of the transmission line (e.g., habitat fragmentation), part of which runs through a park. Environmentalists were far more concerned with indirect impacts associated with mining development (Wild Border Watersheds n.d.; Rivers Without Borders n.d.). Many proposed mining projects are in a subalpine basin that is the source of three wild salmon rivers: the Skeena River, Nass River, and Stikine River. The local First Nations refer to the area as the "Sacred Headwaters." In addition to being an important salmon habitat, the area is also home to other threatened and vulnerable wildlife, including grizzly bears (Suzuki 2013).

One of the most significant projects in the area is Imperial Metal's Red Chris open-pit copper and gold mine. In 2014, Energy and Mines Minister Bill Bennett stated that the mine would not have progressed without the NTL (Penner 2014). It is anticipated that more than 180 million tons of tailings and an estimated 300 million tons of waste rock will be created over the life of the mine, requiring acid-rock drainage treatment for at least 200 years (Pollon 2011). The project will involve damming and diverting streams and turning fish-bearing waters into tailings ponds. In 2010, Ecojustice (a nonprofit environmental law organization) won a case against the federal government in the Supreme Court of Canada about the EIA process for the Red Chris Mine (Tessaro 2013). Although the Court ruled that the government had violated national environmental law, it did not require the Red Chris environmental assessment to be redone.

The mining industry was unquestionably a major driver of the NTL from the outset, with a key interest in obtaining a cheap supply of energy to make mining in a remote area, with known deposits, economically viable. The mining industry is a powerful lobby group in BC, and in Canada more generally. Between 2005 and 2009, the ruling provincial Liberal Party received more than CAD 1.1 million (USD 968 million) in political contributions from one mining company – Teck Cominco, now known as Teck Resources (one of the original proponents of the NTL) – and its subsidiaries alone (Elections BC 2011).

However, it is worth highlighting that there was another obvious option available to the federal government to fund the NTL. The Infrastructure Stimulus Fund was endowed with far more money (CAD 4 billion [USD 3.5 billion]) than the Green Infrastructure Fund and had no "green strings" attached. Why then did the federal government not direct BCTC to apply to that fund instead? The answer appears to be that there was a requirement that Infrastructure Stimulus Fund grants be spent by March 2011. This condition would have ruled out the NTL as a candidate for funding as the project did not have environmental approval until May 2011. Establishing green outcomes for the NTL to fit the parameters of the Green Infrastructure Fund was apparently easier than changing the completion requirements for the Infrastructure Stimulus Fund (which were approved by Parliament).

In summary, the NTL – the recipient of the biggest grant from the Green Infrastructure Fund – will have only a minor direct environmental benefit in terms of greenhouse gas emissions reductions. Further, it will indirectly result in significant harm to a relatively pristine natural environment.

Korea: The Four Major Rivers Project

During his presidential election campaign, Lee Myung-bak proposed a Pan-Korean Grand Waterway involving a series of canals, including one stretching 335.5 miles (540 km) connecting Seoul and Busan (Korea's two largest cities) (Kim 2012). Lee won the election, but this proposal proved very controversial. Polls suggested that more than 80 percent of the country's citizens opposed the project (Kim 2012). In February 2008, college professors across Korea formed the Professors' Organization for Movement against the Grand Korean Canal (POMAC), the membership of which would eventually swell to over 2,500 academics. In the summer of 2008, to regain the public's favor following his incredibly unpopular decision to allow the importation of US beef during the mad cow disease crisis, Lee promised to drop the canal project. Stocks of construction companies across the nation immediately fell (Card 2009).

The GFC peaked soon after and Lee's administration moved to create a Green New Deal. The centerpiece of the Green New Deal was the Four Major Rivers Project, which eventually soaked up more than KRW 22 trillion (USD 20 billion) in taxpayer funds. The project involved dredging 570 billion m^3 of sediment and the creation of 16 dams across the country's four largest rivers. Three dams were built on the Han River, eight on the Nakdong River, three on the Geum River, and two on the Yeosang River. The government framed the project primarily in terms of climate change adaptation (projection against flooding) (Republic of Korea n.d.). While dam construction was the focus of the project, wastewater treatment facilities were also upgraded and land-use changes were made along the river to eliminate farms (which the government argued were illegal and causing pollution). Some riverside recreational space was also created, including bicycle paths.

UNEP (2009d) eagerly praised Korea's Green New Deal when it was released. However, Korean critics immediately pointed out that the Four Major Rivers Project was simply the Pan-Korean Grand Waterway under a different name. The government refuted this claim, but a 2013 report from the Board of Audit and Inspection (an arms-length government body) suggests that the critics were correct. According to the report, when President Lee publicly abandoned the Pan-Korean Grand Waterway, the Ministry of Land, Transport and Maritime Affairs was secretly ordered to develop an alternative plan to revive the project (*The Chosun Ilbo* 2013).

The Four Major Rivers Project proceeded at a phenomenal rate and was officially completed in October 2011. Extensive resources were called upon to finish the project in a short time frame and an astonishing level of cross-government cooperation was employed. The government justified the speed of the project based on the notion that upstream and downstream works had to be conducted at the same time to minimize flood risk and because "it was necessary to come up with the urgent countermeasure against large-scale floods and droughts occurring worldwide due to climate change" (MLTM 2012, 70). However, it is commonly believed that President Lee wanted the project completed within his five-year term.

The speed of the project has been blamed for a high number of injuries and deaths among laborers on the project, as well as structural flaws in the completed bridges and weirs (Chang, Han, and Kim 2012). The Board of Audit and Inspection reported in 2013 that the concrete riverbeds, built to protect the weirs, had subsided or been swept away for 11 out of 16 weirs (Stedman 2013; Lah, Park, and Cho 2015). Korean economists were concerned that the cost of maintaining the system would burden the country's recovering economy (interview with Professor Hong Jong Ho, Seoul, December 5, 2013). It has been estimated that USD 271 million per year will be required for maintenance (Stedman 2013).

The Board of Audit and Inspection also determined that large-scale corruption and collusion had occurred in the bidding process for construction work on the project (*The Chosun Ilbo* 2013). Eight contractors involved in the scheme were fined by the South Korean Fair Trade Commission for bid rigging and in September 2013, the Supreme Prosecutor's Office in Seoul charged 22 individuals at 11 construction companies with bid rigging (Sleight 2013).

Pundits dispute the number of genuine jobs created by the Four Major Rivers Project as opposed to those that already existed and were simply reclassified as part of the project (Chang et al. 2012; Kim et al. 2012). The government aimed to create as many as 340,000 jobs through the project, but Lah et al. (2015) estimated that only 4,162 jobs were actually created (including temporary jobs). Concern has also been expressed about the quality of the jobs created (Yun et al. 2011; Chang et al. 2012; Kim et al. 2012). It has been suggested that the government's much smaller investment in renewable energy created higher-quality jobs than the Four Major Rivers Project did (Chang et al. 2012).

In terms of environmental impact, specific benefits highlighted by the government were flood control, securing sufficient water resources against water scarcity, and improving water quality (MLTM 2012; Cha, Shim, and Kim 2011). The government argued that "repeated flooding and droughts have caused human casualties, ecosystem loss and habitat degradation, property damage and forced displacement of riverine residents" (Cha et al. 2011, 1). However, critics of the project countered that the major rivers in Korea had already been well prepared against floods and that it is along the tributaries of those rivers where most serious flooding now occurs (Chang et al. 2012). In June 2011, Typhoon Meari hit Korea and government officials claimed that the minimal damage that occurred "proved the Four Rivers 'flood-proof' " (Cha et al. 2011, 9). However, locals and environmental group Green Korea United blamed the collapse of a bridge during the typhoon on dredging activities for the Four Major Rivers Project (*The Dong-a Ilbo* 2011a). Interviewees suggested that it is too early to judge the impact of the project on long-term flood management.

It is not in dispute that the project has created greater capacity for water storage. However, critics suggest that doing so was unnecessary because there is no water shortage in Korea, "a country which has sufficient annual rainfall, a number of mountains, and is well-equipped with water supply facilities" (Chang et al. 2012, 157). Experts argue that the problem facing the country is "excessive per capita water consumption" (10.5 gallons [40.02 L] per person daily, which is two to six times the consumption rate of other developed countries) (Chang et al. 2012, 157). The government's own water resource planning document from 2006 suggests that even in a worst-case scenario of dramatic droughts and increased demand, water shortfalls would not have been large enough to justify the scale of the Four Major Rivers Project and could have been addressed through much smaller and simpler management systems (Kim, J-s. 2013).

The issue of water quality is perhaps the most controversial aspect of the project. The government claimed that by 2012, "the water quality of the mainstream will be improved to an average of level two (Biochemical Oxygen Demand less than 3 ppm)" (Cha et al. 2011, 4). The government seems to have hoped that in addition to reducing the introduction of contaminants through new water treatment facilities, it could also rely on the dictum that "the solution to pollution is dilution." The Lee administration claimed that enlarging the "water bowl" through dredging and installing dams would improve water quality by diluting pollutants (Nam 2011). However, the National Institute of Environmental Research found that increased water levels during the dry season and decreased rates of water flow would encourage algae growth in the stagnant water and lead to a reduction in water quality (Nam 2011).

Activists argue that this was exactly what occurred in the summer of 2012, when large algal blooms developed in the Nakdong and Han rivers, leading Seoul's municipal government to advise residents to boil any tap water intended for consumption (Park 2012). The water was so green that locals referred to it as "the green algae latte," after a popular green-tea drink. The government maintained that the blooms were the result of an unusually long heat wave and associated drought and had nothing to do with the Four Major Rivers Project (Park 2012). Some experts agreed that environmental factors had been the main cause of the blooms. However, one interviewee (a water ecology expert working for the government who wished to remain anonymous) contended that the increased stagnation of water had undeniably exacerbated the problem.

As with any major construction works, the Four Major Rivers Project was anticipated to have some negative environmental impacts. An EIA was conducted in 2009. Considerable pressure was placed on the MOE to complete the assessment quickly and a preliminary feasibility study for the project was not conducted (interview with Professor Lee Sang-Don, Seoul, December 3, 2013). The assessment took four months and was completed before the project plans were even finalized. Experts suggest that for such a large project, a proper assessment should have taken at least one year (Ruffin 2010). In 2012, the Busan High Court ruled that the government had broken the law by failing to conduct a preliminary feasibility study (*The Hankyoreh* 2012).

In the EIA, the government acknowledged that the project would negatively affect some wetland areas. The NGO Birds Korea (2010) predicted that 50 bird species would be negatively affected by the project and that the conservation value of at least one Ramsar-listed wetland would be reduced. Since then, the director of Birds Korea has argued that these predictions proved correct, noting that although data are limited, there are indications of a significant decline in the number of water-birds wintering in Korea between 2009 and 2013 (Moores 2013).

In 2012, the World Water Network awarded Korea a "Grey Globe Award" (the award highlights wetlands that are being actively degraded or neglected). The award announcement noted:

> The wetlands are home to many endangered species such as hooded cranes (Globally Vulnerable) whose numbers have declined from 3,000 to 1,000 since the Four Major Rivers Project started in 2009. Established resting sites for white-naped cranes have also been lost, as well as most of the habitats of fresh water clams. The Nakdong Estuary has seen a drop of 75% in its wintering bird populations, despite being nationally designated.
>
> (World Water Network 2012)

In October 2013, a representative of the main opposition party (the Democratic Party) used an Environment Ministry report to argue that 28 protected species had disappeared from the river ecosystem during the implementation of the project (Kim, P 2013).

UNEP became embroiled in the debate about the environmental impacts of the Four Major Rivers Project when it released an interim report assessing Korea's green growth strategy in August 2009, which endorsed the project. The report noted that it was "encouraging to observe" that each of the project's objectives "not only addresses a vital ecological scarcity, but that actions planned will also serve as useful forms of adaptation to the onset of climate change" (UNEP 2009d, 5). Following the release of the interim report, members of POMAC wrote to

UNEP and met with representatives of the organization. In a letter to UNEP Executive Director Achim Steiner, a German professor of hydrology wrote:

> Trying to sell this "4 Rivers Project" as a "river restoration" project fatally reminds us of the flawed argument in favor of one-sided river engineering measures of the past, before the negative experiences and the subsequent protests forced people to rethink. I perceive "river restoration" as something completely different, namely measures leading to the restoration of the free flowing waters, and not to the rearrangement of the rivers with a cascade of dams, which inevitably leads to the destruction of the precious riverscape.
>
> (Bernhart 2011)

Although UNEP's final report was slightly revised (the text quoted above was removed), the overall tone remained positive (UNEP 2010b). The experience left many Korean environmentalists disheartened and highly critical of the organization. Interviewees suggested that UNEP had failed its mandate when it simply accepted the government's views on the project without examining its likely environmental impact (interviews with Professor Lee Sang-Don, Seoul, December 3, 2013 and Professors Yun Sun-Jin and Hong Jong Ho, Seoul, 5 December 2013).

In summary, the Four Major Rivers Project may or may not help Korea adapt to climate change by mitigating floods. However, flood management could have been achieved through other means with a less dramatic impact on the country's riverine ecosystems. It was the construction industry, not the environment, that stood to benefit most from the Four Major Rivers Project, and President Lee had strong ties to that industry as the former CEO of a major construction firm. Speculation over why Lee pursued this project so relentlessly range from the extremely cynical suggestion that he "owed" the construction industry for their help with his election campaign, to the more forgiving argument that he was simply misguided and truly believed that the project would benefit the country (COP15 Korea NGOs Network 2009; interviews by author with Professor Kim Jung-wk, Seoul, December 4, 2013 and Professors Yun Sun-Jin and Hong Jong Ho, Seoul, 5 December 2013).

United States: High-speed rail

It is widely accepted that the US has a major problem when it comes to infrastructure (Frischmann 2012). US investments in infrastructure, which have been funded at roughly the same level for the last 45 years, lag behind those of many developed and developing nations (Brown 2011). Frischmann (2012, x) describes the federal government's approach to infrastructure as "complacent, reactive, piecemeal" and "incredibly short-sighted." In 2009, the American Society for Civil Engineers (ASCE) gave the country's infrastructure an overall grade of "D." This rose to "D+" in the organization's 2013 report, but the cost to restore existing infrastructure to good condition increased from USD 2.2 trillion to USD 3.6 trillion

(ASCE 2013). Brown (2011, 20) argues that the US's relatively low level of investment in infrastructure "may be symptomatic of its general disinvestment in the public realm."

Approximately USD 132 billion of the USD 787 billion ARRA package was apportioned to infrastructure projects. While President Obama (2009) described this as the "most sweeping investment in our infrastructure since President Eisenhower built the interstate highway system in the 1950s," Brown (2011, 21) argues it was a fraction of what is needed and "hardly represents a meaningful 'new deal' for America's public works." She also notes that the money mainly served to underwrite "backlogged, construction-ready projects that reinforce the carbon intensity on which our economy depends" (Brown 2011, 21).

The transportation sector represents about 30 percent of annual greenhouse gas emissions in the US and, since 1990, its contribution has grown rapidly (Clewlow 2012). Approximately 21 percent of ARRA infrastructure funding went to high-ways, bridges, and roadways, while only 13 percent was earmarked for mass transit and rail projects (Urban Land Institute 2009). Nevertheless, the USD 8 billion that intercity passenger rail projects received under ARRA "represented an enormous appropriation in historical terms" (Peterman, Frittelli, and Mallett 2013, 1). The funding was apparently included in the stimulus package "largely at the behest of President Obama," who had made rail a priority of his administra-tion (Peterman et al. 2013, 1). Obama (2009) appeared particularly keen on HSR, remarking that it would be "faster, cheaper and easier" to build such a rail network than to upgrade and expand existing roads and aviation networks. However, this optimism glosses over the fact that HSR requires a significant up-front capital outlay for development of the right-of-way, track, signals, and stations as well as ongoing operating costs (Peterman et al. 2013).

While Obama pitched the expenditure as an investment in the creation of a "world class" system, much of the funding was not allocated to what most experts would classify as HSR. There is, in fact, no single definition of HSR. In Europe, HSR is defined as either separate lines built for speeds of 155 miles per hour (mph) (250 kilometers per hour [km/h]), existing lines upgraded to speeds of 124 mph (200 km/h), or upgraded lines whose speeds are constrained by circumstances such as topography or urban development (Council of the European Union 1996). In contrast, in the US, the Federal Railroad Administration defines HSR in market terms as service that is time-competitive with other forms of transport (namely auto and air) in travel distances between 100 and 500 miles (161–805 km).

There are two main approaches to building HSR (Peterman et al. 2013). First, existing tracks and signaling can be improved to allow trains to reach high speeds. This is generally the cheaper option. Alternatively, new tracks can be dedicated exclusively to HSR services. ARRA provided funding for both types of projects. Money was allocated for upgrades to existing lines in five corridors: Seattle-Portland, Chicago-St. Louis, Chicago-Detroit, the Northeast Corridor, and Charlotte-Washington, DC. New "higher speed" lines between Cleveland and Cincinnati and Milwaukee and Madison were also funded. Finally, USD 3.5 billion went to two dedicated HSR passenger lines in Florida (USD 1.25 billion) and California (USD 2.25 billion). In 2010, following Obama's request for further budgetary appropriations to rail, California received an additional USD 901 million (of which USD 715 million was allocated to the dedicated HSR line) and Florida a further USD 800 million (Lombardi 2010).

Unfortunately for President Obama, the fate of his HSR dreams was in the hands of the state governments. In 2010, newly elected Republican governors in Florida, Ohio, and Wisconsin put the brakes on rail projects and returned the stimulus funding to the federal government. All three argued that although their respective state governments were asked to contribute very little to the construction phase of the projects, they would be responsible for ongoing operating costs. Governor John Walker of Wisconsin argued, "the bottom line is I don't believe long-term the state taxpayers can afford to have the high-speed line between Milwaukee and Madison" (*The Huffington Post* 2010). Governor John Kasich voiced similar concerns about the Cleveland-Cincinnati link and ridiculed the "high-speed" moniker, suggesting trains on the line would only average 39 mph and that the trip would not be able to compete with car travel (Fields 2010).

The quashing of the Orlando-Tampa line was the biggest blow to Obama's aspirations, as this was intended to be in many ways a demonstration project for how HSR could be achieved (Williams 2011). Florida Governor Rick Scott characterized HSR as an expensive boondoggle (*The Economist* 2011). This is despite a report from the Florida Department of Transportation (that the Governor was apparently briefed on before returning the stimulus funding) concluding that approving the line would have been a fiscally sound decision, and that the project would have made an annual surplus of USD 31–45 million within a decade of operation (Jackovics 2011). Senator Bill Nelson, a Florida Democrat, argued that Scott's decision was entirely political: "Florida lost a major new transportation system and 24,000 good-paying jobs simply because of political extremism, a mindset that we had to do it the governor's way or get lost" (Jackovics 2011).

The money returned by the three governors was largely redistributed to other projects, although Congress rescinded USD 400 million from the budget in 2011. As of December 2013, according to the Federal Railroad Administration, 99 percent of high-speed and intercity passenger rail funding appropriated since 2009 had been obligated. However, only about 17 percent of the total funds had been spent (Peterman 2013). By mid-2014, that number had increased to 23 percent (Grunwald 2014). By mid-2016, 37 of the 75 projects were complete, with an additional 19 projects scheduled for completion by the end of 2016 (Feinberg 2016).

With Florida out of the picture, the Los Angeles-San Francisco route became the sole dedicated HSR line to receive funding under ARRA. As of 2016, it was also the largest public-works program underway in the US (*The Economist* 2016). The plan is for trains to reach 220 mph and for the travel time between Los Angeles and San Francisco to be approximately two hours and forty minutes (Lombardi 2010). The California High Speed Rail Authority claimed that the project will create 100,000 jobs each year during construction. A second phase envisions extensions of the line to San Diego (in the south) and Sacramento (in the north). In 2008, California voters approved the sale of USD 9 billion in bonds to partly finance the project.

Despite the initial public support, the project has been plagued by controversy and at the time of writing, its future was still somewhat in doubt. Opponents unsuccessfully tried to put a proposition on the November 2016 election ballot calling for the bonds issued to help pay for the HSR project to be redirected to water projects. According to a piece in *The Economist* (2016), if this proposal had been successful (it was not) it "would have dealt a death blow" to the project by eliminating its biggest single source of funding.

Several court cases related to the line have also been launched. In one of the most serious cases, the Kings County Board of Supervisors and two Central Valley farmers alleged that the rail authority violated restrictions imposed by the original ballot that approved the bond issue to partially fund the project. This case was dismissed in March 2016, but the court left the door open for the case to be reheard at a future date if new evidence arose (*The Economist* 2016). The key complaint in the case and in other challenges to the project is that the estimated cost of the project has skyrocketed. In 2009, the total cost of the building phase for the initial Los Angeles-San Francisco line was estimated at USD 36.4 billion (in 2010 dollars). However, in 2012, the cost for a fully dedicated high-speed system rose to between USD 65.4 billion and USD 74.5 billion. An alternative system that would use some existing passenger rail lines was estimated at between USD 54.9 billion and USD 66.3 billion (both in 2010 dollars). The full high-speed plan was subsequently abandoned because of the hefty price tag. The most recent draft of the business plan has pegged the cost of the first phase at USD 64 billion (*The Economist* 2016).

Another issue of contention has been the choice to build the first segment of the line between Merced and Bakersfield in the Central Valley. While the expediency of building in this less-populated area is advantageous, especially considering the September 2017 statutory deadline for ARRA funds to be spent, the decision has been criticized because there will be little use of the segment if the rest of the line is not built (financing for the entire line has yet to be secured and the federal government has not doled out any money for HSR since 2011). In essence, it would be a "train to nowhere."

While environmentalists generally supported the initial proposal for HSR in California, they became more reluctant as time went on. Part of the reason for this, as Clewlow (2012) pointed out, was the concern that the project would absorb a significant portion of the scarce funds available for environmental initiatives under California's cap-and-trade emissions reduction program. However, it is also the case that some environmentalists question the greenhouse gas emissions reductions that can be achieved through the project. A major problem is the lack of clean energy sources to power the trains (Tutton 2011). Another issue is that claims about emissions reductions tend to rest heavily on assumed high passenger loads (i.e., substantial diversion of road and air traffic to more efficient rail travel). Moreover, predictions about the climate change mitigation impacts of HSR tend to ignore the carbon emissions associated with building railways.

Westin and Kågeson (2012) note that the extensive use of steel and concrete in HSR lines, which are highly energy intensive in their production, means that the greenhouse gas emissions associated with the construction and ongoing maintenance of HSR are often substantial. Chang and Kendall (2011) also stated that tunnels and aerial structures are particularly carbon intensive and can add greatly to the overall carbon footprint of an HSR line.

This does not mean that HSR does not make sense from a climate change mitigation perspective, it simply means that to offset the emissions associated with construction and maintenance, passenger volumes need to be substantial and the diverted traffic should primarily come from aviation (Westin and Kågeson 2012). Chang and Kendall (2011) conducted a life-cycle assessment on the California HSR proposal and concluded that construction emissions would be offset by reductions from diverted travel by about two years after HSR services began operating. The global warming effect (taking into account radiative forcing) would be offset after a further four years. While this seems reasonable, they cautioned that lower rates of ridership than anticipated by the project proponents would result in the lengthening of this recuperation period to 20 years or more.

A key determinant of ridership levels is, of course, the cost of HSR in relation to other modes of travel. This is affected by oil prices, taxes, and other climate change policies. As such, it can be argued that the adoption or rejection of policies that would encourage people to use HSR will strongly determine ridership rates. Other countries support HSR through complementary policies to incentivize rail travel (e.g., connections to public transit) and discourage alternative modes (e.g., high road tolls and high fuel taxes).

Ultimately, the environmental impacts of the California HSR project remain a question for future research. It is fair to conclude that, to date, "the bullet-train rhetoric from Obama and the White House's main train buff, Vice President Joe Biden, has not lived up to the bullet-train reality" (Grunwald 2014). However, the project could yet prove to be significant in the long term in changing how Americans approach domestic travel.

Whether the Obama Administration could have done more on HSR in ARRA is open to debate. There is the question of whether what Grunwald (2014) calls a "spread-it-thin strategy" of providing small grants to many projects is the best policy for this sector. He argues that this strategy "is hard to justify in a vacuum" because "it doesn't make much sense to upgrade trains from slow speeds to semi-slow speeds if they're never going to be able to compete with cars or planes." Others have also been critical of the decision to fund numerous Amtrak upgrades instead of focusing on the bigger HSR plans (Nixon 2014). Conversely, putting all your eggs in one basket is a risky strategy, especially when politics are so polarized that governors are willing to reject billions of dollars of federal funding for the sake of partisanship.

Whichever view one favors, it is indisputable that the lack of long-term federal funding represents a significant obstacle to HSR development in the US (Peterman et al. 2013). Post-ARRA, President Obama requested USD 1 billion per year of additional funding over five years, but only USD 2.5 billion was ever released.

A USD 53 billion proposal in 2011 was abandoned because Republicans gained a majority in the House of Representatives and stopped funding HSR altogether. To put this into perspective, in 2015 alone, China invested USD 126 billion in HSR and intends to spend USD 538 billion more from 2016 to 2020 (Zhaokun 2016). Grunwald (2014) concludes:

> There was never any chance that bullet trains would be whizzing all over America by now, but the reason there's no realistic prospect of that happening anytime soon has nothing to do with executive incompetence and everything to do with politics.

Summary and key policy recommendations

Despite the dire condition of much of the infrastructure in the three countries studied, and the significant long-term consequences of building brown infrastructure that locks in carbon emission trajectories for decades, the cases demonstrate that legitimately green infrastructure was not prioritized in the stimulus packages studied following the GFC.

One observation that cuts across the cases is the lack of a clear definition of green infrastructure. In this respect, Brown's (2011, 19) call for infrastructure that is "aligned with natural systems, integrated into social context, and designed for a changing climate" may provide a more robust definition for states to work with. In terms aligning with natural systems, it may not be possible to ever eliminate the impact of physical infrastructure on the natural environment. Stevens et al. (2006, 14) suggest that there is an "inherent tension" between infrastructure development and sustainability. Infrastructure requires the input of natural resources, creates waste, and competes with natural habitat for space. A goal of green infrastructure must, therefore, be to minimize these negative impacts.

Regarding the second aspect of the definition, Frischmann (2012, xi) argues, "we do not fully appreciate the social value that infrastructures provide." He explains, "infrastructures affect the behaviour of individuals, firms, households and other organisations by providing and shaping the available opportunities of these actors to participate in these systems and to interact with each other." As such, infrastructure that is "integrated into the social context" means infrastructure that is responsive to the needs of the community. An HSR to nowhere does not respond to the needs of the community, represents a waste of resources, and is, therefore, no "greener" than a road to nowhere.

With respect to climate change, the word "designed" is critical to the definition. Otherwise, any infrastructure development with incidental environmental benefits could be labeled green, diminishing the value of the definition. For example, while improved telecommunications infrastructure can reduce the need for land transport and greenhouse gas emissions (Stevens et al. 2006), it is not designed with this purpose in mind. Further, design should ideally aim to contribute to a country's greenhouse gas emission reduction targets and provide resilience to climate change (Rydge, Jacobs, and Granoff 2015). In other words, green infrastructure should both mitigate climate change and help make societies "adaptable to extreme weather conditions and rising sea levels" (Kennedy and Corfee-Morlot 2013, 773).

A further consideration in funding green infrastructure with stimulus money is the importance of a distinction between public works and private infrastructure. Frischmann (2012, xxiii) argues convincingly that "society is better off sharing infrastructure openly." However, if there is a need for private/commercial infrastructure (green or otherwise) that will provide no direct public benefit, then it should be funded by the private sector. This was the case with the NTL. The line primarily benefited a small number of mining companies. The Canadian public would have been better served if the Green Infrastructure Fund's resources had been allocated elsewhere.

If one adopts this type of definition of green infrastructure, it becomes clear that a fair amount of what has been referred to as "green infrastructure" in the context of the 2009 stimulus can be better characterized as green-washed infrastructure. The NTL and the Four Major Rivers Project were clearly not aligned with the natural environment or the needs of the community, or designed for a changing climate. California HSR has a greater claim on the green infrastructure label, although it remains to be seen whether it will live up to expectations.

Another conclusion that can be drawn from this chapter is that politics played a substantial role in decisions about how and where green stimulus funding was allocated. The power of corporate lobby groups drove investment decisions in Canada and Korea, with poor outcomes for the environment. In the US, state–federal power politics hindered the development of HSR. These cases serve as an important reminder to Green Keynesians, that while we may prefer the state to the market, this is in many ways choosing between the lesser of two evils. In most parts of the world, the state has a fairly poor record of promoting environmental protection. Further, decades of neoliberalism have left many sections of government captured by industry. The GFC was an opportunity for states to begin the process of reversing the trend of corporate interests dominating government, but it was never something that was going to happen overnight.

Green Keynesians may have been overly optimistic about what could be achieved in the immediate period following the outbreak of the GFC, but the hope that the state can be reformed to serve the people continues to drive many popular movements, such as that which propelled Senator Bernie Sanders to the limelight in 2016. While it is important to be aware of the current limitations of the state, it is premature to conclude that Green Keynesianism is an unrealistic endeavor. Instead, the key lesson is that the objectives of Green Keynesianism cannot be achieved through green stimulus alone. A broader package of reform, one that goes even further than progressive Green New Deal proposals that were made in the wake of the GFC, is required.

7   Technological innovation and the venture capitalist state

An unofficial global "agreement" was thus reached out of the economic crisis, and that agreement was that the time for clean technologies had come (again). A green energy revolution seemed to be within the realm of possibilities.

Mariana Mazzucato (2015a)

The effect of major economic crises on innovation – the transformation of ideas into new products and services – is not clear-cut. In theory, a downturn can initiate a Schumpeterian process of "creative destruction" that opens new opportunities for innovation (OECD 2012b). However, in practice, it appears that the more significant effect is negative. The drop in demand for products, the potential loss of public funding to support innovation, and the increased risk aversion of private venture capitalists all contributed to a decline in innovation during the GFC (OECD 2012b).

Innovation is recognized both as a lynchpin for economic growth (Rotman 2009; OECD 2010) and critical for tackling climate change, although as noted in Chapter 2, the degree to which new technology can be relied upon in greening the economy is debated. There are also important concerns about the appropriateness of some proposed technological innovations with, for example, CCS viewed by many environmentalists and some scientists as excessively risky because of the potential for stored CO_2 to escape (e.g., Greenpeace International 2008; Zoback and Gorelick 2012).

The energy sector is a particularly important area in which technological advancements are necessary to reduce emissions. However, strong legacy technologies (in coal, oil, and nuclear power) and risk-averse investors tend to impede innovation (Bonvillian and Van Atta 2011). Two financing gaps or "valleys of death" have been deemed responsible for preventing the adoption of many promising new technologies (Jenkins and Mansur 2011; Jenkins et al. 2012). The first is the Technology Valley of Death. This valley sits between the early research stage of technological development and the proof-of-concept stage, in which a working prototype is produced. This valley exists because most private investors view risks as too high and the potential returns as eventuating too far in the future. The second is the Commercialization Valley of Death, which exists between the time a technology is proved in concept and when it is ready for the market. The high costs of bringing design and manufacturing processes to commercial scale combined with the risk that the technology will not be profitable can dissuade private investors at this point in the innovation process.

While these valleys exist for most forms of technology, they are considered particularly difficult to bridge in the energy sector. The energy sector has high capital requirements (especially when compared to, for example, many developments in the information technology sector) and a long period of time is required to bring a new technology to the market (Jenkins and Mansur 2011). Jenkins and Mansur (2011, 7) also point out that "large, risk-averse corporations dominate the energy market" and that the industry has been reluctant to fund innovation because fossil fuels have remained competitive and profitable (in part, due to continued government subsidies). A historical lack of successful venture capital investments in energy has further contributed to risk aversion in the private sector (GAO 2012; Branscomb and Keller 1998). Mazucatto (2015b, 143) describes venture capitalists as "impatient capitalists," unwilling to sustain the risks and costs of technological development over long periods. In her view, which is echoed by others, the "patient capital" that is required is more likely to come from the state (Edenhofer and Stern 2009; Mazucatto 2015a). Mazucatto (2015a) argues that nearly all technological revolutions (e.g., the internet) have involved a massive investment from the state. However, although the idea of an "entrepreneurial" or "venture capitalist" state has become more palatable to many in the wake of the GFC, it remains a controversial proposition.

The idea that governments should fund basic research is not often disputed, but there are still some who question whether it is an appropriate use of fiscal stimulus. Basic research fails the timeliness test because it requires the development of detailed proposals before work can begin, and projects that are already planned are typically hard to scale up quickly due to shortages in skilled labor. Morris, Nivola, and Schultze (2012, 11) note that "research is intrinsically ill-suited for a fiscal stimulus … A major research or demonstration project is unlike, say, a 'shovel-ready' highway project." Another criticism is that investments are unlikely to create many jobs, and because research relies on highly specialized skilled labor, it is also "unlikely to put money into the pockets of people who need it most" (Morris et al. 2012, 11). Viewed from the perspective of researchers, the restrictions of stimulus funding (particularly the temporary criterion) can hamper the long-term requirements of innovation (Rotman 2009).

However, when it comes to the commercialization of a technology, these arguments become less significant. At the same time, debates about the appropriate role of the state in the process become more polarized. Many orthodox economists and conservative politicians prefer to leave the commercial end of the innovation process to the market. They argue that when the government operates in this space, it simply crowds out private venture capital. This is considered suboptimal because the market is much better than the government at "picking winners" (*The Economist* 2010). Summers, a key economic adviser to the White House during the GFC, famously said in an email that government is a "crappy venture capitalist" (Rampton and Hosenball 2011). Others admit that both markets and governments can make poor investment choices, but that "in markets – better at discovering and responding to new information – failures happen more quickly and cheaply" (Less 2012, 9). Those who subscribe to these views but also want to tackle climate change argue that a government-set carbon price will sufficiently drive private-sector investment in technological innovation (McIlveen 2010 in Gross et al. 2012). Such policies are sometimes described as "technology-neutral" because they supposedly promote innovation without picking specific winners (Haley 2017).

However, others argue that technology-neutral policies promote the adoption of near-commercial technologies, but fail to produce new technological options (Haley 2017). Further, it is disputed that government support for new technologies crowds out private venture capitalism. To the contrary, some suggest that it may actually crowd it in. For example, Brander, Du, and Hellmann (2014) argue that there is considerable evidence to demonstrate that government venture capitalism enlarges the total pool of venture capital available. Their study found that most companies that received only government investment would not have received private funding if government funding was unavailable. Those that had mixed funding sources tended to attract more private venture capital than those that had no government funding. Branscomb and Keller (1999) further argue that while governments are held to a higher standard than private investors because they are investing taxpayers' money, there is no evidence that they are worse than private venture capitalists at picking winners. Both public and private sectors have to deal with the problem of having incomplete information on which to base decisions (Haley 2017).

During the GFC, the notion that the state should play a significant role in technological innovation seemed to win out over the traditional market approach. The venture industry was hit hard by the GFC, with new investor commitments to venture capital firms in 2009 falling by nearly 50 percent over the previous year (House Committee on Science and Technology 2010; Block, De Vries, and Sandner 2012). Renewable energy projects were left particularly vulnerable as venture capitalists became more risk averse and less interested in early stage investments (Wessner and Wolff 2012; Wurzelman 2012). In this environment, there was more widespread support for government intervention. However, the technology-neutral/market fundamentalist view would come to dominate again quickly, particularly in the US, after the recovery had begun.

This chapter examines how stimulus measures taken in response to the GFC were used to catalyze technological innovation in the energy sector and increase the deployment and commercialization of existing clean energy technologies. While governments in all five case countries invested some stimulus funding in basic research and engaged in some degree of state venture capitalism, the programs in Australia, Canada, and the US are broadly similar and thus, the easiest to compare. While funding was invested in a variety of technologies in each of these countries, this chapter focuses on the stimulus provided to CCS projects and renewable energy projects.

Cases: Carbon capture and storage

Australia: Carbon Capture and Storage Flagships

Two large-scale demonstration ("flagship") programs were funded in the 2009 Budget – one for CCS and one for solar power generation. As noted in Chapter 1, it is questionable whether the flagship programs should be considered stimulus measures. The government had committed to introducing a Carbon Pollution Reduction Scheme (an emissions trading scheme) prior to the onset of the GFC and these programs complemented that initiative. Nevertheless, the 2009 Budget measures are generally included in calculations of Australia's green stimulus. The flagship programs provide some interesting lessons in terms of government support for technological development. Therefore, they are discussed in this chapter.

The CCS Flagships program received AUD 2 billion (USD 1.6 billion) in new funding in the 2009 Budget, and AUD 425 million (USD 336 million) in re-allocated funding. The aim was to create 1,000 MW of low-emissions power generation and demonstrate a range of technologies to capture carbon dioxide from coal-fired power stations (Styles and Talberg 2009). It was noted by the Australian government that this was in line with the G8 target for 20 industrial-scale CCS projects to be operating by 2020 (Commonwealth of Australia 2010).

The key eligibility requirements for CCS Flagship projects were that they involve (1) multi-user infrastructure (development of storage sites in high-emission regions and/or pipeline infrastructure to transport CO_2 from regional areas); and (2) integrated capture and storage (e.g., coal gasification, post-combustion capture, and oxy-firing) (Department of Industry, Innovation and Science n.d.). The process of selection involved state and territory governments nominating projects they would be prepared to support financially (Harman 2010). After a period of independent assessment, it was expected that projects would be announced in August 2010. Engineering, construction, and commissioning were intended to take place from 2010 to 2015.

Four projects were shortlisted for the program in December 2009: two Integrated Gasification Combined Cycle (IGCC) coal-fired power stations in Queensland (Wandoan and ZeroGen) and two integrated multi-user capture, transport, and storage infrastructure projects in Western Australia (the South West Hub) and in Victoria (CarbonNet) (Department of Industry, Innovation and Science n.d.). The Wandoan project received between AUD 8 and 50 million (USD 6–40 million) in CCS Flagship funding for a project pre-feasibility study and was subsequently canceled (Browne and Swann 2017). The ZeroGen project also received funding (AUD 38.5 million [USD 30.4 million]) for a pre-feasibility study, but did not progress beyond this stage. The proponents of that project failed to locate a suitable underground storage site for the captured CO_2. The unlikelihood that the "degree of public funding support required for both development and ongoing operational phases" would be available was also cited as a key reason for the termination of the project (Garnett, Greig, and Oettinger 2014, 61). It has been estimated that the project would have cost AUD 6.9 billion (USD 5.5 billion) (Herzog 2016).

The South West Hub, which received AUD 52 million (USD 41 million) (the first installment of AUD 330 million [USD 261] million that was allocated to the project) from CCS Flagships, involved an initial four-year period of research to determine whether the proposed region (the Collie Basin) was suitable for CO_2 storage. As of mid-2017, it was still unclear if the project would proceed. A major obstacle for the project was that the partner intended to act as the primary source of CO_2 was unable to secure a supply of coal. All other partners that could have supplied CO_2 pulled out of the project in 2015 (Browne and Swann 2017). If the project does finally proceed, it is unlikely to be operational before 2025, ten years later than originally mandated by the CCS Flagships program. Finally, the CarbonNet project, which has received AUD 95 million (USD 75 million) from CCS Flagships, was still active but running several years behind schedule at the time of writing (Department of Industry, Innovation, Science, Research and Tertiary Education 2012). The proponents aim to have a storage formation declared and an injection license secured for CarbonNet by 2020 (five years after the project was meant to be up and running).

Funding for CCS Flagships was cut in almost every successive budget after it was first announced, to under AUD 300 million (USD 237 million) as of the 2016 Budget (Browne and Swann 2017). The 2017–2018 Budget flagged CCS Flagships for termination in 2018–2019 (Commonwealth of Australia 2017).

The CCS Flagships program has been criticized by outsiders and those directly involved in the process. One major factor in the failure of the program is that over the period it was running, political circumstances dramatically changed, which affected the business case for CCS in Australia. The emissions trading scheme that the flagship programs were meant to complement was never passed into law and Rudd lost his position as prime minister and leader of the Labor government in 2010. Eventually, another Labor government passed a carbon-pricing scheme into law in 2011 under the leadership of Julia Gillard. However, the Liberal-National Coalition led by Tony Abbott was elected to office in 2013 on an "axe the (carbon) tax" platform. When the carbon-pricing scheme was repealed in 2014, only two years after it first came into effect, it left little reason for industry to invest in CCS. The design of the CCS Flagships program required significant industry buy-in for projects to be successful. However, even if the scheme has been left in place, it arguably did not set a high enough price on carbon to motivate private investors to invest in extremely costly CCS technology.

There have also been other issues identified with the design of CCS Flagships that made the program problematic even when separated from the broader political context. For example, Garnett et al. (2014, 446), who led the ZeroGen project, argue that the time frame of the program (2010–2015) caused "deployment risk," which would have required major investments in the plant while exploration for a suitable storage site was still in progress. They suggest that this was akin to "starting to develop a gas-fired power station before any gas is discovered" (Garnett et al. 2014, 446). They also argue that having start-date qualifying conditions created a "disincentive for candour from project proponents with respect to actual project maturity and cost and schedule risk" (Garnett et al. 2014, 11).

Further, they propose that having a competitive bidding process for CCS Flagships "drove proponents to commit to accelerated environmental assessment schedules" and that trying to speed up such processes is high risk, especially for first-of-a-kind projects, because it "can cause distrust and suspicion among certain stakeholders and the community" and "requires some impacts to be considered in generic terms only leaving residual permitting and approval risks that cannot be resolved prior to the commitment of substantial project funds" (Garnett et al. 2014, 26).

Canada: Clean Energy Fund

The Government of Canada announced the CAD 1 billion (USD 880 million) Clean Energy Fund as part of the 2009 stimulus to support cutting-edge technologies that can reduce greenhouse gas and other air emissions in energy production. Funding was allocated in three areas: large-scale CCS demonstration projects (CAD 650 million [USD 572 million]), Renewable Energy and Clean Energy Systems projects (CAD 200 million [USD 176 million]), and clean energy R&D within federal government departments (CAD 150 million [USD 132 million]). As noted in Chapter 1, in 2010, the CAD 1 billion (USD 880 million) budget for the Clean Energy Fund was reduced when CAD 205 million (USD 180 million) was transferred to the ecoENERGY Retrofit – Homes initiative (discussed in Chapter 4). As a result, the funding available for each program was reduced to CAD 610 million (CAD 537 million) for CCS, CAD 146 million (USD 128 million) for Renewable Energy and Clean Energy Systems, and CAD 24 million (USD 21 million) for R&D.

In the end, only CAD 150 million (USD 132 million) was spent on CCS. The majority of this (CAD 120 million [USD 106 million]) was invested in Shell Canada's Quest CCS facility to capture CO_2 from the Athabasca Oil Sands project near Edmonton. Alberta's oil sands, also known as tar sands, are one of the world's largest petroleum reservoirs. Historically, it was too expensive to extract oil from the mixture of sand, clay, and water found there, but advances in technology have made it feasible provided the global oil price remains above a certain level (which differs depending on the type of extraction technology used). Throughout much of the first decade of the twenty-first century, the oil price remained high (with a dip during the GFC). As a result, Canada became a major petroleum-producing country. Since 2014, this has changed as oil prices have dropped substantially.

In addition to costing more, extracting bitumen and other heavy crude oil requires more energy than the production of lighter and more accessible forms of crude oil. Consequently, oil sands production produces about 1.6 times more emissions than conventional production per barrel of oil produced (Handwerk 2011). This makes it an obvious candidate for CCS technology, but there has been little interest demonstrated by industry. Shell Canada, a subsidiary of Royal Dutch Shell, was at one point a major player in Alberta's oil sands as the majority shareholder and operator of the Athabasca Oil Sands project. The Quest CCS facility, which cost over CAD 1.3 billion (USD 1.1 billion), captures CO_2 from the Scotford Upgrader, which is part of the Athabasca Oil Sands project.

The upgrading process is considered the "low-hanging fruit" of CCS in the oil sands context because it produces a nearly pure CO_2 stream (Handwerk 2011).

In addition to being awarded funding from the federal government under the Clean Energy Fund, Shell Canada received CAD 745 million (USD 656 million) from the Province of Alberta for the Quest CCS facility. Shell Canada will also receive two-for-one carbon credits for ten years from the Alberta government under the Specified Gas Emitters Regulation (i.e., the company gets two tons worth of credits for every ton of CO_2 it buries). The credits were originally valued at CAD 15/ton (USD 13/ton), increasing to CAD 30/ton (USD 26/ton) by 2017 (Pembina Institute 2015). It is worth noting that the Pembina Institute, which is generally supportive of CCS playing a role in reducing greenhouse gas emissions, argues that this additional subsidy undermines the overall goal of the project because it allows total allowable emissions from industrial emitters to increase, and at great expense to the Canadian taxpayer (Stewart 2012).

Shell began the planning and preliminary design of the Quest facility in late 2009. Construction of the capture system followed in 2012 and work on the pipeline that would transport the CO_2 to the storage site began in late 2013. The Quest project began commercial operations in November 2015. Shell divested most of its oil sands interests in 2017, but remains the operator of the Quest CCS facility (Shell Canada 2017).

Within a year of commencing operations, the Quest facility had successfully captured and stored one million tons of CO_2. While this may sound like a lot, it is only 35 percent of the emissions from one stage of the extraction process (known as upgrading) for a single oil sands project. This stage generally only makes up 40 percent of emissions from the total process, so the Quest project only eliminates 14 percent of overall emissions from the Athabasca Oil Sands project. Further, as noted above, upgrading is the cheapest and easiest stage at which to apply CCS; doing so at the other stages of oil sands extraction would be even more costly. Nevertheless, NRCAN has lauded the project, claiming that the "success of Quest proves that the technology is feasible and functioning and can be applied in industries such as oil and gas, fertilizer, chemicals, cement, and other large emission sources" (NRCAN 2016b).

A second project funded by the Clean Energy Fund – the Alberta Carbon Trunk Line – received CAD 30 million (USD 26 million) in addition to CAD 33 million (USD 29 million) from another federal government program and CAD495 million (USD436 million) from the Province of Alberta. The total project cost was estimated to be CAD 1.2 billion (USD 1.1 billion). After several delays, construction was expected to begin in 2017. It is worth noting that this is an enhanced oil recovery project. Once completed, the Carbon Trunk Line will capture CO_2 from various industrial sources, transport it through a 240-km pipeline, inject it into depleted oil reservoirs to help extract light oil, and finally store it. The project aims to transport and store 14.6 million ton of CO_2 annually. As noted on the project proponent's website, the process of extracting oil from depleted reserves using captured CO_2 has been used throughout North America for over 30 years. In other words, it is not technologically innovative. Additionally, it is hard to argue that it is a "clean energy" technology, given that it is being used to extract further fossil fuels from the ground.

An additional project, proposed by TransAlta Corp and dubbed "Pioneer," was allocated CAD 342 million (USD 301 million) from the federal government, of which CAD 316 million (USD 278 million) was from the Clean Energy Fund, and CAD 436 million (USD 384 million) from the Province of Alberta. The proposal was for a CCS project connected to the Keephills 3 coal-fired power station. TransAlta planned to sell the captured CO_2 to oil and gas companies for use in enhanced oil recovery (Tait 2012). The company canceled the project in 2012 because "the market for CO_2 sales and the value of emissions reductions in Alberta and Canada are not sufficient" (Lopoukhine 2014).

United States: Carbon capture and storage demonstration projects

The US has been conducting R&D on CCS since the late 1990s, through the DOE's Clean Coal Program. However, this program was not intended to support demonstration projects. Another program – the Clean Coal Power Initiative (CCPI) – was set up in the early 2000s for this purpose, providing up to 50 percent of costs for projects (Herzog 2016). Of the USD 3.4 billion allocated to CCS under ARRA, USD 800 million went into the CCPI to help fund to six projects (see Table 7.1). An industrial CCS program was allocated USD 1.52 billion in stimulus, which was earmarked for three industrial CCS demonstration projects. An additional project known as FutureGen 2.0 (discussed below) was allocated USD 1 billion. USD 50 million went into site characterization activities in geologic formations, while USD 20 million was spent on training and research grants. Finally, USD 10 million was invested in program direction (DOE n.d.a).

Of the six CCPI projects funded, five were canceled. The project that was not canceled, Petra Nova, began commercial operations in 2017. At that time, it was the world's largest working post-combustion CO_2 capture system (Global CCS Institute 2017). The captured CO_2 is used for enhanced oil recovery. As for the industrial CCS projects funded under ARRA, one (Leucadia Energy) was canceled due to rising costs and two are currently operational (Air Products and Illinois Industrial). Air Products is an enhanced oil recovery project. Illinois Industrial involves CO_2 capture from an ethanol production plant.

FutureGen 2.0 is perhaps the most well-known CCS demonstration project in the US. This project has a long history, with its first iteration announced in 2003. At that point, an alliance of coal companies and coal power providers came together to build a power plant with CCS for the purposes of R&D. The US government was to contribute up to USD 1 billion. This project was canceled in 2008.

In August 2010, FutureGen 2.0 emerged as a USD 1.65 billion project with USD 1 billion covered by ARRA. The alliance of proponents was somewhat different, and the plan was changed to a retrofit of an existing coal-fired power station as opposed to a new build. The aim was to capture 90 percent of CO_2 emissions from the plant, which would amount to approximately 1 MMT CO_2–e/yr (National Energy Technology Laboratory 2017). At the time, it was one of the

Table 7.1 CCS projects that received stimulus funding

Proponent (project name)	Stimulus (USD million)	Status
AUSTRALIA		
Glencore (Wandoan)	6–40	Canceled
Queensland government (ZeroGen)	30.4	Canceled
Western Australian government (SouthWest Hub)	41	Possibly proceeding
Victorian government (CarbonNet)	75	Possibly proceeding
CANADA		
Shell Canada (Quest)	106	Began commercial operations in 2015
Enhance Energy (Alberta Trunk Line)	26.4	Under construction
TransAlta (Pioneer)	301	Canceled
UNITED STATES		
FutureGen 2.0	1,000	Canceled
Basin Electric (Antelope Valley)	100 (CCPI)	Canceled
Hydrogen Energy (HECA)	408 (CCPI)	Canceled
AEP (Mountaineer)	334 (CCPI)	Canceled
Southern (Plant Barry)	295 (CCPI)	Canceled
NRG Energy (Petra Nova)	167 (CCPI)	Began commercial operations in 2017
Summit Power (Texas Clean Energy Project)	450 (CCPI) *reduced to 346 when ARRA funds expired	Canceled
Leucadia Energy	261	Canceled
Air Products & Chemicals	284	Began commercial operations in 2013
Archer Daniels Midland (ADM) (IL Industrial CCS Project)	141	Began commercial operations in 2017

Source: Compiled by the author from data provided in Browne and Swann (2017), NRCAN (2016b), Herzog (2016), and DOE (n.d.a.).

largest CCS projects in the world (Tollefson 2015). Progress on FutureGen 2.0 was impeded by the lack of a storage site (the site identified in FutureGen 1.0 was withdrawn because the owners of the site were not interested in the new plan, which did not involve the construction of a new plant on location), the owner of the power plant to be retrofitted withdrew from the project, and the project faced a lawsuit from the Sierra Club over the lack of a federal permit under the *Clean Air Act* (only a state permit had been issued by Illinois) (Herzog 2016). As a result, the project proponents were unable to meet the ARRA funding deadline of September 2015 and the DOE canceled the project. The CEO of the FutureGen 2.0 alliance, Ken Humphreys, argued that were it not for the deadline, the project would have been successful. He has also argued that the Sierra Club legal challenge created a cloud over the project, dissuading potential investors and creating the substantial delays that ultimately killed the project (Herzog 2016). However, others do not see anything unique about FutureGen's downfall. Burton (2015) suggests:

> The demise of FutureGen has followed the same old pattern that has bedevilled numerous other CCS projects. Initial hype and generous public support have been followed by cost overruns, engineering problems, wariness of lenders and public and utility opposition.

For Exelon, one of the nation's largest utilities, which dropped out of FutureGen 2.0 in 2013, the problem with the project (and CCS more generally) is that "customers should not be forced to pay enormous above-market charges for electricity" (quoted in Martin 2015).

Cases: Renewable energy

Australia: Solar Flagships

The 2009 Budget allocated AUD 1.6 billion (USD 1.3 billion) over six years for the development and demonstration of large-scale solar technologies. Most of the funding was new, although AUD 135 million (USD 107 million) of the budget was transferred from the existing AUD 435 million (USD 344 million) Renewable Energy Demonstration Program. AUD 370 million (USD 292 million) was cut from the Solar Flagship's budget in 2011. Ironically, some of this money was redirected to assist flood-affected areas in Queensland following tropical Cyclone Yasi (as noted in Chapter 1, cyclones are expected to become more intense with climate change).

The Solar Flagships program was created within the Department of Resources, Energy and Tourism and overseen by the Australian Solar Institute. The program provided financial support to large solar projects with a generation capacity of at least 150 MW that would be completed no later than the end of 2015 (Department of Industry, Innovation, Science, Research and Tertiary Education 2012). The program also had a rather lengthy list of other eligibility criteria. The project proponent had to have a research partner that was on a list of eligible higher education institutions, research institutions, or vocational education and training institutions (Department of Industry, Innovation, Science, Research and Tertiary Education 2012). The government in the state or territory where the project was to be built also had to have already approved it. More onerously, the proponent had to prove that they had funding from other sources at a ratio of two-to-one (i.e., two dollars from other sources for every one dollar of Solar Flagship funding) and had secured an off-take agreement (power purchase agreement) with a utility or third-party energy user.

By 2011, 52 projects had been proposed under the first round of the program, but only two were set to receive any funding and a second round of funding was cast into doubt. The two projects were the Solar Dawn project and the Moree Solar Farm. AUD 464 million (USD 367 million) was allocated to the Solar Dawn project, a 250-MW solar thermal power plant that was to be built near Chinchilla in South West Queensland. However, in June 2012 the Queensland Liberal-National (conservative) government terminated its AUD 75 million (USD 59 million) investment in the project, and consequently, the proponents were no longer able to meet the Solar Flagship deadline for financial close (Kelly 2012). The project was also unable to secure a power purchase agreement (the same was true for Moree).

In 2012, the Solar Flagships program was reopened for new applications. Three projects – from AGL, Infigen-Suntech, and TRUenergy (later renamed EnergyAustralia) – were shortlisted along with a revised version of the Moree Solar Farm. Oversight of the program was transferred from the Australian Solar Institute to the newly formed Australian Renewable Energy Agency (ARENA) in July 2012. While the shortlisted Solar Flagship projects were referred to ARENA for consideration, this essentially marked the end of the program. Solar Flagships funding went into ARENA's general funding pool to be allocated in accordance with ARENA's General Funding Strategy (personal communication with E. Vickery, ARENA, June 30, 2017).

In the end, ARENA provided the Nyngan and Broken Hill Solar farms, owned by energy company AGL, with AUD 166.7 million (USD 132 million), and these projects are often referred to as the first and only Solar Flagships. The Nyngan plant generates 102 MW (enough to power 39,000 homes) and the Broken Hill plant generates 53 MW (enough to power 20,000 homes). These projects were considered eligible for Solar Flagships funding only because they had an aggregate nominal capacity of 150 MW. The Moree Solar Farm eventually secured AUD 101.7 million (USD 80 million) from ARENA (as well as debt on commercial terms from the government's Clean Energy Finance Corporation) for a revised and substantially smaller version of the original project. It was built in 2015–2016 and now powers 15,000 homes. The Solar Dawn project was terminated in 2012.

The Solar Flagships program was not as controversial in Australia as the pink batts insulation scheme discussed in Chapter 4. Nevertheless, it had a fair number of critics from both ends of the political spectrum. The main criticism leveled at the government was that the program had failed to get projects off the ground. Parkinson (2012) argues that it was "a shocking indictment on the government" that it would:

> go to the 2013 election with not a single panel or heliostat installed from its $1.5 billion Solar Flagships program, despite more than 50 projects worth some $80 billion jostling for a bite of the action when it was first announced in 2009.

Both the federal Liberal-National Coalition and the Greens questioned the project selection process under Solar Flagships and why proposals without power purchase agreements were selected over ones that had secured them.

McConnell (2012) notes that there were two main difficulties for project proponents seeking to obtain power purchase agreements. First, there is a soft market for renewable energy certificates in Australia. Under the large-scale renewable energy target, retailers are obliged to purchase certificates produced by a renewable source. In a previous certificate scheme, a combination of factors resulted in solar PV creating an excess of certificates (ultimately collapsing the scheme). Retailers "banked" these excess certificates, and subsequently there has been little need for retailers to enter into new agreements with renewable energy generators. Second, renewable energy developers are almost entirely reliant on securing a power purchase agreement with one of the "big three" retailers (AGL, EnergyAustralia, and Origin Energy). The big retailers are now developing their own renewable energy projects (e.g., AGL received Solar Flagship funding and EnergyAustralia applied for it), removing the need to involve third parties and sign power purchase agreements with other developers.

The scale of the projects that Solar Flagships focused on has also been identified as a problem. At the time of the program, sites with sufficient capacity for 150-MW projects within the grid were limited (ARENA 2017). The only funded projects were smaller (with only an aggregate capacity of 150 MW). AGL (2013) argues that this is preferable for a number of reasons: small solar plants require a smaller area of land that would have less impact on flora and fauna than a larger site; the local community is likely to be more accepting of a small solar plant than a large solar plant; smaller plants are faster to build; multiple plants provide the opportunity to better manage increasing peak demands during summer in multiple locations, rather than at only one location; geographic diversity reduces weather risk (sites are unlikely to be affected by unfavorable conditions at the same time); and job creation, skills transfer, and economic development occur in multiple areas, rather than only one.

Canada: Clean Energy Fund

Eighteen small-scale projects, covering a wide variety of technologies, were funded under the "Renewable Energy and Clean Energy Systems" section of Canada's Clean Energy Fund. The average allocation of funding was CAD 6.3 million (USD 5.5 million) and the average total project cost was CAD 17.2 million (USD 15.1 million). The Clean Energy Fund provided, on average, 37 percent of required funding. Table 7.2 outlines the projects funded by the Clean Energy Fund.

There was a mix of success and failure in the program's portfolio, as can be expected in any program of this nature. It is not possible to describe all the projects here, but it is worth highlighting one success story, because it provides an interesting contrast to the Canadian case presented in Chapter 6, where a hugely expensive transmission line was justified as "green infrastructure" on the basis that it allowed a remote First Nations community to stop using diesel electricity generation. It was argued in Chapter 6 that the community of Iskut in Northern BC, now serviced by the NTL, could have been taken off diesel power with the development of local small-scale renewable energy projects. This is precisely what occurred with the Cowessess First Nation Wind and Storage Demonstration

Table 7.2 Renewable energy projects in Canada's Clean Energy Fund

Project title	Proponent	Clean energy funding (CAD million)	Total project cost (CAD million)	Key outcomes
Advanced Biomass Gasification for Heat and Power Demonstration Project	University of British Columbia	10.8	28	Should displace over 9,000 tons of fossil fuel-based CO_2 annually by 2017
Bioenergy Optimization Program Demonstration	Manitoba Hydro	2.8	6	Problems encountered with the various technologies being demonstrated, but some interest in further deployment
Urban Waste to Electricity Generation	Harvest Power	5	22.5	Construction of the first "high solids anaerobic digester" in Canada and demonstration of its commercial viability
Biomass-Based Urban Central Heating Demonstration	SSQ, Société Immobilière Inc.	4.7	13.3	Residential development using 30% less energy than conventional developments
Cold-Climate Air Source Heat Pump Demonstration	Ecologix Heating Technologies Inc.	4.5	13	Over 50 heat pumps installed; potential for this company to be the first to bring this technology to the market
Solar Colwood	City of Colwood	2.1	11.9	Modeled energy savings of 4.96 million kWh/year, greenhouse gas reductions of 651 tons of CO_2e/year, and total cost savings for the residents of Colwood of $525,552 per year at utility prices at the time of the project
Energy OASIS (Open Access to Sustainable Intermittent Sources) Project	British Columbia Institute of Technology	4.4	9.1	Demonstration of integration of renewables, storage, electric vehicle charging loads, and intelligent controls in a fully islandable and smart microgrid environment
Electricity Load Demonstration Project	New Brunswick Power Corporation	15.6	32	Demonstrated the technical feasibility of customer load shifting through an Intelligent Load Management system

(Continued)

Table 7.2 (Continued)

Project title	Proponent	Clean energy funding (CAD million)	Total project cost (CAD million)	Key outcomes
Energy Management Business Intelligence Platform Development and Demonstration	Power Measurement Ltd	3.6	10	Demonstrated the capabilities of a software platform to provide insight into the energy consumption of commercial buildings based on data provided by intelligent electric meters
Interactive Smart Grid Zone Demonstration in Québec	Hydro Québec	7.5	49.8	48 vehicle-charging stations installed and 30 electrical vehicles launched; 5,800 new-generation residential smart meters installed
Clean Power by Waste Heat Recovery from Reciprocating Engines	Great Northern Power Corporation	0.98	3.2	Some problems experienced with the technology; field testing ongoing
Community-Based Geothermal Demonstration in Remote First Nations Community	Borealis Geopower Inc.	0.47	1.1	Existence of significant geothermal energy reserves identified, but as of April 2013, the proponent was unable to obtain a power purchase agreement
Tidal Energy Project in the Bay of Fundy	Fundy Ocean Research Center for Energy (FORCE)	23	50.7	North America's first in-stream tidal energy demonstration facility was established
Water Wall Turbine Dent Island Tidal Power Generation Project	Water Wall Turbine Inc.	2.3	5.2	Demonstration of the potential for commercial development of tidal energy
Wind and Storage Demonstration in a First Nations Community, Cowessess First Nation	Cowessess First Nation	2.8	6.9	See below

(Continued)

Table 7.2 (Continued)

Project title	Proponent	Clean energy funding (CAD million)	Total project cost (CAD million)	Key outcomes
Wind Energy R&D Park and Storage System for Innovation in Grid Integration	Wind Energy Institute of Canada (WEICan)	12	24.8	Demonstration of the practical application of an energy storage system
Energy Storage and Demand Response for improved reliability in an outage-prone community	BC Hydro	6.5	13.5	Demonstration of clean back-up power through battery storage; avoided greenhouse gas emissions
Utility Scale Electricity Storage Demonstration Using New and Re-purposed Lithium Ion Automotive Batteries	Electrovaya	3.7	7.6	Demonstration of advanced battery technology
Total		113	309	

Source: Compiled by the author from data provided in NRCAN (2016c).

in Saskatchewan, which was allocated CAD 2.8 million (USD 2.5 million) from the Clean Energy Fund. This is an example of how remote communities can reduce their emissions at relatively low cost and with enduring social benefits. The Cowessess First Nation designed, developed, and arranged financing for a wind-storage system that is now owned and operated by its members. A power purchase agreement was secured with SaskPower, which now pays approximately CAD 100/MWh (USD 88/MWh) for the electricity generated. This provided CAD 215,800 (USD 189,904) in revenue to the community in 2014–2015 (Saskatchewan Research Council 2017). The community now intends to expand the capabilities of the site to include a 200-kW solar array. By displacing natural gas power generation, greenhouse gas emissions have been reduced by an estimated 969 MT CO_2-e/yr.

In 2017, the Green Budget Coalition (comprising 19 Canadian environmental organizations) recommended that the federal government provide CAD 1 billion (USD 880 million) annually to maintain the Clean Energy Fund, highlighting the importance of this particular project, noting that "previous investments by the federal government in this area have made a meaningful difference in communities like the Cowessess First Nation in Saskatchewan" (Green Budget Coalition 2017, 13).

Although this project is widely considered a success, other projects in the program did not fare as well. An evaluation of the program conducted by NRCAN (2014) found that the reporting and accountability requirements of the program were onerous and the time frame for projects was too short. Some project proponents also had difficulty obtaining power purchase agreements, as was the case with Australia's Solar Flagships program.

United States: Advanced Research Projects Agency – Energy

In 2007, the National Academies released a report entitled "Rising Above the Gathering Storm: Energizing and Employing America for a Brighter Economic Future." This report argued that the US government needed to stimulate innovation and develop clean, affordable, and reliable energy. The sole recommendation of the report was the creation of a new government organization – the Advanced Research Projects Agency – Energy (ARPA-E) (National Academy of Sciences, National Academy of Engineering, and Institute of Medicine 2007). ARPA-E was founded in 2007 under the *America COMPETES Act* but the first time it received funding (USD 400 million) was under ARRA in 2009. The agency's mission is to catalyze technological development that will result in (1) reduced energy imports, (2) reduced greenhouse gases emissions, and (3) improved energy efficiency across all sectors of the US economy (Manser et al. 2016).

ARPA-E was modeled on the highly successful Defense Advanced Research Projects Agency (DARPA) program, which is a small arm of the federal government tasked in 1958 with preventing "technological surprises" (like Sputnik) that would threaten national security (Fuchs 2010; Bonvillian and Van Atta 2011). It has had an important role in history-altering inventions such as lasers, the internet, and the personal computer (Fuchs 2010). Like DARPA, ARPA-E utilizes "technology visioning," which involves developing a vision for innovation first and then building a research program to achieve the vision, rather than choosing research to fund based on a standard peer-review process. Bonvillian and Van Atta (2011, 471) describe this as a "dramatically new model in the energy innovation space." ARPA-E's first Funding Opportunity Announcement did not set a specific goal and was open to all energy ideas and technologies. However, subsequent announcements were narrowed to more specific topics.

There are crucial differences between ARPA-E and DARPA. One is funding. Denniston (2010) points out that when DARPA was created in 1958, it received an initial budget of USD 500 million, which in current dollars would be equivalent to USD 3.5 billion (almost nine times the budget of ARPA-E). Another critical difference is that DARPA can, to a large extent, rely on Defense Department procurement to form initial markets for technologies that have been successfully demonstrated (Bonvillan and Van Atta 2011). ARPA-E cannot rely on the DOE in the same fashion, and programs that attempt to bridge the Commercialization Valley of Death (such as the loans programs discussed in the next section) may have ended by the time that the innovations nurtured by ARPA-E are ready to be scaled up. Further, when DARPA has launched innovations into the civilian sector, it has been into "open space," not into a firmly established "legacy sector" (Bonvillian and Weiss 2009).

As of 2016, ARPA-E had invested USD 1.3 billion in 475 projects led by a variety of proponents (universities, businesses, national labs, and nonprofit organizations). ARPA-E provides a team of "tech-to-market" advisers that assists developers to connect with private-sector funders. By 2016, 45 recipients of ARPA-E grants had attracted USD 1.25 billion in private financing and 36 projects had formed new companies (ARPA-E 2016). Only 23 projects had been canceled. Kelly-Detwiler (2016) argues that beyond the simple numbers, the agency has provided huge spillover benefits in advancing applied science and educating innovators and entrepreneurs about how to bring technologies to market.

ARPA-E has invested in a wide range of technologies. Much of the investment in renewable energy is focused on grid storage and distribution issues. In terms of renewable energy generation, ARPA-E does not have programs specifically focused on wind power and all solar power programs were commenced after 2011. However, several applications for wind and solar projects were made in the initial "open round" in 2009. One of these was from 1366 Technologies, a spin-off company from the Massachusetts Institute of Technology (MIT). The company was awarded USD 4 million for a project aiming to substantially reduce the cost of creating silicon wafers for solar panels. 1366 Technologies received an additional USD 70 million from private investors. Although the global price for silicon solar panels fell substantially over the duration of the project, the process developed by 1366 Technologies still managed to provide a 20 percent reduction in cost (ARPA-E 2016). Notably, the company also received a USD 150 million DOE loan guarantee (this program is discussed below) in 2011 to aid the construction of a manufacturing plant in New York to produce the new low-cost wafers. This demonstrates how the ARPA-E and the DOE loan programs were able to complement one another and bridge both valleys of death for at least some technologies. In June 2017, the company announced that a small solar power plant in Hyogo, Japan would be the first commercial user of its new wafer technology (Osborne 2017).

Despite bipartisan support for ARPA-E, Republicans have expressed concerns that it will "focus on late-stage technology development and commercialization efforts that are better left for the private sector" and "eventually crowd-out private investment and get the government into the business of picking 'winners and losers' among competing companies and technologies rather than let the market make these decisions" (Broun 2012, 1). However, a report by the Government Accountability Office (GAO 2012, 2) found that "most ARPA-E projects could not have been funded solely by private investors." Further, venture capitalists do not seem to share concerns about crowding out and actively supported the creation of ARPA-E (House Subcommittee on Energy and the Environment 2007). The agency's selection process is considered robust and sends a signal to private venture capital firms that a project would make a good investment (GAO 2012). In a Congressional hearing in 2012, Director of ARPA-E, Dr Arun Majumdar, defended the agency in a Congressional hearing, arguing "we're not picking winners, we're creating the competition" (House Subcommittees on Energy and Oversight, Committee on Science, Space, and Technology 2012). Majumdar was repeatedly asked about Solyndra despite the lack of connection between ARPA-E and the failed solar company (which received a 1705 loan guarantee, discussed in the next section). Some have expressed concern that the failure of some projects funded under the 1705 Loans program, even though this was not within ARPA-E's purview, led to pressure on the agency to demonstrate results. This, in turn, may have led ARPA-E to become more risk averse (Bullis 2014).

ARPA-E's future remains uncertain. In 2014, the House of Representatives passed a bill that would have slashed the ARPA-E budget to USD 50 million. Negotiations with the Senate led to a final appropriation of USD 280 million. Funding has hovered around that level since then. However, the election of President Trump means that the agency has lost its chief advocate in the White House. In a 2018 Budget Request, President Trump proposed that the program be eliminated entirely (DOE 2017a).

United States: Cash Grants and Loan Programs

ARPA-E, while generally lauded by the scientific community, has its limitations. Notably, it was never intended to move innovations beyond the initial proof-of-concept stage. In other words, it cannot aid in bridging the Commercialization Valley of Death. However, there was additional funding under ARRA for programs that aimed to do just that. Some of this funding went to truly innovative technologies, but most was "allocated to the development of off-the-shelf technologies" (Mundaca and Richter 2015, 1177).

The program with the largest allocation of renewable energy funding under ARRA was the 1603 Cash Grants program, with USD 25 billion. This program took the existing tax credit programs for renewable energy and allowed companies to instead apply for a cash grant equivalent to 30 percent of total eligible costs for most types of projects (Steinberg et al. 2012). The rationale for this program was that many renewable energy companies are too small to take advantage of tax credits. Therefore, they have to rely on third-party tax equity investors (primarily large banks and insurance companies) to purchase the tax credits. However, during the GFC, the pool of such investors was limited, which threatened to hamper further renewable energy developments (Bolinger, Wiser, and Darghouth 2010; Aldy 2013).

The Section 1603 program began accepting applications on July 31, 2009. Projects had to be generating electricity before they could receive the grant. The program was originally intended to expire in 2010, but was extended for a further year. Projects that began construction before the end of 2011 remained eligible to obtain the grant if they became operational before 2017.

Qualifying technologies for the program included biomass, combined heat and power, fuel cells, geothermal, incremental hydropower, landfill gas, marine hydrokinetic, microturbine, municipal solid waste, solar, and wind (United States Treasury 2017). However, the most funded projects were in the wind energy sector. As of the end of March 2017, 105,972 projects had been funded for a total of USD 25.7 billion (United States Treasury 2017). The total installed capacity was 34.5 GW, with annual electricity generation from funded projects estimated to be able to power approximately 8.4 million homes (United States Treasury 2017). Steinberg et al. (2012) estimated that during the operational period of the program (2009–2011), 52,000–75,000 direct and indirect jobs were supported per year. Additionally, the annual operation and maintenance of the PV and wind systems installed will support over 5,000 jobs per year on an ongoing basis for 20–30 years (Steinberg et al. 2012).

For some commentators (e.g., Dickerson 2011), the only problem with the Section 1603 program was that it did not last long enough to provide continued certainty for the sector. However, others have pointed out that most grants went to large foreign corporations rather than to local companies and the projects primarily supported manufacturing overseas because there were no domestic content requirements (Choma 2010). The use of imported wind turbines was particularly contentious.

In addition to cash grants, ARRA also appropriated USD 6 billion for energy loan guarantees. Congress rescinded a large portion of this (in part to replenish the Cash for Clunkers scheme discussed in Chapter 5), leaving the DOE Loans Programs with only USD 2.5 billion. The DOE Loans Programs include the so-called Section 1703 and 1705 loan programs. The 1703 Program was first developed in 2005 under the *Energy Policy Act*. The program was reauthorized and revised under ARRA with the addition of Section 1705 to the Act (DOE n.d.b).

With loan guarantees, project proponents borrow from the private sector, but if they are unable to repay a loan, the federal government intervenes on their behalf. Project proponents benefit by obtaining finance, often at a much better rate than they would otherwise be able to obtain (Krugman 2010c). Under the 1705 Program, some applicants were eligible for a "full loan guarantee," meaning that the actual loan also came from the government, through the Federal Financing Bank (Kao 2013).

To be eligible for a loan guarantee under the 1703 Program, a project had to demonstrate that it would avoid, reduce, or sequester greenhouse gases and employ an innovative or significantly improved energy technology. Such projects were also eligible for the 1705 Program, but additionally, this program would accept proposals for commercial-scale developments of existing technology (Kao 2013). Although broader in this sense, the 1705 Program had a narrower scope than 1703 in terms of the types of technologies supported. Whereas the 1703 Program funded nuclear and CCS technology (among others), 1705 funding could only be directed to renewable energy, electric power transmission, and biofuel projects (Kao 2013). This section will focus primarily on the 1705 Program, as this is where loans for the solar industry were concentrated. Most projects funded were large-scale renewable energy generation (primarily solar) installations (House Committee on Oversight and Government Reform 2012). All projects had to begin construction before September 30, 2011, at which point the 1705 Loan Program expired (DOE n.d.c).

Controversy arose over the 1705 Loan Program primarily because of the widely publicized failure of a small number of projects, most famously Solyndra. Solyndra was founded in 2005, with the aim of manufacturing a cylindrical solar panel that was easier to install than traditional flat panels. Solyndra's photovoltaic system contained much less silicon, making it more cost effective to manufacture. The company grew rapidly and began to sell its product commercially in 2008 (Kao 2013). The full loan guarantee of USD 535 million that Solyndra success-fully applied for under the 1705 Program was to build a second manufacturing facility in California. The project was high profile from the beginning and was touted by the White House as a prime example of how well the clean energy stim-ulus was working. However, the company soon ran into financial difficulties and had to restructure in 2011. One aspect of the restructuring involved new investors gaining a senior secured position, meaning they would be paid back before the federal government (Kao 2013). This element of the deal would later be attacked by Congressional Republicans.

Solyndra filed for bankruptcy on September 6, 2011. The main reason for the company's downfall was the unexpected collapse in the price of silicon solar pan-els, which in part resulted from a massive investment in the technology by the Chinese government (Kats 2012; Wessner and Wolff 2012). The global market for solar panels was also drastically reduced by the reduction or elimination of gov-ernment incentives for purchasers in the wake of the GFC, especially in Europe (Kao 2013). However, there were also some mistakes made by the company.

The fallout of Solyndra's bankruptcy has been considerable. There have been several Congressional hearings on the matter, scrutiny from the Federal Bureau of Investigation, and the passage of the "No More Solyndra's" bill (Kasperowicz and German 2012). There have been allegations of crony capitalism (because one of the company's largest shareholders was an Obama campaign donor), which could have been avoided if the governance of the 1705 Loans Program had been more transparent (Primack 2013). However, critics would still have made claims about the government being poor at "picking winners," as these arguments are primarily based on an ideological concern about government interference in the market and a disdain for the renewable energy industry (Kao 2013). As Kao (2013, 428) notes, "Solyndra has become the poster child for critics of federal involvement in and support of renewable energy." In fact, Solyndra continues to be brought up frequently in political discussions more than five years after it went bankrupt. Trump even alluded to Solyndra in the first presidential debate with Hilary Clinton, stating "we invested in a solar company, our country. That was a disaster. They lost plenty of money on that one" (Fehrenbacher 2016).

In fact, the 1705 Loan program performed remarkably well in pure economic terms, with a loss ratio of only 2.3 percent, which according to the Loan Office's Executive Director Mark McCall is "a rate that would be viewed favorably even in the private sector for a portfolio of a similar type" (quoted in Casey 2016). There were always expected to be some defaults, and this was factored into the design of the program. In addition to not having exceeded its budget for defaulted loans, the Department had also brought in about USD 1.65 billion in interest payments up to the end of 2016 (Eckhouse and Roston 2016).

Further, while Solyndra has received the bulk of media attention, the DOE funded a wide range of projects that were very successful, including the first five utility-scale PV solar facilities in the US larger than 100 MW and one of the largest wind farms in the world (Mundaca and Richter 2015; DOE 2016). By April 2015, most projects in DOE's portfolio were in full operation (GAO 2015). The solar and wind energy projects supported through 1705 Loans provide an annual reduction in greenhouse gas emissions of approximately 6 MMT CO_2-e (see Table 7.3). Loans to solar and wind projects supported more than 8000 construction jobs and 500 permanent jobs (see Table 7.3). The DOE (2016) argues that its loan guarantees have "helped transform U.S. energy production and paved the way for the fastest growing sector of the solar industry."

However, some supporters of renewable energy investment remain skeptical. Aldy (2013, 149) suggests that the "1705 loan guarantee program has been much less successful than the 1603 grant program and has not had a meaningful impact on the US power sector." British economist Mariana Muzzucato (2015) offers a different critique, arguing that while there is no problem with governments providing loan guarantees in principle, there should be a move to socialize rewards as well as risks. In other words, it is fine for taxpayers to be on the hook when a company like Solyndra goes bust, provided they also receive a share of rewards when a funded company turns a profit. While it is the case that the US government receives interest on loans in the 1705 Program, arguably it could have received a greater return on investment by acquiring a stake in the companies and receiving a share of profits.

Table 7.3 Wind and solar projects that received 1705 loans

Company	Energy type	Loan guarantee (USD M)	Number of jobs		Emission reductions (MT CO₂-e/yr)
			Construction	Permanent	
1366 Technologies	Solar	150	50	70	1,100,000
Abound Solar	Solar	400	Canceled		
Agua Caliente	Solar	967	400	10	312,000
Alamosa	Solar	90.6	75	5	34,000
Antelope Valley	Solar	646	350	20	279,000
California Valley	Solar	1,200	350	11	370,000
Crescent Dunes	Solar	737	600	45	279,000
Desert Sunlight	Solar	1,500	550	15	614,000
Genesis	Solar	852	800	47	322,000
Granite Reliable	Wind	169	198	6	130,000
Ivanpah	Solar	1,600	1,000	61	500,000
Kahuku	Wind	117	200	6	39,000
Mesquite 1	Solar	337	300	12	190,000
Mojave	Solar	1,200	830	70	329,000
Record Hill	Wind	102	200	8	56,000
Shepherds Flat	Wind	1,300	400	45	1,000,000
Solana	Solar	1,450	1,700	90	480,000
Solyndra	Solar	535	Canceled		
TOTAL		**13,353**	**8,003**	**521**	**6,034,000**

Source: Compiled by the author from data provided in DOE (2017b).

Summary and key policy recommendations

In each of the three countries examined in this chapter, the government allocated far more stimulus funding to the development and/or commercial deployment of CCS technology than to renewable energy generation technology. This was widely criticized by environmentalists in these countries at the time. Arguably, CCS projects should have never been classified as "green stimulus" by the HSBC team or anyone else. CCS is undesirable, not just because of the risk associated with failures, but also because of the massive environmental damage and health issues that result from coal mining (e.g., mountain top removal, the resurgence of black lung disease in Australia) and oil drilling (particularly as more accessible reserves dry up and companies begin to explore remote and pristine environments, for example in the Arctic and in the Southern Ocean off the coast of Australia). It is particularly egregious to suggest that CCS is green when it is being used for enhanced oil recovery.

As it happens, CCS also turned out to be a bad bet. Of the 17 CCS projects allocated funding under stimulus packages across the three countries studied, ten were eventually canceled and a further two remain in doubt. Part of the problem, at least in the US and Australia, was that the capital provided by the state was "impatient," with stimulus funding deadlines that were unrealistic. Another factor was the failure of each government to implement a price on carbon that would incentivize industry participation in CCS. However, it is also evident that several projects faced insurmountable challenges related to excessively high costs and availability of storage sites. While governments should certainly be permitted to make bad investments (a natural part of the innovation process), it is worth interrogating why so much public investment was made in this particular technology. It was evident to many at the time that CCS was risky and extremely expensive and could only become economic if a very high carbon price was adopted. Thus, the industry itself has been reluctant to provide funding for CCS projects. Despite this, governments forged ahead for largely political reasons. The coal lobby is very powerful in Australia and the US, as is the oil industry in Canada. CCS has been pushed by these industries, largely to delay the uptake of cleaner energy alternatives such as wind and solar. Marshall (2016, 289) describes CCS as a "technologically based fantasy," and argues that in Australia "the main impetus for policy around CCS has been to protect coal and the ways of life associated with coal power."

The political influence of the fossil fuel lobby is also evident in the disproportionate reactions by politicians to the failure of renewable energy projects compared with the failure of CCS projects. This is clearest in the limited response from Congress to the demise of FutureGen 2.0, which received a billion-dollar grant, in comparison with the seemingly never-ending discussion of Solyndra, which defaulted on a USD 535 million loan. The reaction to Solyndra can, therefore, not simply be explained as neoliberal opposition to state intervention in the market and the issue of "picking winners." This certainly played a role, and arguably the White House failed to adequately defend the notion that the state should be involved in innovation. However, the inconsistency in reaction clearly demonstrates that politicians are more than happy to pick winners when those winners are traditional allies and sources of campaign funds.

While many governments have since given up on the "fantasy" of CCS, the experience of the 2008–2009 stimulus funding should somewhat temper the optimism of those who promote the entrepreneurial state as a path to a green economy. Provided the fossil fuel lobby retains significant political power, decisions made by the state about investments in technological innovation will not necessarily be more environmentally beneficial than those made in the market by private actors.

The experience with stimulus for renewable energy generation projects was much more variable than for CCS. Australia aimed to fund large-scale demonstration projects and ran into difficulties with proponents being unable to obtain power purchase agreements to supply the grid. This demonstrates the fact that green stimulus measures cannot be developed without consideration of the broader regulatory environment. This was less of a problem in the US, where several large-scale generation projects were successful. Renewable energy manufacturing projects, which are considered higher risk than generation projects but also create a greater number of permanent, high-quality jobs, were funded to a lesser extent in the US, with varying degrees of success. Solyndra – the victim of a rapidly changing global market in renewable energy technology – cast a shadow over what was an otherwise successful loan program. In Canada, very little stimulus was directed to innovation or commercial deployment of renewable technology. However, one small-scale project demonstrated that community-run projects are effective both in reducing emissions and providing local economic benefits. These types of projects also avoid the issues that Mazzucato is concerned about, with respect to socializing risk while privatizing reward, because the reward is socialized (at least for the immediate community).

ARPA-E represented the most interesting policy innovation of all cases, because it moved away from a model in which the private sector sets the technological agenda and the government simply provides funding. According to Goldstein and Tyfield (2017), a private sector-driven model, which they call state venture capitalism, is faithful to the neoliberal commitment to the market. In contrast, ARPA-E's technological visioning approach suggests a move toward a more significant role for the state in steering technological innovation, and is more in line with Mazzucato's vision for the entrepreneurial state. However, even in the case of ARPA-E, CCS and nuclear projects were funded, suggesting that the organization is not free from political influence and has not taken on board a precautionary approach that would consider whether these technologies are appropriate even if proven viable.

The question of technological "appropriateness" suggests the need to move beyond the notion of the entrepreneurial state. In addition to the idea that the government sets the path for technological innovation, there must also be the qualification that investments should be viable by social and ecological criteria (Eskelinen 2015).

Part III
Conclusions

8 A waste of a good crisis?

> The difficulty lies, not in the new ideas, but in escaping from the old ones.
> John Maynard Keynes (1997)

In the aftermath of Cyclone Nargis, generals from Myanmar's military regime swooped into the worst affected region, the Irrawaddy Delta. However, according to Mutter (2015), they did so not to assist in recovery efforts, but to seize vacated land. As suggested in Chapter 1, crises present opportunities. But the experience in Myanmar (and countless other disaster-stricken countries and communities) serves as an important reminder that opportunities are not capitalized on solely or even primarily by progressives hoping to advance the public interest. As Naomi Klein (2007) has documented, neoliberals are quite adept at exploiting crises for capital gain.

Such profiteering occurred in the wake of the GFC, although not as blatantly as in the case of Cyclone Nargis or other instances of "disaster capitalism" (Mutter 2015). Corporate interests, in particular, took the opportunity in 2008–2009 to lap up government bailouts and argue for the removal of "red" and "green tape" (e.g., EIAs), purportedly to hasten economic recovery. They also lobbied to secure stimulus funding, sometimes under the pretense that their projects were "green." States were, in many cases, too willing to facilitate the transfer of public funds to private coffers, even when the case for economic or environmental benefits was weak. Subsidies for the purchase of "eco" products (see Chapter 5) and large-scale "green" infrastructure projects (see Chapter 6) were particularly problematic. Investments in CCS (see Chapter 7) were an unfortunate and unnecessary waste of public money.

In some of the countries studied, such outcomes are not particularly surprising when one considers prevailing power relations and the leaders in office at the time. These factors are particularly relevant given the tendency for power to be concentrated during periods of crisis (Peters 2011). Stephen Harper – a staunch neoliberal with little interest in addressing climate change – led the Canadian government during the GFC. In Japan, where the leadership changed several times over the course of 2008–2009, the government's energy policy has long been captured by vested interests in the utilities and nuclear industry. A primary focus on energy efficiency strategies in Japan's green stimulus also pleased the influential high-tech industries (Moe 2012). That the "greenest" stimulus package (Korea's) was significantly less green than initially claimed may seem surprising in light of the rhetoric expressed by President Lee Myung-bak about green growth. However, once again, corporate influence (wielded in this case by the construction industry) played a dominant role.

It is more difficult to account for the outcomes in the US and Australia. In both countries, newly elected progressive leaders, who had campaigned heavily on the promise of tackling climate change, failed to deliver transformational change. To some degree, political opponents can be blamed for hampering the green stimulus efforts of the governing parties (e.g., Republican governors returning stimulus funding for HSR [see Chapter 6]) and creating a toxic environment in which any misstep in the rollout of spending programs was amplified and exploited for political gain (e.g., insulation in Australia [see Chapter 4] and Solyndra in the US [see Chapter 7]). However, this alone does not explain the overall lack of vision in either country's stimulus package. The first section of this chapter examines one factor that helps to account for this, which was not anticipated by proponents of Green Keynesianism: the resilience of neoliberalism.

While it is difficult to conclude that the green stimulus measures implemented in 2008–2009 marked a substantial green shift in government spending or a significant improvement in actual environmental conditions, some of the cases in the preceding chapters do provide reason for optimism about the potential of Green Keynesianism. When spending measures are carefully designed and directed to appropriate sectors, they can have beneficial results for the environment and employment. Weatherization programs in three of the countries studied in Chapter 4 were largely effective, and investments in renewable energy technology, particularly in the US (see Chapter 7), were also successful. Notably, these were the areas of investment that were the focus of progressive proposals for a Green New Deal in 2008 and 2009 (e.g., GNDG 2008).

The second section of this chapter collects lessons from the cases – both positive and negative – and incorporates them into a set of criteria for evaluating whether a stimulus measure should qualify for a "green" label. These criteria will hopefully assist governments in determining where to direct stimulus money in the future to maximize environmental benefits. The criteria should also assist nongovernment actors in scrutinizing claims that a particular stimulus measure is green.

The third section of this chapter returns to the discussion that first arose in Chapter 2 about the need for Green Keynesianism to be further developed as a more comprehensive policy framework and economic philosophy. It is argued that more work is needed to incorporate approaches from post-Keynesian and ecological economics into a Green Keynesian framework that moves beyond recommendations for stimulus measures in times of crisis and addresses the need for degrowth in advanced economies. The chapter closes with some reflections on what Green Keynesians can do to prepare for the next economic crisis.

Neoliberalism is dead, long live neoliberalism

In Chapter 1, it was noted that the GFC presented environmentalists with two opportunities: (1) to direct stimulus spending to environmental projects, and (2) to push for the adoption of a new ecological macroeconomic framework. While the outcomes of the 2008–2009 stimulus spending were mixed, it is beyond doubt that the second opportunity was missed. Neoliberal market fundamentalism was not overturned in favor of a more ecologically sustainable economic paradigm in the wake of the GFC. There are many possible explanations for this. One is that the opportunities presented by crises may be more limited than is commonly assumed and that the optimism about the potential for crises to catalyze paradigmatic change may be unwarranted. Oliver and Pemberton (2004, 415) argue that "paradigm failure does not necessarily lead to wholesale paradigm replacement." Instead, there is often a battle to institutionalize a new policy framework in which a subset of the defeated policy framework is incorporated into the prevailing paradigm. Starke, Kaasch, and Van Hooren (2013, 184) examined developments in social policy following several crises, including the GFC, and found that "the link between crisis and path-breaking change may be much weaker than previously thought" and that "missed opportunities may well be much more common." They argue that one reason for this is that during moments of crisis, people "tend to stick to what they know best." Thus, governments are likely to draw on established "policy routines" when developing a response (Starke et al. 2013, 10). The policy routines of the governments studied in this book were established under neoliberalism.

Neoliberalism has certainly proven remarkably resilient (Overbeek and Apeldoorn 2012; Peck 2013). Colin Crouch (2011, 179) argues that what is left of neoliberalism after the GFC is "virtually everything." According to Peck (2013, 137), despite the "evident culpability of the bankers and (de)regulators" in creating the GFC, it turned out that "this conjuncture was not immediately propitious for ideological regime change." The neoliberal model has "been undeniably tarnished" in the eyes of the public, but "the social structure on which the program was predicated ... is still largely intact" (Peck 2013, 137).

The deeply embedded nature of neoliberalism is reflected throughout this book. It is evident in the swift return that global organizations made to calls for fiscal consolidation and austerity after 2009 (see Chapter 3), and in the design and implementation of the stimulus measures themselves. Most of the stimulus packages came in the form of tax cuts rather than public investments. Direct investments, even those labeled "green," were largely channeled to established corporate interests – car companies, electronics manufacturing firms, construction companies, and even the mining and fossil fuel industries. The 2008–2009 stimulus was a far cry from the public-works programs in the New Deal, which, for all their problems, were predominantly devoted to creating public infrastructure and other public goods (e.g., parks and recreational facilities) that could be enjoyed by all. The prevailing response to the GFC could even be described as "neoliberal stimulus" rather than Keynesian stimulus (Parker 2013, 278).

The resilience of neoliberalism is also evident in the discursive battles that were fought over the stimulus. Of the countries examined in this book, this was most evident in Australia and the US. In each case, a progressive (but not unreservedly Keynesian) leader implemented green stimulus programs that experienced some difficulties. These problems were blown out of proportion by political rivals who exploited the opportunity to create a narrative that suggested that the government was incompetent, and that all governments should refrain from "picking winners" and interfering in the market. For neoliberals, Solyndra in the US and "pink batts" in Australia continue to be symbolic of everything that is wrong with Keynesianism and climate-focused energy policy. Grunwald (2012, 272) remarks, "Solyndra has become Republican shorthand for ineptitude, cronyism and the failure of green industrial policy." In Australia, it has been noted that public confidence in the ability of governments to run large-scale energy efficiency programs has been affected by the insulation scandal (Dowling 2012; Crawford and Stephan 2014). Consequently, it less likely that future federal governments will embark upon large investment programs of this nature (Dovers 2013). The failure of each government to effectively defend the role of state investment in an energy transition has helped breathe life back into neoliberalism.

It is fair for Goldstein and Tyfield (2017, 4) to suggest that Green Keynesians have been reluctant to acknowledge that the state has been fundamentally transformed by neoliberalism. This is something that cannot be undone overnight, in a rush to embrace the state "as a potential ecological savior." However, as argued in Chapter 1, to simply give up on the state either in favor of global governance or devolution of power to the local level is equally misguided. As demonstrated in Chapter 3, global organizations suffer from the same neoliberal tendencies as states and no champion for Green Keynesianism is in sight. While localization is an amiable goal (that does not have to be incompatible with Green Keynesianism), states remain the only actors with the capacity to mobilize the resources necessary, in the time available, to combat the global environmental crisis. Therefore, the question that remains paramount, and cannot be answered here, is how progressives can win back and rehabilitate the state.

It's pretty easy being (labeled) green

Mazzucato (2015a), a strong advocate of government involvement in technological innovation, finds fault with Keynes primarily because, in her view, his theory can be used to advocate for "useless" government spending. The classic notion of a man digging a hole and then filling it in again is rightfully offensive to Mazzucato, especially given the current dire need for investment in areas such as clean energy. Arguably, Green Keynesians have tried to rectify this problem by stipulating that funding should be targeted to projects that would create jobs *and* deliver environmental dividends. Unfortunately, as is often the case with anything labeled "green," a substantial amount of ambiguity remained. While Kermit the Frog may be correct that actually being green is "not easy," policymakers and policy analysts tend to throw the label around with little consideration for what it means.

It has been demonstrated throughout this book that the oft-quoted values attached to green stimulus programs in 2008–2009, that were initially reported by a research team at HSBC (Robins et al. 2009a, 2009b), are a substantial over-estimation. This is partly because many governments reduced their initial green stimulus pledges after 2009, reallocated funds, or simply failed to spend the money that was earmarked because of difficulties in implementing the programs (e.g., Australia's 'flagship' programs discussed in Chapter 7). However, a second and more critical issue is that the scope of what was considered green by the HSBC team was overly broad. There is no universally accepted definition of "green stimulus," which is not a problem unique to this area of study; for example, Goods (2011) outlines similar difficulties in defining "green jobs." Barbier (2010, 294) is one of the few who has attempted to define green stimulus, seeing it as comprising:

> Fiscal stimulus measures that are targeted to reducing carbon dependency and to other environmental improvements – e.g., supporting renewable energy development, carbon capture and sequestration, energy efficiency, public transport and rail; improving or modernizing electrical grid transmission and river basin management; and improving freshwater supplies and ecosystem management.

However, this definition mainly serves to list examples of projects that might or might not be legitimately "green" depending on the circumstances. Notably, Barbier explicitly includes CCS, which, as argued in Chapter 7, from the critical perspective adopted in this book, does not have a valid claim to the label.

Instead of defining green stimulus, the approach taken here is to provide a modified version of the "three Ts" of "good" stimulus (outlined in Chapter 1). The modification is intended to both remove the problematic aspects of the original criteria that have been identified through the case studies and to add further elements to account for the additional aim of green stimulus (i.e., to combat the global environmental crisis).

Timely

The original criterion of timeliness, which suggested that stimulus funds should be distributed as quickly as possible, turned out to be less important than originally anticipated in the context of the GFC. As Grunwald (2012) suggests, the definition of what was "timely" could be stretched when it was clear the recession would be bigger and longer than predicted. Nevertheless, this criterion heavily influenced the design and rollout of the 2008–2009 stimulus.

As the preceding chapters have highlighted, there is a tension between this criterion and the environmental objectives of Green Keynesianism. Timeliness translated into "shovel-ready" brown projects getting priority over green ones. Grunwald (2012, 17) argues that priority should have been given to "shovel-worthy" projects over shovel-ready ones. The haste with which governments tried to get money out the door also contributed to poor policy design, most notably in the case of the home insulation scheme in Australia (see Chapter 4). Stephen Harper's conservative government in Canada further demonstrated that the time-liness criterion could be used as a convenient excuse to pare back or eliminate important regulatory processes, like EIAs, that can slow down the rollout of the stimulus. In Korea, time pressures also resulted in a hasty and incomplete envi-ronmental assessment of the Four Major Rivers Project.

Given these issues, the timely criterion should be modified. Measures should still be implemented in a timely manner; there is, after all, as much urgency asso-ciated with addressing climate change as with any economic downturn. However, speed should not take precedence over the need for investment measures to be thoughtfully considered, appropriately designed, and regulated by existing frame-works that have been put in place to protect the public and the environment.

Targeted

The original reason given by economists for the targeted criterion is that low-income earners are more likely to spend any money that they save through stimu-lus programs, creating a larger multiplier effect in the economy. However, there is also a broader moral case to be made for addressing inequality through gov-ernment investment. As Davidson (2009, 6) notes, Keynes believed that one of the major faults of the capitalist system was its "arbitrary and inequitable distri-bution of income and wealth." Further, as demonstrated in Chapter 4, targeting low-income households also has beneficial impacts from a purely environmental perspective. At least in the case of home retrofits, targeting low-income earners effectively eliminates the problem of free riding because individuals are unable to make energy efficiency improvements in the absence of a subsidy.

While the targeted criterion should be retained, its meaning should also be expanded to take two additional issues into consideration: (1) public money should primarily be targeted to public projects, and (2) regions that are hard-est hit by the transition away from fossil fuels should receive more govern-ment support.

In terms of directing investment to the public sphere, an example, as suggested in Chapter 6, is that public infrastructure should receive government funding whereas effectively private infrastructure (e.g., a transmission line to provide cheap energy to mining companies) should not. There may be a reasonable case for governments providing concessional loans and other assistance to private companies that are developing or commercializing clean technologies. However, as Mazzucato (2015a) suggests, in these cases, the state should receive a return on successful investments. Importantly, greater funding should be directed to community-led projects. The contrast between the NTL (see Chapter 6), a CAD 130 million investment in mining "sold" to the public as a project to transition a small remote community from diesel power to clean energy, and the Cowessess First Nation Wind and Storage Demonstration project (see Chapter 7), which brought not only clean energy but also revenue to a similar community at a fraction of the cost (CAD 2.8 million), exemplifies the notion that very often, small is beautiful.

Targeting regions hit hardest by the transition away from fossil fuels is recommended for both moral and political reasons. It is widely acknowledged that there will inevitably be winners and losers in the transition to a more ecologically sound economy. This must be addressed, because one aim of Green Keynesianism should be a more equal society. However, as the Construction, Forestry, Mining and Energy Union in Australia (2016, 28) points out, ignoring the "losers" also creates political opposition to a transition:

> If we want to achieve major change that mitigates global warming, the social impacts must not be treated as a secondary issue. To the extent that climate policy creates losers, it will be resisted (and this is especially so if opportunistic politicians seek to exploit the fear of loss).

Here, the concept of a "just transition," which links ecological sustainability with issues of work and social justice, is potentially useful. The term was originally conceived through an initiative of the former Oil, Chemical and Atomic Workers union in North America. Although it originated in the labor movement, the just transition frame is used by an increasing number of organizing networks, grassroots organizations, and environmental groups. While, as Snell and Fairbrother (2013, 158) note, it is defined in multiple and contested ways, at the heart of most notions of a just transition "is a basic principle of fairness advocating that the cost of policies that aim to benefit society should not be disproportionately borne by those who are hurt by them." The preamble of the Paris Climate Agreement mentions that the parties take into account "the imperatives of a just transition of the workforce and the creation of decent work and quality jobs in accordance with nationally defined development priorities" (UNFCCC 2015, preamble).

Like Green Keynesianism, a just transition challenges the notion that market-based solutions are the only option for economic revitalization and implies a return to industrial planning (Snell and Fairbrother 2013). The instruments required to ensure a just transition include employment diversification policies, job training/retraining programs and educational programs, and social protection measures (social insurance, access to health services, etc.) (International Trade Union Confederation 2009). There are also more radical policies, like universal basic income, that are increasingly being explored by post-Keynesian economists and even some governments, that could help to facilitate a just transition. Within the specific context of the criteria for green stimulus, incorporating the notion of a just transition would require targeting government investment to regions that are traditionally reliant on employment in the fossil fuel industries. Further, it would suggest that strong roles in the development and implementation of stimulus programs be assigned to unions, employees, and local communities. These groups should be able to work in collaboration with government to design appropriate stimulus measures rather than merely being on the receiving end of government funding.

Temporary

In the countries studied in this book, the governments interpreted the temporary criterion to mean that all funding should be spent by a prespecified deadline, usually within a few years of the stimulus package's release. As with timeliness, the temporary criterion lost much of its relevance when the Great Recession continued for longer than predicted.

As noted in previous chapters, the temporary criterion had a negative impact in some of the cases. The spending deadlines set by governments tended to be arbitrary and too short for some new technologies and industries to mature (see Chapter 7). To put it in Mazzucato's (2015a) language, temporary implies "impatient capital," when the opposite is needed. Short timeframes for stimulus also created boom and bust scenarios for industries (see Chapter 4).

Despite this, simply discarding the temporary criterion would give the wrong impression about the purpose of green stimulus. After all, the argument here is not that specific measures should stay in place indefinitely, especially given economic factors such as the rapidly declining cost of renewable energy (i.e., solar companies will not need subsidies forever). Therefore, it is proposed that the temporary criterion should be replaced by the requirement that investments be "transitional." Transitional investments are those that are in place long enough to provide the certainty and stability required for new sectors to become established. However, "transitional" also indicates something further in relation to a key objective of green stimulus, which is to steer the economy in a new direction rather than to a return to a pre-crisis status quo. In this regard, transitional suggests that stimulus measures should provide substantial "bang for the buck" in terms of environmental benefits such as greenhouse gas emissions reductions. It also encapsulates the idea that policymakers should consider rebound effects, life-cycle impacts, and indirect environmental harms when designing stimulus measures. Long term, these factors can negate any environmental benefits accrued from the investment in the short term. Cato (2013, 24) suggests:

> Investment can be justified as "transitional" if, although requiring the use of more energy in the short-term, in the long run it would ensure greater well-being with the investment of less energy. By this definition the insulation of homes is clearly transitional investment, whereas the installation of a system of recharging points for electric vehicles would be much harder to justify.

Energy usage is given emphasis by Cato, but there are other factors to be considered (e.g., creation of waste, contribution to biodiversity loss). For example, an investment in CCS is not "transitional" because even if it reduces greenhouse gas emissions, it helps perpetuate the old fossil fuel economy that relies on environmentally destructive extractive activities.

Table 8.1 sums up the differences between the established three Ts for traditional stimulus – timely, targeted, and temporary – and the proposed three Ts for green stimulus – timely, targeted, and transitional. The intention in making this

Table 8.1 Original and modified "3 Ts"

3 Ts of traditional stimulus		3 Ts of green stimulus	
Characteristic	Meaning	Characteristic	Meaning
Timely	Measures are implemented quickly in response to an economic crisis	Timely	Measures are implemented quickly in response to an economic crisis but not at the expense of careful design and consideration for environmental impacts
Targeted	Greatest benefits go to low-income earners	Targeted	Greatest benefits go to low-income earners and regions hardest hit by green transition Public money flows predominantly to public projects
Temporary	Measures have a fixed deadline to signal to the market that they will not become permanent	Transitional	Measures are in place long enough to provide stability and certainty to the sector Reductions in CO_2 emissions or other environmental benefits are prioritized and substantial Measures are appropriately designed to minimize rebound effects, free riding, life-cycle impacts and indirect environmental impacts

distinction is not to frame green stimulus as a minor subset of a more general category of "regular" stimulus. Indeed, given the investments in clean energy required to meet the commitments of the Paris Agreement, green stimulus should be considered the dominant measure in any future government stimulus packages. Proposals from environmentalists recommending 20 percent of stimulus should be green may reflect a desire for pragmatism. However, the reality is that the environmental gains made with that 20 percent of stimulus that is green would be overtaken several times over by the other 80 percent that is "brown." The only nongreen stimulus that should be accepted by environmentalists is investment in environmentally "neutral" activities (i.e., activities that do not cause substantial environmental harm), such as health care and the arts.

In addition to the modified three Ts, decisions about where to invest should also be guided by the precautionary principle. As noted in Chapter 2, Keynes was quite concerned with uncertainty, and the precautionary principle fits well with his views (Berr 2015). Applying a precautionary approach in stimulus decisions requires that investments be considered viable by social and ecological criteria and that technology that poses substantial risks (e.g. CCS and nuclear power) not be funded.

Finally, it is also important to consider that green stimulus measures do not exist in a vacuum; success or failure of a program may depend on the existence of complementary policies or the removal of contradictory ones. Discontinuing fossil fuel subsidies is an obvious measure that can usefully supplement investment programs aimed at promoting clean technology. In contrast, it is counterproductive to incentivize fuel efficiency through subsidies for "eco-cars" but then encourage individuals to drive more by reducing taxes and road tolls (see Chapter 5).

Beyond stimulus

Most of this book has focused on learning from the experiences of stimulus measures taken in response to the GFC. It is hoped that the lessons provided will inform the content and design of future government stimulus packages. However, Green Keynesianism does not have to be limited to when we are "in a foxhole." Jeffrey Sachs (2013) argues that Keynesianism is not just about "quick and dirty" stimulus measures. He suggests that this is "crude Keynesianism." Instead, we need "consistent, planned, decade-long boost in public investments in people, technology, and infrastructure."

The criteria for green stimulus set out above can equally be applied to government investment in periods of relative economic stability (although it should be self-evident that the timeliness criterion becomes less relevant). Further, Green Keynesianism does not have to be defined solely by one type of policy measure. As noted in Chapter 2, some Green New Deal proposals also included measures aimed at constraining the power of the financial sector and increasing taxes on resource extraction.

McBride and Merolli (2013) argue that the Keynesian economic paradigm that preceded neoliberalism had several instruments to achieve full employment other than government-funded programs. They suggest that a new paradigm modeled after Keynesianism might promote (1) controls on capital mobility; (2) managed rather than free trade; (3) a stronger public sector through stricter regulation of market processes, and higher taxes and spending; (4) a more pragmatic view of budget deficits; (5) a return to policies of greater equality and social justice; and (6) intervention in the labor market to establish social and employment protection. In a Green Keynesian paradigm, policies must be developed to manage the need to transition to a no-growth or degrowth economic model in advanced economies.

Skidelsky (2009, 168–169) argues that the GFC represented an "intellectual failure of mainstream economics" but also "a moral failure: that of a system built on money values. At the heart of the moral failure is the worship of economic growth for its own sake, rather than to achieve the 'good life'." As noted in Chapter 2, Keynes was not an advocate of growth for its own sake. However, a core tenant of Keynesianism (the multiplier effect) is that government spending will benefit areas of the economy other than the specific one targeted, because people (especially those at the lower end of the tax bracket) will spend the money they earn/save through the government program in other parts of the economy. As Borgnäs (2015) points out, the money earned/saved by participants in green stimulus programs will very likely be spent on goods and services in the "brown" economy.

In other words, the profitability (in Keynesian terms) of green investments depends on nongreen sectors expanding. Thus, even if government investments are "transitional," as recommended above, there is the question is what is happening in the broader economy.

Part of this problem can be addressed if, as Victor (2008, 214) suggests, government investments "reflect and support" a shift to increased leisure and recreation time, a renewed focus on family and community, and public, rather than private, goods. However, other policies will also be required. Post-Keynesian and ecological economists have begun to grapple with the question of how issues such as overconsumption can be addressed without creating unemployment and social hardship (e.g., a shorter working week, universal basic income). There is also increasing interest from politicians in proposals of this nature, even in the absence of any "green" tendencies. This is because, quite separately from environmental concerns about growth, technological changes and increased automation in many industries are rapidly changing the nature and availability of work (Arntz, Gregory, and Zierahn 2016).

Another question that inevitably arises is how governments will pay for green investments and other public programs if the taxable economy is shrinking in a degrowth model (Borgnäs 2015). Røpke (2016) argues that tax reform is part of the solution; increased taxes on resources, financial transactions, high incomes, and so on can compensate for the overall decline in taxable income. However, tax reform would have to be accompanied by changes in global economic governance to reduce the risk of capital flight.

These issues are complex and demonstrate that there is considerable work to be done to develop a progressive model of Green Keynesianism that moves beyond a set of recommendations for government investment. Nevertheless, there is a great deal of promise in the increasing cross-pollination of ideas between the post-Keynesian and ecological economics schools.

An ecological state

A key idea that emerged in chapter 2, and that has been revisited in the 3Ts of green stimulus discussed above, is that Green Keynesianism should be viewed as a transitional project. This begs the question of what the ultimate aim of Green Keynesianism should be. In other words, what kind of paradigm is the world meant to be transitioning to?

An "ecological state" is briefly sketched here as a potential alternative to both the (market-focused/neoliberal) "green economy" and the traditional (Keynesian) welfare state. Inspiration is drawn from Meadowcroft (2005, 4), who describes this type of state as one "where ecologically-oriented intervention comes to constitute – and is generally acknowledged to constitute legitimately – an essential responsibility of the public power" and is "predicated on a recognition that environmental systems are critical to long term social welfare, and that their protection and enhancement require conscious and continuous adjustment by the public power."

Figure 8.1 Contrasting the ecological state with other economic models

As should be clear from these passages, the ecological state is a strong inter-ventionist state, consistent with a post-Keynesian approach. This distinguishes it from the green economy, which would (at best) fall in the "neoclassical synthesis" end of the spectrum of Keynesianism (see Chapter 2). The ecological state can be distinguished from the welfare state (the traditional focus of post-Keynesian economists) by the recognition of planetary boundaries. As Meadowcroft (2005, 5) explains, the acknowledgment of "limits is implicit in the idea of an ecological state" and "ensuring that environmental impacts do not breach such limits, and so undermine the foundations for human economic and social well being, would be an essential objective of an ecological state." As noted in Chapter 1, in 2009 research-ers developed the planetary boundaries framework, which "defines a safe operating space for humanity based on the intrinsic biophysical processes that regulate the stability of the Earth System" (Steffen et al. 2015). The nine planetary boundaries identified in that framework define the limits for the ecological state proposed here.

Figure 8.1 illustrates how the ecological state can be distinguished from the other models. Notably, the box symbolizing the ecological state is smaller than the others, to demonstrate the need for degrowth to remain within plane-tary boundaries.

The next opportunity?

In the decade since the GFC first erupted, there have been near-constant predic-tions that the next economic crisis is just around the corner and that we remain woefully unprepared for it. Environmentalists are no more eager for an economic crisis than anyone else, but it appears almost inevitable that one will erupt in the near future. While there is no reason to wait for the next crisis to push Green Keynesian proposals, it is sensible to prepare crisis-specific plans to make the most of any opportunity that should arise. As suggested earlier in this chapter, the opportunity may not be for paradigmatic change. However, even a limited

opportunity for channeling government investment and making small environmental gains must be seized.

One area for action to lay the groundwork for a Green Keynesian response to
the next crisis is to try to shift the mindset in global organizations that have an
influence on state economic policy. As noted in Chapter 3, the OECD and IMF
have indicated that they are more open to Keynesianism now than they have been
in the recent past. Efforts by scholars and think tanks to nudge these organizations further in the direction of Green Keynesianism would be beneficial. Further,
reform of other organizations – namely the WTO and G20 – would also be welcome, although this is unlikely to occur in the short term.

At the state and local level, supporters of Green Keynesianism would be wise
to begin to identify regions in need of particular support (in line with the targeted/
just transition criterion for green stimulus). In those regions, studies that indicate
how government investment could best be utilized, in terms of supporting new
industries and job training, will help lay the groundwork for near "shovel-ready"
plans and programs. Indeed, developing lists of "shovel-worthy" projects currently lacking funding, regardless of where they are located, would also be useful.
When the crisis does hit, Green Keynesians need to be quick to respond. Not just
with proposals based on the areas outlined above, but with clear guidance about
how green stimulus should be defined and the kinds of projects that should defi-
nitely not be funded.

Finally, Green Keynesians need to work hard to counter narratives about the
state that are perpetuated by neoliberals. Were there legitimate problems with
the 2008–2009 stimulus packages? Absolutely. But the myths about "scandal-
ous investments" that neoliberals have promulgated are not actually related to
those problems.

A substantial amount of damage to the public's perception of the Keynesian
model has been done by the perpetuation of these myths. Nevertheless, there is an
opportunity to undo some of this damage at the moment, particularly in Australia
and the US, where these myths are particularly influential. The governments currently in power in these countries – the Turnbull government in Australia and the
Trump administration/Republican Congress in the US – are so desperate to prop
up the dying fossil fuel industries that they are increasingly offering (to coal companies in particular) large and very publicly visible subsidies. This undermines
the notion that the political right is ideologically committed to "letting the market
decide." There is an opening for Green Keynesians to highlight this hypocrisy and
demonstrate that the opposition from neoliberals to "picking winners" is simply
opposition to a clean energy transition and a commitment to vested interests.

Importantly, environmentalists need to ensure that in doing so, they do not
focus the public debate solely on what the current governments should not do,
but also emphasize what could be achieved by a progressive state. It needs to
be clear to the public that there are good reasons for governments to invest in
some areas and not in others. In other words, how we talk about the state matters.
This study has adopted a predominantly critical perspective on the 2008–2009
stimulus packages. However, the narrative has not proceeded so far down the

path of critique as to conclude that putting faith in the state is a fool's errand. The state, in its current "zombie neoliberal" form, is certainly no ecological savior. Nevertheless, reforming and rehabilitating the state presents the clearest avenue to address the global environmental crisis. Giving up on the state is giving up on humanity's best chance for survival.

Bibliography

ABC News. 2009. "Initial Praise for Govt Stimulus Package." February 3. http://www.abc. net.au/news/2009-02-03/initial-praise-for-govt-stimulus-package/282008.

AGL. 2013. *Environmental Impact Statement: Nyngan Solar Plant*. https://www.agl.com. au/-/media/AGL/About-AGL/Documents/How-We-Source-Energy/Solar-Environment/Nyngan-Solar-Plant/Assessments-and-Reports/2013/March/Nyngan-Solar-Plant-Environmental-Impact-Statement-Main-Report.pdf?la=en.

Alcott, B. 2005. "Jevons' Paradox." *Ecological Economics* 54: 9–21.

Aldred, R. and D. Tepe. 2011. "Framing Scrappage in Germany and the UK: From Climate Discourse to Recession Talk?" *Journal of Transport Geography* 19: 1563–1569.

Aldy, J. E. 2013. "A Preliminary Assessment of the American Recovery and Reinvestment Act's Clean Energy Package." *Review of Environmental Economics and Policy* 7 (1): 136–155.

Alexander, S. 2012. "Planned Economic Contraction: The Emerging Case for Degrowth." *Environmental Politics* 21 (3): 349–368.

Alhulail, I. and K. Takeuchi. 2014. "Effects of Tax Incentives on Sales of Eco-Friendly Vehicles: Evidence from Japan." Discussion Paper no. 1412, Graduate School of Economics, Kobe University, Japan.

Allcott, H. and S. Mullainathan. 2010. "Behavior and Energy Policy." *Science* 327: 1204–1205.

ACEEE. 2009. *Accelerated Retirement of Fuel-Inefficient Vehicles Through Incentives for the Purchase of Fuel-Efficient Vehicles*. White Paper, January 13. Washington, DC: ACEEE. http://aceee.org/white-paper/accelerated-retirement-fuel-inefficiency-vehicles-through-.

Andresen, S. 2007. "The Effectiveness of UN Environmental Institutions." *International Environmental Agreements: Politics, Law and Economics* 7: 317–336.

Aoshima, M. 2010. *Analysis of the Energy Consumption Savings Resulting from the Introduction of the Domestic Appliance Eco Points Program*. Tokyo: Institute of Energy Economics Japan.

Aoshima, Y. and H. Shimizu. 2012. *A Pitfall of Environmental Policy: An Analysis of "Eco-Point Program" in Japan and Its Application to the Renewable Energy Policy*. Tokyo: Institute of Innovation Research Hitotsubashi University.

Arimura, T. H. and K. Iwata. 2015. *An Evaluation of Japanese Environmental Regulations, Quantitative Approaches from Environmental Economics*. Dordrecht: Springer.

Arimura, T. H. and M. Morita. 2015. "A Policy Evaluation of the Eco-Point Program: The Program's Impact on CO2 Reductions and the Replacement of Home Appliances."

In *Environmental Subsidies to Consumers: How Did They Work in the Japanese Market?*, edited by S. Matsumoto, 91–110. New York: Routledge.

Army Corps of Engineers. n.d. "Civil Works Project Lists." Accessed February 22, 2017. http://www.usace.army.mil/Recovery/Civil-Works-Project-Lists/.

Arntz, M., T. Gregory, and U. Zierahn. 2016. "The Risk of Automation for Jobs in OECD Countries: A Comparative Analysis." Paris: OECD.

ARPA-E. 2016. *Project Impact Sheet: Direct Manufacturing of Silicon Wafers Reduces Cost and Improves Performance.* US Department of Energy. https://arpa-e.energy.gov/sites/default/files/documents/files/1366Technologies-Open%202009%20External%20Impact%20Sheet_FINAL.pdf

ASCE. 2013. *2013 Report Card for America's Infrastructure.* https://www.infrastructure reportcard.org/making-the-grade/report-card-history/2013-report-card/.

Asmelash, H. B. 2015. "Energy Subsidies and WTO Dispute Settlement: Why Only Renewable Energy Subsidies Are Challenged." *Journal of International Economic Law* 18: 261–285.

Australian Conservation Foundation, Australian Council of Trade Unions, Australian Council of Social Service, The Climate Institute, Australian Institute of Superannuation Trustees, Property Council of Australia, and the Australian Green Infrastructure Council. 2008. "Towards a Green New Deal: Economic Stimulus and Policy Action for the Double Crunch." News release. http://www.actu.org.au/Images/Dynamic/attachments/6252/Green%20New%20Deal%20statement%20-%20081202.pdf.

Australian National Audit Office. 2010. *The Home Insulation Program.* Canberra: Australian National Audit Office.

Australian Renewable Energy Agency (ARENA). 2017. Lessons Learned in the Development of Moree Solar Farm. Fotowatio Renewable Ventures. https://arena.gov.au/assets/2017/05/MSF-Lessons-Learned-FINAL.pdf.

Ayres, R. U. 2014. *The Bubble Economy: Is Sustainable Growth Possible?* Cambridge, MA: MIT Press.

Babb, S. 2013. "The Washington Consensus as Transnational Policy Paradigm: Its Origins, Trajectory and Likely Successor." *Review of International Political Economy* 20: 268–297.

Backhouse, R. E. and B. W. Bateman. 2008. "Keynesianism." In *The New Palgrave Dictionary of Economics.* 2nd ed. (online), edited by S. N. Durlauf and L. E. Blume. New York: Palgrave Macmillan. http://www.dictionaryofeconomics.com/dictionary.

Bäckstrand, K. and A. Kronsell. 2015. "The Green State Revisited." In *Rethinking the Green State: Environmental Governance toward Climate and Sustainability Transitions*, edited by S. N. Durlauf and L. E. Blume, 1–24. London: Routledge.

Ban, C. and K. Gallagher. 2015. "Recalibrating Policy Orthodoxy: The IMF Since the Great Recession." *Governance: An International Journal of Policy, Administration, and Institutions* 28: 131–146.

Ban, K.-M. 2008. *Secretary-General Ban Ki-Moon's Opening Statement to the High-Level Segment of the United Nations Climate Change Conference.* Poznan, Poland: United Nations Framework Convention on Climate Change.

Ban, K. and A. Gore. 2009. "Green Growth is Essential to any Stimulus." *Financial Times*, February 16.

Banktrack. 2012. "BankTrack Position on the Natural Capital Declaration." Last accessed September 5, 2012. https://www.banktrack.org/show/news/banktrack_position_on_the_natural_capital_declaration.

Barbier, E. 2010. *A Global Green New Deal: Rethinking the Economic Recovery.* Cambridge: Cambridge University Press.

Barry, J. and R. Eckersley. 2005. "An Introduction to Reinstating the State." In *The State and the Global Ecological Crisis*, edited by J. Barry and R. Eckersley, ix–xxv. Cambridge, MA: MIT Press.

BC Environmental Assessment Office. n.d. "Northwest Transmission Line: Project Timeline." Last accessed August 5, 2017. https://projects.eao.gov.bc.ca/p/northwest-transmission-line/detail.

BC Hydro. n.d. "Energy in BC: Northwest Transmission Line Project." Last accessed November 30, 2016. https://www.bchydro.com/energy-in-bc/projects/ntl.html.

BCTC. 2009. Northwest Transmission Line Proposal: Green Infrastructure Fund (on file with author).

Beattie, A. and J. Chaffin. 2012. "China Takes Solar Power Dispute to WTO." *Financial Times*, November 5. https://www.ft.com/content/b5b8a1cc-2768-11e2-8c4f-00144feabdc0.

Belluz, J. 2011. "Home Renovation Free Ride: Do Energy Rebates Help the Environment or Fund Home Makeovers That Would Have Happened Anyway?" *Maclean's Magazine*, April 4.

Berkhout, P. H. G., J. C. Muskens, and J. W. Velthuijsen. 2000. "Defining the Rebound Effect." *Energy Policy* 28: 425–432.

Bernard, S., S. Asokan, H. Warrell, and J. Lemer. 2009. "The Greenest Bail-Out?" *Financial Times*, August 17.

Bernhart, H. 2011. "Letter from Prof H. H. Bernhart to Achim Steiner." May 4. http://www.hanamana.de/dul/sites/hanamana.de.dul/files/briefsteiner04_05_2011english.pdf.

Berr, E. 2009. "Keynes and Sustainable Development." *International Journal of Political Economy* 38 (3): 22–39.

Berr, E. 2015. "Sustainable Development in a Post Keynesian Perspective: Why Eco-Development is Relevant to Post Keynesian Economics." *Journal of Post Keynesian Economics* 37 (3): 459–480.

Biermann, F. and S. Bauer, eds. 2005. *A World Environment Organization: Solution or Threat for Effective International Environmental Governance?* London: Ashgate.

Binswanger, M. 2001. "Technological Progress and Sustainable Development: What About the Rebound Effect?" *Ecological Economics* 36: 119–132.

Birds Korea. 2010. *The Anticipated Impacts of the Four Rivers Project (Republic of Korea) on Waterbirds*. Birds Korea Preliminary Report. Busan: Birds Korea. http://birdskorea.org/Habitats/4-Rivers/Downloads/Birds-Korea-4-River-Report-March-12-2010.pdf.

Blackwater, B. 2012. "Two Cheers for Environmental Keynesianism." *Capitalism Nature Socialism* 23 (2): 51–74.

Blackwell, R. 2011. "Temporary Green Policies Leave Businesses in Limbo." *The Globe and Mail*, March 23. http://www.theglobeandmail.com/report-on-business/industry-news/energy-and-resources/temporary-green-policies-leave-businesses-in-limbo/article1954145/.

Blanchard, O. J. 2008. "Neoclassical Synthesis." In *The New Palgrave Dictionary of Economics*. 2nd ed. (online), edited by S. N. Durlauf and L. E. Blume. New York: Palgrave Macmillan. http://www.dictionaryofeconomics.com/dictionary.

Blinder, A. 2008. "A Modest Proposal: Eco-Friendly Stimulus." *New York Times*, July 27. http://www.nytimes.com/2008/07/27/business/27view.html.

Block, J., G. De Vries, and P. Sandner. 2012. "Venture Capital and the Financial Crisis: An Empirical Study across Industries and Countries." In *The Oxford Handbook of Venture Capital*, edited by D. Cumming, 37–60. Oxford: Oxford University Press.

Blok, K., H. L. F. de Groot, E. E. M. Luiten, and M. G. Rietbergen. 2004. *The Effectiveness of Policy Instruments for Energy-Efficiency Improvement in Firms: The Dutch Experience.* Vol. 15 of *Eco-Efficiency in Industry and Science.* Dordrecht: Springer.

Board of Audit. 2012. *Regarding the Results of Measures and Subsidies to Increase the use of Green Home Appliances.* Report based on Article 30–2 of the *Accounting and Audit Institution Act*, October.

Bolinger, M., R. Wiser, and N. Darghouth. 2010. "Preliminary Evaluation of the Section 1603 Treasury Grant Program for Renewable Power Projects in the United States." *Energy Policy* 38: 6804–6819.

Bonvillian, W. B. and R. V. Atta. 2011. "ARPA-E and DARPA: Applying the DARPA Model to Energy Innovation." *The Journal of Technology Transfer* 36 (5): 469.

Bonvillian, W. B. and C. Weiss. 2009. "Taking Covered Wagons East: A New Innovation Theory for Energy and Other Established Technology Sectors." *Innovations* 4 (4): 289–300.

Borger, J. and F. Carus. 2009. "Climate Change the Biggest Loser of G20 Summit, Warn Environmental Groups." *The Guardian*, April 3. http://www.theguardian.com/environ ment/2009/apr/03/g20-climate-change-stimulus-package.

Borgnäs, K. 2015. "Marxist Crisis Theory and the Global Environmental Challenge." In *The Politics of Ecosocialism: Transforming Welfare*, edited by K. Borgnäs, T. Eskelinen, J. Perkiö, and R. Warlenius. London: Routledge.

Boughton, J. M. 2002. Why White, Not Keynes? Inventing the Postwar International Monetary System. International Monetary Fund Working Paper No. 02/52. https:// www.imf.org/en/Publications/WP/Issues/2016/12/30/Why-White-Not-Keynes-Invent ing-the-Post-War-International-Monetary-System-15718.

Bowen, A. and N. Stern. 2010. "Environmental Policy and the Economic Downturn." *Oxford Review of Economic Policy* 26 (2): 137–163.

Bowen, A., S. Fankhauser, N. Stern, and D. Zenghelis. 2009. "An Outline of the Case for a 'Green' Stimulus." Policy Brief, London: Grantham Research Institute on Climate Change and the Environment and Centre for Climate Change Economics and Policy.

Boyle, T. 2007. "Renovators Hail Energy Retrofit Plan." *The Star*, January 27. https:// www.thestar.com/news/2007/01/27/renovators_hail_energy_retrofit_plan.html.

Brahmbhatt, M. 2014. "Criticizing Green Stimulus." *WIREs Climate Change* 5: 15–21.

Bramley, M. and P. J. Partington. 2009. *Evaluation of the Government of Canada's Greenhouse Gas Reduction Policies, Prepared for the Climate Change Performance Index 2010.* Vancouver: The Pembina Institute.

Brand, U. 2012. "Green Economy: The Next Oxymoron?" *GAIA* 21 (1): 28–32.

Brander, J. A., Q. Du, and T. Hellmann. 2014. "The Effects of Government-Sponsored Venture Capital: International Evidence." *Review of Finance* 19 (2): 571–618.

Branscomb, L. M. and J. H. Keller. 1998. *Investing in Innovation: Creating a Research and Innovation Policy That Works.* Cambridge, MA: MIT Press.

Broder, J. 2008. "Obama Confirms Climate Change Goals." *New York Times*, 18 November. http://www.nytimes.com/2008/11/19/us/politics/19climate.html.

Broome, A. 2010. "The International Monetary Fund, Crisis Management and the Credit Crunch." *Australian Journal of International Affairs* 64: 37–54.

Broome, A. 2015. "Back to Basics: The Great Recession and the Narrowing of IMF Policy Advice." *Governance* 28 (2): 147–165.

Broun, P. 2012. Statement by Representative Paul C. Broun, Chairman, Subcommittee on Investigations and Oversight, Committee on Science, Space, and Technology, U.S. House of Representatives. A Review of the Advanced Research Projects Agency-Energy,

Hearing Before the Subcommittee on Investigations and Oversight, Committee on Science, Space, and Technology, U.S. House of Representatives, 112th Congress, 2nd Session, January 24, 2012. https://www.gpo.gov/fdsys/pkg/CHRG-112hhrg72379/html/CHRG-112hhrg72379.htm.

Brown, H. 2011. "Eco-Logical Principles for Next-Generation Infrastructure." *The Bridge* 41 (1): 19–26.

Browne, B. and T. Swann. 2017. *Money for Nothing*. Discussion Paper, the Australia Institute. http://www.tai.org.au/sites/defualt/files/P357%20Money%20for%20nothing_0.pdf.

Brownlee, M. 2013. *Financing Residential Energy Savings: Assessing Key Features of Residential Energy Retrofit Financing Programs*. Policy Brief, Ottawa: Sustainable Prosperity.

Bullis, K. 2014. "ARPA-E's Strategy for Survival." *MIT Technology Review*, February 24. https://www.technologyreview.com/s/524901/arpa-es-strategy-for-survival/.

Burton, B. 2015. "FutureGen's Demise Another Blow to CCS." *Renew Economy*, February 5. http://reneweconomy.com.au/futuregens-demise-another-blow-to-ccs-48915/.

Business-Expert Task Force on Low Carbon Economic Prosperity. 2009. An Open Letter to G20 Leaders. March 31. World Economic Forum. http://www.weforum.org/pdf/climate/G20_ProsperityTaskForceLetter.pdf.

Canada and BC. 2009. Draft Green Infrastructure Fund Agreement for Northwest Transmission Line Project. http://thetyee.ca/News/2011/07/17/GIF-NTL-Contribution-Agreement.pdf.

Canis, B., J. J. Grimmett, M. D. Platzer, and B. D. Yacobucci. 2010. *Accelerated Vehicle Retirement Programs in Japan and South Korea: Background for Congress*. CRS Report for Congress, Congressional Research Service. https://www.everycrsreport.com/reports/R41462.html.

Capoccia, G. and R. D. Kelemen. 2007. "The Study of Critical Junctures: Theory, Narrative, and Counterfactuals in Historical Institutionalism." *World Politics* 59 (3): 341–369.

Capozza, I. 2011. "Greening Growth in Japan." OECD Environment Working Papers No. 28. Paris: OECD.

Card, J. 2009. "Korea's Four Rivers Project: Economic Boost or Boondoggle?" *Yale Environment 360* (blog), September 21. http://e360.yale.edu/features/koreas_four_rivers_project_economic_boost_or_boondoggle.

Cariboni, D. 2012. "Rio + 20: Developing Countries Accept Green Economy." *Inter Press Service News Agency*, June 17. http://www.ipsnews.net/2012/06/rio20-developing-countries-accept-green-economy/.

Carin, B. and D. Shorr. 2013. *The G20 as a Lever for Progress*. CIGI G20 Papers No. 7, Waterloo, ON: Centre for International Governance Innovation. https://www.cigionline.org/sites/default/files/g20no7_0.pdf.

Casey, M. 2008. "Why the Cyclone in Myanmar Was So Deadly." *National Geographic News*, May 8. http://news.nationalgeographic.com/news/2008/05/080508-AP-the-perfect.html.

Casey, T. 2016. "7.5 MW of New Rooftop Solar in One Blow for US Navy." *CleanTechnica*, March 18. https://cleantechnica.com/2016/03/18/7-5-mw-new-rooftop-solar-one-blow-us-navy/.

Cato, M. 2013. *The Paradox of Green Keynesianism*. Weymouth, UK: Green House.

CCPA. 2009. *Federal Budget 2009: CCPA Analysis*. Ottawa: CPPA. http://www.policyalternatives.ca/publications/reports/federal-budget-2009.

CELA. 2011. *Healthy Retrofits: The Case for Better Integration of Children's Environmental Health Protection into Energy Efficient Programs.* Toronto, ON: Canadian Environmental Law Association.

Center for American Progress Action Fund and SmartTransportation.org. 2008. *Cash for Clunkers.* Washington, DC: Center for American Progress. https://cdn.american progress.org/wp-content/uploads/issues/2008/pdf/cash_for_clunkers.pdf.

Cha, Y. J., M. P. Shim, and S. K. Kim. 2011. "The Four Major Rivers Restoration Project." Paper presented at the UN Water International Conference, Zaragoza, October 3–5. http://www.un.org/waterforlifedecade/green_economy_2011/pdf/session_8_water_planning_cases_korea.pdf.

Chaddock, G. R. 2009. "Obama Wins His Economic Stimulus Package, but without the Bipartisanship He Sought." *The Christian Science Monitor*, February 14. https://www.csmonitor.com/USA/Politics/2009/0214/obama-wins-his-economic-stimulus-package-but-without-the-bipartisanship-he-sought.

Chang, B. and A. Kendall. 2011. "Life Cycle Greenhouse Gas Assessment of Infrastructure Construction for California's High-Speed Rail System." *Transportation Research Part D*, 16: 429–434.

Chang, Y.-B., J.-K. Han, and H.-W. Kim. 2012. "Green Growth and Green New Deal Policies in the Republic of Korea." *International Journal of Labour Research* 4 (2): 151–171.

Charnovitz, S. 1993. "The Environment vs. Trade Rules: Defogging the Debate." *Environmental Law* 23: 475–517.

Charnovitz, S. 2012. "Organizing for the Green Economy: What an International Green Economy Organization Could Add." *Journal of Environment and Development* 21: 44–47.

Charnovitz, S. and C. Fischer. 2014. *Canada-Renewable Energy: Implications for WTO Law on Green and Not-So-Green Subsidies.* Washington DC: Resources for the Future.

Cho, H., J. Leitner, J. Lee, and S. Heo. 2014. "Korean Green Growth: A Paradigm Shift in Sustainability Policy, and its International Implications." *Journal of Korean Law* 13: 301–333.

Choma, R. 2010. "Most Wind Grants Go to Overseas Farms." *Investigative Reporting Workshop.* American University School of Communication, February 8. http://investigativereportingworkshop.org/investigations/wind-energy-funds-going-overseas/story/most-wind-grants-go-overseas-firms/.

Chu, B. 2016. "OECD Pushes for Global Keynesian Fiscal Stimulus to Spring Low-Growth Trap." *Independent*, November 28.

Christoff, P. and R. Eckersley. 2013. *Globalization and the Environment.* Maryland, US: Rowman & Littlefield Publishers Inc.

Clapp, J. 2014. "International Political Economy and the Environment." In *Advances in International Environmental Politics*, edited by M. Betsill, K. Hochstetler, and D. Stevis, 107–136. New York: Palgrave Macmillan.

Clapp, J. and P. Dauvergne. 2005. *Paths to a Green World: The Political Economy of the Global Environment.* Cambridge, MA: MIT Press.

Clapp, J. and E. Helleiner. 2012. "International Political Economy and the Environment: Back to the Basics?" *International Affairs* 88 (3): 485–501.

Clewlow, R. R. 2012. *An Analysis of the Energy and Climate Impacts of High-Speed Rail and Aviation in the United States.* Cambridge, MA: Union of Concerned Scientists.

Commonwealth of Australia. 2009. *Nation Building for the Future.* http://www.budget.gov.au/2009-10/content/glossy/infrastructure/download/infrastructure_overview.pdf.

Commonwealth of Australia. 2010. "Investing in Australia's Clean Energy Future." *2009–10 Budget Overview*, http://www.budget.gov.au/2009-10/content/overview/html/over view_14.htm.

Commonwealth of Australia. 2017. Budget Paper No. 1 2017–18: Statement 6 Expenses and Capital Investments, 1–53, http://budget.gov.au/2017-18/content/bp1/download/bp1_bs6.pdf.

Connell, S. 2013. "From Paradox to Paradigm: Korea's Green Growth Approach." *2nd Green Revolution* (blog), February 17. http://2ndgreenrevolution.com/2013/05/07/from-paradox-to-paradigm-koreas-green-growth-approach.

Conner, S. 2010. "Cash for Clunkers: Can Cash in the Pocket Create Concerned Consumers?" In *Advances in Marketing: Annual Meeting of the Association of Collegiate Marketing Educators*, edited by V. Lukosius and G. Aguirre, 37–38. Dallas, TX.

Construction, Forestry, Mining and Energy Union in Australia. 2016. "Just Transition for Coal Power Workers." Submission to the Senate Environment and Communications Reference Committee Inquiry on Retirement of Coal Power Stations. http://www.aph.gov.au/DocumentStore.ashx?id=7a64820f-7c06-4695-b7f2-5861d543cfc3&subId=459942.

Cook, S. and K. Smith. 2012. "Introduction: Green Economy and Sustainable Development: Bringing Back the Social." *Development* 55 (1): 5–9.

Cooper, A. 2010. "The G20 as an Improvised Crisis Committee and/or a Contested 'Steering Committee' for the World." *International Affairs* 86: 741–757.

Cooper, A. and V. Pouliot. 2015. "How Much is Global Governance Changing? The G20 as International Practice." *Cooperation and Conflict* 50: 334–350.

Cooper, G. 2008. *The Origin of Financial Crises: Central Banks, Credit Bubbles and the Efficient Market Fallacy*. Petersfield, UK: Harriman House.

COP15 Korea NGOs Network. 2009. "Green Growth Policy of the Korean Government and Its Critics." December 7. http://green-korea.tistory.com/101.

Copeland, A. and J. Kahn. 2013. "The Production Impact of 'Cash-for-Clunkers': Implications for Stabilisation Policy." *Economic Inquiry* 51 (1): 288–303.

Copenhagen Climate Council. 2009. "Open Letter to the G20 London Summit, 2009." http://www.endseurope.com/docs/90401e.pdf.

Cosbey, A. 2011. "Renewable Energy Subsidies and the WTO: The Wrong Law and the Wrong Venue." *Subsidy Watch*. Global Subsidies Initiative, (1).

Cosbey, A. and P. C. Mavroidis. 2014. "A Turquoise Mess: Green Subsidies, Blue Industrial Policy and Renewable Energy: The Case for Redrafting the Subsidies Agreement of the WTO." *Journal of International Economic Law* 0: 1–37.

Cosbey, A., K. Kulovesi, L. Casier, and A. V. Moltke. 2014. *Trade and Green Economy: A Handbook*. 3rd ed. Geneva: International Institute for Sustainable Development and United Nations Environment Programme.

Council of Economic Advisers. 2010. *The Economic Impact of the American Recovery and Reinvestment Act of 2009*. Executive Office of the President, Second Quarterly Report. https://obamawhitehouse.archives.gov/sites/default/files/microsites/100113-economic-impact-arra-second-quarterly-report.pdf.

Council of Economic Advisers. 2014. *2014 Economic Report of the President*, Washington DC: Executive Office of the President. https://www.gpo.gov/fdsys/pkg/ERP-2014/content-detail.html.

Council of the European Union. 1996. "Council Directive 96/48/EC of 23 July 1996 on the interoperability of the trans-European high-speed rail system European Union." http://eur-lex.europa.eu/legal-content/EN/TXT/?uri=LEGISSUM:l24095.

Crawford, R. and A. Stephan. 2012. "Pink Batts: Not a Scandal, but Not as Good as Claimed." *The Conversation*, October 31. https://theconversation.com/pink-batts-not-a-scandal-but-not-as-good-as-claimed-10213.

Crawford, R. and A. Stephan. 2014. "Pink Batts: What Did It Teach Us About Building Better Buildings?" *The Conversation*, February 4. https://theconversation.com/pink-batts-what-did-it-teach-us-about-building-better-buildings-21644.

Croft, A. 2009. "G20 Should Send Clear Signal on Climate Change: Denmark." *Reuters*, February 19. http://www.reuters.com/article/us-g20-environment-idUSTRE51H5B220 090218.

Crouch, C. 2011. *The Strange Non-Death of Neoliberalism*. Cambridge: Polity Press

Custers, P. 2010. "The Tasks of Keynesianism Today: Green New Deals as Transition Towards a Zero Growth Economy?" *New Political Science* 32 (2): 173–191.

Daley, J. and T. Edis. 2011. *Learning the Hard Way: Australia's Policies to Reduce Emissions*. Canberra: Grattan Institute.

Daly, H. 1991. "Sustainable Development: From Concept and Theory to Operational Principles." In *Resources, Environment, and Population: Present Knowledge, Future Options*, edited by Davis, K. and M. Berstam, 25–43. Oxford: Oxford University Press.

David Suzuki Foundation. 2009. "2009 Federal Budget Analysis," January 28. http://www.davidsuzuki.org/media/news/2009/01/2009-federal-budget-analysis/.

David Suzuki Foundation. 2011. *Property Assessed Payments for Energy Retrofits and Other Financing Options*. Vancouver, BC: David Suzuki Foundation.

Davis, L.W., A. Fuchs, and A. Gertler. 2014. "Cash for Coolers: Evaluating a Large-Scale Appliance Replacement Program in Mexico." *American Economic Journal: Economic Policy* 6 (4): 207–238.

Davidson, P. 2009. *The Keynes Solution: The Path to Global Economic Prosperity*. New York: Palgrave Macmillan.

De Graaf, J. and D. K. Batker. 2011. *What's the Economy for, Anyway?* New York: Bloomsbury Press.

Department of Climate Change and Energy Efficiency. 2011. "Factsheet Home Insulation Program: Emissions Reductions." http://www.climatechange.gov.au/sites/climatechange/files/files/climate-change/factsheet-hisp-emissions-reductions.pdf.

DOE (US). n.d.a. "FE Implementation of the Recovery Act." Washington, DC: Office of Fossil Energy. Last accessed January 30, 2017. https://energy.gov/fe/fe-implementation-recovery-act.

DOE (US). n.d.b. "US Department of Energy – Loan Guarantee Program." Washington, DC: Office of Fossil Energy. Last accessed September 20, 2017. https://energy.gov/savings/us-department-energy-loan-guarantee-program.

DOE (US). n.d.c. "Section 1705 Loan Program." Last accessed September 20, 2017. https://energy.gov/lpo/services/section-1705-loan-program.

DOE (US). 2009. "Secretary Chu Announces Nearly $300 Million Rebate Program to Encourage Purchases of Energy Efficient Appliances." July 14. https://energy.gov/articles/secretary-chu-announces-nearly-300-million-rebate-program-encourage-purchases-energy.

DOE (US). 2012. "Successes of the Recovery Act." https://www.energy.gov/downloads/successes-recovery-act-january-2012.

DOE (US). 2016. "5 Big Wins in Clean Energy from the Loan Programs Office." February 17. https://energy.gov/articles/5-big-wins-clean-energy-loan-programs-office.

DOE (US). 2017a. "FY 2018 Congressional Budget Request: Budget in Brief." Office of Chief Financial Officer. https://energy.gov/sites/prod/files/2017/05/f34/FY2018 BudgetinBrief_0.pdf.

DOE (US). 2017b. "Portfolio Projects." Last accessed August 5, 2017. https://energy.gov/lpo/portfolio/portfolio-projects.

Department of Industry, Innovation and Science (Australia). n.d. "Carbon Capture and Storage Flagships Program." Last accessed October 15, 2017. https://industry.gov.au/resource/LowEmissionsFossilFuelTech/Pages/Carbon-Capture-Storage-Flagships.aspx.

Department of Industry, Innovation, Science, Research and Tertiary Education (Australia). 2012. *Solar Flagships: Questions on Notice*. Economics Legislation Committee, Budget Estimates Hearing 2012–13, May 28–29.

Detrow, S. 2015. "Weatherization and Other Energy-Efficiency Efforts May Not be Worth the Cost, According to a New Study." *Scientific American*, June 24. https://www.scientificamerican.com/article/energy-efficiency-efforts-may-not-pay-off/.

Deutsche Bank Advisors. 2008. *Economic Stimulus: The Case for "Green" Infrastructure, Energy Security and "Green" Jobs*. Deutsche Bank Group. https://institutional.deutscheam.com/content/_media/1113_GreenEconomicStimulus.pdf.

Dhar, S. 2014. *IMF Macroeconomic Policy Advice in the Financial Crisis Aftermath. Background Paper*, Washington, DC: Independent Evaluation Office of the International Monetary Fund.

Dickerson, P. 2011. "The (Too Short) Extension of Section 1603 Renewable Energy Cash Grants." *The Electricity Journal* 24 (2): 27–33.

Docena, H. 2012. "From Culprits to Saviors: The Triumph of Green Capital at the Rio + 20." *Global Dialogue: Newsletter for the International Sociological Association*. Madrid: International Sociological Association.

Dovers, S. 2013. "The Australian Environmental Policy Agenda." *Australian Journal of Public Administration* 72 (2): 114–128.

Dowling, J. 2012. "Revamp for Insulation Guidelines." *Sydney Morning Herald*, February 22. http://www.smh.com.au/federal-politics/political-news/revamp-for-insulation-guidelines-20120221-1tlu2?deviceType=text.

Dreher, A., S. Marchesi, and J. R. Vreeland. 2008. "The Political Economy of IMF Forecasts." *Public Choice* 137: 145–171.

Duca, J. V. 2013. "Subprime Mortgage Crisis." *Federal Reserve History*, November 22. http://www.federalreservehistory.org/Events/DetailView/55.

Eckhouse, B. and E. Roston. 2016. "Trump Can't Kill Solyndra Loan Office That Outperforms Banks." *Bloomsberg*, November 30. https://www.bloomberg.com/news/articles/2016-11-28/trump-can-t-kill-solyndra-loan-program-that-outperforms-banks.

Edenhofer, O. and N. Stern. 2009. *Towards a Global Green Recovery: Recommendations for Immediate G20 Action*. Report submitted to the G20 London Summit, Potsdam: Potsdam Institute for Climate Impact Research and Grantham Research Institute on Climate Change and the Environment at the London School of Economics.

Elections BC. 2011. "Financial Reports and Political Contributions System." Last accessed September 28, 2016. http://contributions.electionsbc.gov.bc.ca/pcs/.

Elmendorf, D. and J. Furman. 2008. "Three Keys to Effective Fiscal Stimulus." *The Washington Post*, January 25. https://www.brookings.edu/opinions/three-keys-to-effective-fiscal-stimulus/.

Energy Efficient Strategies. 2011. *The Value of Ceiling Insulation: Impacts of Retrofitting Ceiling Insulation to Residential Dwellings in Australia*. Report for the Insulation Council of Australia and New Zealand (ICANZ), version 4.0.

Energy Information Administration. n.d. "Total Carbon Dioxide Emissions from the Consumption of Energy 2014." Last accessed January 30, 2017. http://www.eia.gov/cfapps/ipdbproject/IEDIndex3.cfm?tid=90&pid=44&aid=8.

Energy Information Administration (US). 2012. "RECS Data Show Decreased Energy Consumption Per Household." Residential Energy Consumption Survey. Last accessed January 30, 2017. https://www.eia.gov/consumption/residential/reports/2009/consump tion-down.php?src=%E2%80%B9%20Consumption%20%20%20%20%20%20 Residential%20Energy%20Consumption%20Survey%20(RECS)-f5.

Energy Information Administration. 2013. "Use of Energy in the United States: Explained Energy Use in Homes." Last accessed January 30, 2017. https://www.eia.gov/energy explained/index.cfm?page=us_energy_homes.

Environment Canada. 2011. *A Climate Change Plan for the Purposes of the Kyoto Protocol Implementation Act*. Ottawa: Environment Canada.

Environment Canada. 2014. *Canada's Emissions Trends*. Ottawa: Environment Canada.

Environment Communications and the Arts References Committee (Australia). 2010. "Energy Efficient Homes Package (Ceiling Insulation)." https://www.aph.gov.au/bina ries/senate/committee/eca_ctte/eehp/report/report.pdf.

Environmental Protection Agency (US). n.d. "EPA Programs that Implement the Recovery Act." Last accessed January 30, 2017. https://archive.epa.gov/recovery/web/html/pro grams.html.

Environmental Protection Agency (US). 2006. *Life Cycle Assessment: Principles and Practice*. Virginia, US: Scientific Applications International Corporation.

Eskelinen, T. 2015. "Possibilities and Limits of Green Keynesianism." In *The Politics of Ecosocialism: Transforming Welfare*, edited by K. Borgnäs, T. Eskelinen, J. Perkiö, and R. Warlenius, 101–115. London: Routledge.

Etsy, D. C. 1994. *Greening the GATT: Trade, Environment, and the Future*. Washington, DC: Peterson Institute for International Economics.

European Greens. n.d. "Green New Deal." Last accessed October 15, 2017. https://euro peangreens.eu/content/green-new-deal.

European Greens. 2010. *Why We Need a Green New Deal*. Brussels: The Greens/EFA in the European Parliament.

Eyraud, L., A. Wane, C. Zhang, and B. Clements. 2011. *Who's Going Green and Why? Trends and Determinants of Green Investment*. International Monetary Fund Working Paper, Washington, DC: International Monetary Fund.

Fehrenbacher, K. 2016. "Donald Trump Goes Solar on Hillary Clinton During the First Debate." *Fortune*, September 27. http://fortune.com/2016/09/26/trump-solyndra-debate/.

Feinberg, S. 2016. "Lagging Behind: The State of High Speed Rail in the U.S." Written Statement of Sarah Feinberg Administrator, Federal Railroad Administration, US Department of Transportation Before the House Committee on Oversight and Government Reform Subcommittee on Transportation and Public Assets. https://oversight.house. gov/hearing/lagging-behind-the-state-of-high-speed-rail-in-the-united-states/.

Feindt, P. H. and R. Cowell. 2010. "The Recession, Environmental Policy and Ecological Modernization – What's New About the Green New Deal?" *International Planning Studies* 15 (3): 191–211.

Fields, R. 2010. "Ohio Gov.-Elect John Kasich Rejects Passenger Train He Says Will Travel an Average Speed of 39 mph." *POLITIFACT Ohio*, December 8. http://www. politifact.com/ohio/statements/2010/dec/08/john-kasich/ohio-gov-elect-john-kasich-rejects-passenger-train/.

Financial Times. n.d. "Definition of Fiscal Stimulus." *Financial Times Lexicon*. Last accessed October 26, 2017. http://lexicon.ft.com/Term?term=fiscal-stimulus&mhq5j=e6.

Finnemore, M. and K. Sikkink. 1998. "International Norm Dynamics and Political Change." *International Organisation* 42: 887–917.

Flynn, S. 2009. "America's Infrastructure Crisis." *CNN AC360°* (blog), January 28. http://ac360.blogs.cnn.com/2009/01/28/america%E2%80%99s-infrastructure-crisis/.

Fontana, G. and M. Sawyer. 2016. "Towards Post-Keynesian Ecological Macroeconomics." *Ecological Economics* 121: 186–195.

ForestEthics. 2009. "NorthWest Transmission Line Anything But 'Green'." *Pacific Free Press*, September 18. http://www.pacificfreepress.com/2009/09/18/opinion/northwest-transmission-line-anything-but-qgreenq.html.

Foster, J. B. 2002. *Ecology Against Capitalism*. New York: Monthly Review Press.

Foster, J. B., R. York, and B. Clark. 2011. *The Ecological Rift: Capitalism's War on the Earth*. New York: Monthly Review Press.

Foster, J. D. 2009. "Keynesian Fiscal Stimulus Policies Stimulate Debt – Not the Economy." July 27. http://www.heritage.org/report/keynesian-fiscal-stimulus-policies-stimulate-debt-not-the-economy.

Fowlie, M., M. Greenstone, and C. Wolfram. 2015. *Do Energy Efficiency Investments Deliver? Evidence from the Weatherization Assistance Program*. Cambridge, MA: National Bureau of Economic Research.

Fox, J. 2008. "The Comeback Keynes." TIME, October 23. http://content.time.com/time/magazine/article/0,9171,1853302,00.html.

French, H., M. Renner, and G. Gardner. 2009. *Toward a Transatlantic Green New Deal*. Brussels: Heinrich Böll Foundation.

Friedman, T. 2007a. "A Warning from the Garden." *The New York Times*, January 19. http://www.nytimes.com/2007/01/19/opinion/19friedman.html.

Friedman, T. 2007b. "The Power of Green." *The New York Times*, April 15. http://www.nytimes.com/2007/04/15/opinion/15iht-web-0415edgreen-full.5291830.html.

Friedman, T. 2009. "The Inflection is Near?" *The New York Times*, March 7. http://www.nytimes.com/2009/03/08/opinion/08friedman.html.

Frischmann, B. M. 2012. *Infrastructure: The Social Value of Shared Resources*. Oxford: Oxford University Press.

Fuchs, D. A. and S. Lorek. 2005. "Sustainable Consumption Governance: A History of Promises and Failures." *Journal of Consumer Policy* 28: 261–288.

Fuchs, E. R. H. 2010. "Rethinking the Role of the State in Technology Development: DARPA and the Case for Embedded Network Governance." *Research Policy* 39: 1133–1147.

Fukada, T. 2009. "Aso Unveils Record Stimulus: Latest Package Brings Total Cost to ¥57 Trillion." *The Japan Times*, April 11.

G20. 2009a. "London Summit – Leaders' Statement." Presented at G20 London Summit 2009, University of Toronto, Canada, April 1–2. http://www.g20.utoronto.ca/summits/2009london.html.

G20. 2009b. "Pittsburg Summit – Leaders' Statement." Presented at G20 Pittsburg Summit, David L. Lawrence Convention Center, September 24–25. http://www.g20.utoronto.ca/summits/2009pittsburgh.html.

G20. 2010a. "G20 Toronto Summit Declaration." Presented at G20 Toronto Summit 2010, Metro Toronto Convention Center, June 26–27. http://www.g20.utoronto.ca/summits/2010toronto.html.

G20. 2010b. "Seoul Summit Document." Presented at G20 Seoul Summit 2010, COEX Convention and Exhibition Center, November 11–12. http://www.g20.utoronto.ca/2010/g20seoul-doc.html.

Gamtessa, S. F. 2013. "An Explanation of Residential Energy-Efficiency Retrofit Behavior in Canada." *Energy and Buildings* 57: 155–164.

GAO (US). 2012. *Advanced Research Projects Agency–Energy Could Benefit from Information on Applicants' Prior Funding*. Washington, DC: US Department of Energy.

GAO (US). 2015. *DOE Loans Programs: Current Estimated Net Costs Include $2.2 Billion in Credit Subsidy, Plus Administrative Costs*. Report to Congressional Committees, Washington, DC.

Garnett, A. J., C. R. Greig, and M. Oettinger. 2014. *ZeroGen ICGG with CCS, A Case History*. 2nd ed. Brisbane: University of Queensland.

Gayer, T. and E. Parker. 2013. *Cash for Clunkers: An Evaluation of the Car Allowance Rebate System*. Washington, DC: Brookings Institution. https://www.brookings.edu/research/cash-for-clunkers-an-evaluation-of-the-car-allowance-rebate-system/.

GGI. n.d. "About GGGI: Programs & History." Last accessed July 20, 2017. http://gggi.org/about-gggi/programs-plan-history/.

Gilbert, N. 2009. "World Leaders Fail to Kick-start Green Economy." *Nature*, April 3. http://www.nature.com/news/2009/090403/full/news.2009.236.html.

Gill, S. 2011. "Organic Crisis, Global Leadership and Progressive Alternatives." In *Global Crises and the Crisis of Global Leadership*, edited by S. Gill, 233–254. Cambridge: Cambridge University Press.

Global CCS Institute. 2017. "Projects Database: Petra Nova Carbon Capture." Last accessed September 1, 2017. https://www.globalccsinstitute.com/projects/petra-nova-carbon-capture-project.

GNDP. 2008. *A Green New Deal: Joined-up Policies to Solve the Triple Crunch of the Credit Crisis, Climate Change and High Oil Prices*. London: New Economics Foundation.

Gnos, C. and L.-P. Rochon. 2008. *The Keynesian Multiplier*. London: Routledge.

Goldstein, J. and D. Tyfield. 2017. "Green Keynesianism: Bringing the Entrepreneurial State Back in(to Question)?" *Science as Culture* 1–24. http://www.tandfonline.com/doi/abs/10.1080/09505431.2017.1346598?journalCode=csac20).

Goodman, J. 2012. "Beyond the 'Green Economy': Contradictions of Ecosystem Pricing." Presented at Life & Debt: Living through the Financialisation of the Biosphere Conference, University of Technology Sydney, July 24–25.

Goods, C. 2011. "Labour Unions, the Environment and 'Green Jobs'." *The Journal of Australian Political Economy* 67: 47–67.

Gore, C. 2010. "The Global Recession of 2009 in a Long-Term Development Perspective." *Journal of International Development* 22 (6): 714–738.

Government of Canada. 2009. *Building Infrastructure to Create Jobs*. Canada's Economic Action Plan, (3rd report). Ottawa.

Government of Canada. 2012. *A Final Report to Canadians: The Stimulus Phase of Canada's Economic Action Plan*. Ottawa.

Grabel, I. 2011. "Not Your Grandfather's IMF: Global Crisis, 'Productive Incoherence' and Developmental Policy Space." *Cambridge Journal of Economics* 35: 805–830.

Grabell, M. 2012. *Money Well Spent? The Truth Behind the Trillion-Dollar Stimulus, the Biggest Economic Recovery Plan in History*. New York: PublicAffairs.

Green, A. 2006. "You Can't Pay Them Enough: Subsidies, Environmental Law, and Social Norms." *Harvard Environmental Law Review* 30: 407–440.

Green Budget Coalition. 2016. *Recommendations for Budget 2016*. Ottawa: Green Budget Coalition. http://greenbudget.ca/wp-content/uploads/2016/01/Full-Recommendations-Budget-2016.pdf.

Green Budget Coalition. 2017. "Recommendations for Budget 2017." http://greenbudget.ca/wp-content/uploads/2016/11/Renewable-Energy-Energy-Efficiency-GBC-Rec-for-Budget-2017.pdf.

Greenpeace Canada. 2009. "Harper Wrong to Support False Energy Solutions and Under-fund Green Economy." January 26. http://www.greenpeace.org/canada/en/recent/harper-wrong-to-support-false/.

Greenpeace International. 2008. *False Hope: Why Carbon Capture and Storage Won't Save the Climate.* Amsterdam: Greenpeace.

Greenpeace International. 2012. "Greenpeace Comment on State of Rio + 20 Negotiations Text for Adoption." June 19. http://www.greenpeace.org/international/en/press/releases/2012/Greenpeace-comment-on-state-of-Rio20-negotiations-text-for-adoption/.

Greenpeace USA. 2009. *Highlights of ICF International Analysis: "GHG Impact of Economic Stimulus Package."* Washington, DC: Greenpeace.

Gross, R., J. Stern, C. Charles, J. Nicholls, C. Candelise, P. Heptonstall, and P. Greenacre. 2012. *On Picking Winners: The Need for Targeted Support for Renewable Energy, ICEPT.* Working Paper, London: Imperial College.

Grunwald, M. 2012. *The New New Deal: The Hidden Story of Change in the Obama Era.* New York: Simon & Schuster.

Grunwald, M. 2014. "The Truth About Obama's High-Speed Rail Program." *TIME,* August 11. http://time.com/3100248/high-speed-rail-barack-obama/.

Güven, A. B. 2012. "The IMF, the World Bank, and the Global Economic Crisis: Exploring Paradigm Continuity." *Development and Change* 43 (4): 869–898.

Haley, B. 2017. "Designing the Public Sector to Promote Sustainability Transitions: Institutional Principles and a Case Study of ARPA-E." *Environmental Innovation and Societal Transitions* 25: 107–121.

Hall, L. 2010. "Peter Garrett Demoted After Botched Insulation Program." *Sydney Morning Herald,* February 26. http://www.smh.com.au/environment/energy-smart/peter-garrett-demoted-after-botched-insulation-program-20100226-p8jn.html.

Hamilton, B. 2010. *A Comparison of Energy Efficiency Programmes for Existing Homes in Eleven Countries. Prepared for the Department of Energy and Climate Change United Kingdom,* the Regulatory Assistance Project. Brussels: Regulatory Assistance Project. http://www.raponline.org/wp-content/uploads/2016/05/rap-hamilton-internationalcomparisonresidential-2010-02-19.pdf.

Hampson, F. and P. Heinbecker. 2011. "The 'New' Multilateralism of the Twenty-First Century." *Global Governance* 17: 299–310.

Han, P. 2010. "Sustainable and Green Tourism Korea's Green New Deal and 4 Rivers Restoration Project." Presentation to the OECD Workshop on Sustainable Development Strategies and Tourism, June 18. https://www.oecd.org/cfe/tourism/45558102.pdf.

Handwerk, B. 2011. "A Quest to Clean Up Canada's Oil Sands Carbon." *National Geographic News,* August 20. http://news.nationalgeographic.com/news/energy/2011/08/110818-quest-carbon-capture-canada-oil-sands/.

Hanger, I. 2014. *Report of the Royal Commission into the Home Insulation Program.* Canberra: Commonwealth of Australia.

Harding, R. and J. Soble. 2009. "Eco-Points Scheme Off to Slow Start." *Financial Times,* May 20. https://www.ft.com/content/832e5bea-448e-11de-82d6-00144feabdc0.

Harman, K. 2010. "Carbon Capture and Storage: Australian Government Policy Initiatives," Australian Government Department of Resources Energy and Tourism. http://www.cagsinfo.net/__data/assets/pdf_file/0017/845/session3-1.pdf.

Harris, J. 2013. "Green Keynesianism: Beyond Standard Growth Paradigms." In *Building a Green Economy: Perspectives from Ecological Economics,* edited by R. Richardson, 69–82. East Lansing: Michigan State University Press.

Hartcher, P. 2009. "Toey Liberals Spoiling for an Election Fight Are Just Plain Batty." *Sydney Morning Herald,* 23 May.

Hawke, A. 2010. Review of the Administration of the Home Insulation Program, April 6. http://www.homeinsulationroyalcommission.gov.au/hearings/Documents/Evidence31 March2014/AGS.002.039.1149.pdf.

Heinberg, R. 2011. *The End of Growth: Adapting to Our New Economic Reality.* Gabriola Island: New Society Publishers.

Hepburn, C. and A. Bowen. 2012. *Prosperity with Growth: Economic Growth, Climate Change and Environmental Limits.* London: Grantham Research Institute on Climate Change and the Environment. http://www.lse.ac.uk/GranthamInstitute/publication/prosperity-with-growth-economic-growth-climate-change-and-environmental-limits-working-paper-92/.

Hernández, D. and S. Bird. 2010. "Energy Burden and the Need for Integrated Low-Income Housing and Energy Policy." *Poverty & Public Policy* 2 (4): 5–25.

Herzog, H. 2016. *Lessons Learned from CCS Demonstration and Large Pilot Projects.* Working Paper, Cambridge, MA: MIT Energy Initiative. https://sequestration.mit.edu/bibliography/CCS%20Demos.pdf.

Hess, D. 2012. *Good Green Jobs in a Global Economy.* Cambridge, MA: MIT Press.

Hewes, W. 2008. *Creating Jobs and Stimulating the Economy through Investment in Green Water Infrastructure.* Washington, DC: American Rivers and Alliance for Water Efficiency.

Hinterleitner, M., F. Sager, and E. Thomann. 2016. "The Politics of External Approval: Explaining the IMF's Evaluation of Austerity Programmes." *European Journal of Political Research* 55: 549–567.

Holroyd, C. 2014. "Japan's Green Growth Policies: Domestic Engagement, Global Possibilities." *The Japanese Political Economy* 40 (3–4): 3–36.

Horie, M. 2015. "Budgeting in Japan After the Global Financial Crisis: Postponing Decisions on Crucial Issues." In *The Global Financial Crisis and its Budget Impacts in OECD Nations: Fiscal Responses and Future Challenges*, edited by J. Wanna, E. A. Lindquist, and J. de Vries, 118–144. Cheltenham, UK: Edward Elgar Publishing.

Houde, S. and J. E. Aldy. 2014. *Belt and Suspenders and More: The Incremental Impact of Energy Efficiency Subsidies in the Presence of Existing Policy Instruments.* Working Paper no. 20541, Cambridge, MA: National Bureau of Economic Research.

House Committee on Oversight and Government Reform (US). 2012. *Statement of Gregory H. Kats, President of Capital E*, May 16.

House Committee on Science and Technology (US). 2010. *Testimony of John Denniston, Partner, Kleiner Perkins Caufield & Byers*, January 27.

House Subcommittee on Energy and the Environment (US). 2007. *Testimony of John Denniston, Partner, Kleiner Perkins Caufield & Byers.* Establishing the Advanced Research Projects Agency-Energy (ARPA-E), April 26.

House Subcommittees on Energy and Oversight, Committee on Science, Space, and Technology (US). 2016. *Statement of Dr. Arun Majumadar, Director, Advanced Research Projects Agency-Energy*, Department of Energy, 24 January.

Houser, T., S. Mohan, and R. Heilmayr. 2009. *A Green Global Recovery? Assessing US Economic Stimulus and the Prospects for International Coordination.* Policy Brief, February, Washington, DC: Peterson Institute for International Economics and World Resources Institute.

Hoicka, C. E., P. Parker, and J. Andrey. 2014. "Residential Energy Efficiency Retrofits: How Program Design Affects Participation and Outcomes." *Energy Policy* 65: 594–607.

Huberty, M., H. Gao, and J. Mandell. 2011. *Shaping the Green Growth Economy.* Berkeley: Berkeley Roundtable on the International Economy.

Hughes, G. 2011. *The Myth of Green Jobs*. London: Global Warming Policy Foundation.

IISD. 2009. "UNEP Releases Policy Brief on Global Green New Deal in Advance of G20." March 20. http://energy-l.iisd.org/news/unep-releases-policy-brief-on-global-green-new-deal-in-advance-of-g20/.

Illing, S. D. 2015. "The Earth is Too Big to Fail." *The Huffington Post*. June 22. http://www.huffingtonpost.co.uk/sean-d-illing-/earth-day_b_7116402.html.

ILO. 2010. *Global Unemployment Trends*. Geneva: ILO.

IMF. 2009. *World Economic Outlook: Crisis and Recovery*. Washington, DC: IMF.

IMF. 2010. *World Economic Outlook Update: A Policy-Driven Multispeed Recovery*. Washington, DC: IMF.

IMF. 2011. *World Economic Outlook Outlook: Slowing Growth, Rising Risks*, Washington, DC: IMF.

IMF. 2013. *Reassessing the Role and Modalities of Fiscal Policy in Advanced Economies*. Policy Paper, Washington, DC: IMF. https://www.imf.org/external/np/pp/eng/2013/072113.pdf.

Infrastructure Canada. n.d.a. "Reliable, Cleaner Energy for Underserved Areas in British Columbia." Last accessed February 10, 2014. http://www.infrastructure.gc.ca/prog/gif-fiv-eng.html.

Infrastructure Canada. n.d.b. "Producing Renewable Energy from Organic Waste." Last accessed February 10, 2014. http://www.infrastructure.gc.ca/prog/gif-fiv-eng.html.

Infrastructure Canada. 2016. *Evaluation of the Green Infrastructure Fund*. Ottawa: Government of Canada. http://www.infrastructure.gc.ca/alt-format/pdf/other-autre/GIF-evaluation-eng.pdf.

Inomata, T. 2008. *Management Review of Environmental Governance within the United Nations System. Joint Inspection Unit*. Geneva: United Nations.

International Centre for Trade and Sustainable Development. 2016. "India Files WTO Challenge Against US State Programmes for Renewable Energy." *Bridges*, September 15.

International Energy Agency. 2013. "ecoENERGY Retrofit – Homes. Energy Efficiency," http://hera.iea.org/policy/ecoenergy-retrofit-homes.

International Trade Union Confederation. 2009. "What is a Just Transition?" https://www.ituc-csi.org/IMG/pdf/01-Depliant-Transition5.pdf.

Irwin, N. and Z. A. Goldfarb. 2008. "U.S. Seizes Control Of Mortgage Giants." *Washington Post*, September 8. http://www.washingtonpost.com/wp-dyn/content/article/2008/09/07/AR2008090700259.html.

Ivanova, M. 2007. "Moving Forward by Looking Back: Learning from UNEP's History." In *Global Environmental Governance: Perspectives on the Current Debate*, edited by L. Swart and E. Perry, 26–47. New York: Centre for UN Reform Education.

Ivison, J. 2011. "John Ivison: Tories calling NDP's Bluff on Budget." *National Post*, March 21. http://nationalpost.com/full-comment/john-ivison-tories-calling-ndps-bluff-on-budget/.

Iwata, K., H. Katayama, and T. H. Arimura. 2015. "Do Households Misperceive the Benefits of Energy-Saving Actions? Evidence from a Japanese Household Survey." *Energy for Sustainable Development* 25: 27–33.

Jackovics, T. 2011. "Florida's Rail Billions Go Elsewhere." *Tampa Bay Times*, May 10. http://www.tbo.com/news/floridas-rail-billions-go-elsewhere-206173.

Jackson, T. 2009. *Prosperity Without Growth: Economics for a Finite Planet*. London: Earthscan.

Jacobs, M. 2012. *Green Growth: Economic Theory and Political Discourse*. Policy Working Paper No. 108, Leeds: Centre for Climate Change Economics and Policy.

Jenkins, J. and S. Mansur. 2011. *Bridging the Clean Energy Valleys of Death: Helping American Entrepreneurs Meet the Nation's Energy Innovation Imperative.* Oakland, CA: Breakthrough Institute.

Jenkins, J., M. Muro, T. Nordhaus, M. Shellenberger, L. Tawney, and A. Trembath. 2012. *Beyond Boom & Bust: Putting Clean Tech on a Path to Subsidy Independence.* Washington, DC: Brookings Institute.

Jenkins, T. and A. Simms. 2012. *The Green Economy.* London: Global Transition.

Jessup, P. 2011. "Japan's Eco-Point Program Transforms Market for LED Lamps." *LEDS Magazine,* July 18. http://www.ledsmagazine.com/articles/2011/07/japan-s-eco-point-program-transforms-market-for-led-lamps-magazine.html.

Jevons, W.S. 1865. *The Coal Question.* 2nd ed. London: Macmillan and Co.

Jiménez, J. L., J. Perdiguero, and C. García. 2016. "Evaluation of Subsidies Programs to Sell Green Cars: Impact on Prices, Quantities and Efficiency." *Transport Policy* 47: 105–118.

Jones, B. and M. Keen. 2009. "Climate Policy and Recovery." IMF Staff Position Note, Washington, DC: IMF.

Jones, R. S. and B. Yoo. 2010. "Korea's Green Growth Strategy: Mitigating Climate Change and Developing New Growth Engines." OECD Economics Department Working Paper no. 798. http://www.oecd.org/officialdocuments/displaydocumentpdf/?cote=ECO/WKP%282010%2954&doclanguage=en.

Jones, V. 2009. "Recovery Act Funds Old and New Technology to Conserve Energy, Create Green Jobs." *The Seattle Times,* July 15.

Jun, K. 2010. *Beyond the Crisis: Korea's Emergence from the Global Financial Storm of 2008.* Seoul: Seoul Selection.

Kamin, S. B. and L. P. DeMarco. 2010. *How Did a Domestic Housing Slump Turn into a Global Financial Crisis?* Board of Governors of the Federal Reserve System International Finance Discussion Paper no. 994. Washington, DC: Federal Reserve. https://www.federalreserve.gov/pubs/ifdp/2010/994/ifdp994.pdf.

Kao, H. 2013. "Beyond Solyndra: Examining the Department of Energy's Loan Guarantee Program." *Environmental Law and Policy Review* 37: 425–509.

Kasperowicz, P. and B. German. 2012. "House Approves 'No More Solyndras Act'." *The Hill,* September 14. http://thehill.com/policy/energy-environment/249555-house-passes-no-more-solyndras-act.

Katada, S. N. 2013. "Financial Crisis Fatigue? Politics Behind Japan's Post-Global Financial Crisis Economic Contraction." *Japanese Journal of Political Science* 14 (2): 223–242.

Kawai, M. and S. Takagi. 2011. "Why Was Japan Hit so Hard by the Global Financial Crisis?" In *The Impact of the Economic Crisis on East Asia: Policy Responses from Four Economies,* edited by D. Shaw and B. J. Liu, 131–148. Cheltenham, UK: Edward Elgar Publishing.

Kelly, J. 2012. "Darkness Falls on $1.2bn Solar Dawn Project." *The Australian,* November 13. http://www.theaustralian.com.au/national-affairs/climate/solar-dawn-facility-in-queens land-fails-to-deliver/news-story/76fa037a383fa27e9643adfb129e6734.

Kelly-Detwiler, P. 2016. "ARPA-E: What Role Should the Government Play in Commercializing New Energy Technologies?" *Forbes,* May 17. https://www.forbes.com/sites/peterdetwiler/2016/05/17/arpa-e-what-role-should-the-government-play-in-commercializing-new-energy-technologies/2/#75e6ef5af446.

Kenis, A. and M. Lievens. 2015. *The Limits of the Green Economy: From Reinventing Capitalism to Repoliticising the Present.* London: Routledge.

Kennedy, C. and J. Corfee-Morlot. 2013. "Past Performance and Future Needs for Low Carbon Climate Resilient Infrastructure – An Investment Perspective." *Energy Policy* 59: 773–783.

Keynes, J. M. 1997. *General Theory of Employment, Interest and Money*. New York: Prometheus Books

Keynes, J. M. 2016. *The Essential Keynes*. Edited by Robert Skidelsky. London: Penguin Classics.

Kharas, H. and D. Lombardi. 2012. *The Group of Twenty: Origins, Prospects and Challenges for Global Governance*. Washington, DC: Brookings Institution.

Kim, H., J. Han, and J.-H. Park. 2012. *Green Growth and Green Jobs in Korea: Potentials and Perspectives*. Seoul: Energy and Climate Policy Institute for Just Transition.

Kim, J-w. 2012. "Four Major River Project and Environmental Ordeal under the Lee Myung-bak Government in South Korea." In *Democratization, Decentralization, and Environmental Governance in Asia*, edited by A. Mori, 72–85. Kyoto: Kyoto University Press.

Kim, J.-s. 2013. "The Environmental Fallout of the Four Major Rivers Project." *The Hankyoreh*, August 3. http://www.hani.co.kr/arti/english_edition/e_national/598190. html.

Kim, P. 2013. "28 Endangered Species Gone Due to 4-River Project." *The Korea Observer*, October 21. http://www.koreaobserver.com/dozens-endangered-species-perish-follow ing-river-project-8163/.

King, J. E. 2008. "Post Keynesian Economics." In *The New Palgrave Dictionary of Economics*. 2nd ed. (online), edited by S. N. Durlauf and L. E. Blume. New York: Palgrave Macmillan. http://www.dictionaryofeconomics.com/dictionary.

Kirton, J. 2013. *G20 Governance for a Globalized World*. Burlington, VT: Ashgate.

Kirton, J. and E. Kokotsis. 2015. *The Global Governance of Climate Change: G7, G20, and UN Leadership*. Burlington, VT: Ashgate.

Klein, N. 2007. *The Shock Doctrine: The Rise of Disaster Capitalism*. New York: Picador.

Klein, N. 2008. "Naomi Klein: Wall St. Crisis Should Be for Neoliberalism What Fall of Berlin Wall Was for Communism." *Democracy Now!*, October 6. https://www. democracynow.org/2008/10/6/naomi_klein.

Kobayashi, H. 2012. *Both a Hit for Environmentally 'Eco' and Economically 'Eco': The Eco-Point Strategy*. Tokyo: Japan Centre for Economic Research.

Koch, M. 2013. "Welfare After Growth: Theoretical Discussion and Policy Implications." *International Journal of Social Quality* 3 (1): 4–20.

Kojima, A. 2009. "Japan's Economy and the Global Financial Crisis." *Asia-Pacific Review* 16 (2): 15–25.

Kojima, S. 2010. "Green Growth and Green Economy in Japan." Paper presented at NISD Conference on "Green Growth and Green Economy, November 25–26, Seoul: Institute for Global Environmental Strategies.

Komine, T. 2010. "The Japanese Economy and Economic Policy After the Lehman Shock." *Hosei University Economic Review* 77 (3): 5–24.

Krugman, P. 2008. "Let's Get Fiscal." *The New York Times*, October 16. http://www. nytimes.com/2008/10/17/opinion/17krugman.html.

Krugman, P. 2010a. "Lost Decade, Here We Come." *The New York Times*, June 6. https:// krugman.blogs.nytimes.com/2010/06/06/lost-decade-here-we-come/.

Krugman, P. 2010b. "The Pain Caucus." *The New York Times*, May 30. http://www. nytimes.com/2010/05/31/opinion/31krugman.html.

Krugman, P. 2010c. "Green Economics: How We Can Afford to Tackle Climate Change." *The New York Times Magazine*, April 7. http://www.nytimes.com/2010/04/11/magaz ine/11Economy-t.html?mcubz=0.

Krugman, P. 2012. *End this Depression Now!* New York: W.W. Norton & Company.

Krugman, P. 2013. "The Japan Story. (blog)" *The New York Times*, February 5. https:// krugman.blogs.nytimes.com/?s=japan.

Krugman, P. 2014. "Keynes Is Slowly Winning." *The New York Times*, November 26. https://krugman.blogs.nytimes.com/2014/11/26/keynes-is-slowly-winning/.

Kuntze, J.-C. and T. Moerenhout. 2013. *Local Content Requirements and the Renewable Energy Industry – A Good Match?* Geneva: International Centre for Trade and Sustainable Development.

Kushler, M. 2015. "Residential Energy Efficiency Works. Don't Make a Mountain Out of the E2e Molehill." American Council for Energy Efficient Economy (blog), June 25. http:// aceee.org/blog/2015/06/residential-energy-efficiency-works#.VYxwaxu3vgg.twitter.

Ladislaw, S. O. and N. Goldberger. 2010. *Assessing the Global Green Stimulus*. Washington DC: Center for Strategic and International Studies.

Lah, T. J., Y. Park, and Y. J. Cho. 2015. "The Four Major Rivers Restoration Project of South Korea: An Assessment of Its Process, Program, and Political Dimensions." *Journal of Environment and Development* 24 (4): 375–394.

Lander, E. 2011. *The Green Economy: The Wolf in Sheep's Clothing*, Amsterdam: Transnational Institute.

Lean, G. 2009a. "Chancellor Vetoes Green Revolution in Snub to Mandelson." *The Independent*, March 8.

Lean, G. 2009b. "Hopes for Climate Treaty Set Back by G20's Weasel Word." *The Independent*, April 5.

Lee, M. and K. I. Carlaw. 2010. *Climate Justice, Green Jobs and Sustainable Production in BC*. Ottawa: Canadian Centre for Policy Alternatives.

Lee, M. and A. Card. 2012. *A Green Industrial Revolution*. Ottawa: Canadian Centre for Policy Alternatives.

Leighninger, R. 2007. *Long-Range Public Investment: The Forgotten Legacy of the New Deal Columbia*. South Carolina: University of South Carolina Press.

Lenski, S. M., G. A. Keoleian, and K. M. Bolon. 2010. "The Impact of 'Cash for Clunkers' on Greenhouse Gas Emissions: A Life Cycle Perspective." *Environmental Research Letters* 5: 1–8.

Lenski, S. M., G. A. Keoleian, and M. R. Moore. 2013. "An Assessment of Two Environmental and Economic Benefits of 'Cash for Clunkers'." *Ecological Economics* 96: 173–180.

Less, S. 2012. *Greening the Economy – Not 'Green Economy'*. Research Note. London: Policy Exchange.

Li, S., J. Linn, and E. Spiller. 2013. "Evaluating 'Cash for Clunkers': Program Effects on Auto Sales and the Environment." *Journal of Environmental Economics and Management* 65: 175–193.

Lodefalk, M. and J. Whalley. 2002. "Reviewing Proposals for a World Environmental Organization." *The World Economy* 25: 601–617.

Lombardi, C. 2010. "US Govt Awards $2.4 Billion for High-Speed Rail." *CNET*, November 3. https://www.cnet.com/news/u-s-govt-awards-2-4-billion-for-high-speed-rail/.

Lopoukhine, R. 2014. "CCS Series: Government Subsidies Keep Alberta's CCS Pipe Dream Afloat." *Desmog Canada*, February 21.

Luckhurst, J. 2016. *G20 Since the Global Crisis*. New York: Palgrave Macmillan.

Lütz, S. 2015. "From Washington Consensus to Flexible Keynesianiasm? The International Monetary Fund After the Financial Crisis." *Journal of International Organizations Studies* 6 (2): 85–98.

MacNeil, R. 2014. "Canadian Environmental Policy Under Conservative Majority Rule." *Environmental Politics* 23 (1): 174–178.

McBride, S. and J. Merolli. 2013. "Alternatives to Austerity? Post-Crisis Policy Advice from Global Institutions." *Global Social Policy* 13: 299–320.

McCarthy, S. 2012. "Energy-Saving Program Shut Down Too Early, Millions in Rebates Never Paid Out." *The Globe and Mail*, September 28. https://beta.theglobeandmail.com/news/politics/energy-saving-program-shut-down-too-early-millions-in-rebates-never-paid-out/article4575763/?ref=http://www.theglobeandmail.com&.

McConnell, D. 2012. "Not Dead Yet: Flagship 'Collapse' Only Part of Australia's Solar Story." *The Conversation*, February 10. https://theconversation.com/not-dead-yet-flagship-collapse-only-part-of-australias-solar-story-5288.

McKie, D. 2013. "EcoEnergy Home Retrofits' Early End Left Funds Unspent." *CBC News*, December 3. http://www.cbc.ca/news/politics/ecoenergy-home-retrofits-early-end-left-funds-unspent-1.2447081.

Maher, N. 2008. *Nature's New Deal: The Civilian Conservation Corps and the Roots of the American Environmental Movement*. Oxford: Oxford University Press.

Mahon, R. 2008. "Babies and Bosses: Gendering the OECD's Social Policy Discourse." In *The OECD and Transnational Governance*, edited by Mahon, R. and S. McBride, 260–275. Washington: University of Washington Press.

Mahon, R. and S. McBride. 2008. "Introduction." In *The OECD and Transnational Governance*, edited by Mahon, R. and S. McBride, 3–22. Washington: University of Washington Press.

Manser, J. S., J. A. Rollin, K. E. Brown, and E. A. Rohlfing. 2016. "ARPA-E: Accelerating U.S. Energy Innovation." *ACS Energy Letters*. Washington, DC: ACS Publications.

Marcussen, M. 2001. "The OECD in Search of a Role: Playing the Idea Game." *European Consortium for Political Research 29th Joint Sessions of Workshops*. Grenoble, France.

Marghescu, T. 2009. "Economic Meltdown and the Rise of Nature – Investing in Green Infrastructure." International Union for the Conservation of Nature (IUCN), February 9. https://www.iucn.org/content/economic-meltdown-and-rise-nature-investing-green-infrastructure-0.

Marshall, J. P. 2016. "Disordering Fantasies of Coal and Technology: Carbon Capture and Storage in Australia." *Energy Policy* 99: 288–298.

Martin, R. 2015. "As the Feds Pull Out, Dreams of 'Clean Coal' Fade." *Fortune*, February 6. http://fortune.com/2015/02/06/as-the-feds-pull-out-dreams-of-clean-coal-fade/.

Matsumoto, S. 2015a. "Environmental Subsidies to Consumers as Policy Instruments." In *Environmental Subsidies to Consumers: How Did They Work in the Japanese Market?*, edited by S. Matsumoto, 8–26. New York: Routledge.

Matsumoto, S. 2015b. "The Japanese Motor Vehicle Market." In *Environmental Subsidies to Consumers: How Did They Work in the Japanese Market?*, edited by S. Matsumoto, 155–164. New York: Routledge.

Mayring, P. 2000. "Qualitative Content Analysis." *Forum Qualitative Sozialforschung/ Forum: Qualitative Social Research* 1 (2). http://www.qualitative-research.net/index.php/fqs/article/viewArticle/1089/2385.

Mazzetti, M. 2012. "Assessing South Korea's National Strategy for Green Economic Growth." In *US–Korea 2011 Yearbook*, Maryland: U.S.–Korea Institute at SAIS, John

Hopkins University. http://uskoreainstitute.org/wp-content/uploads/2013/10/Mazzetti_YB2011.pdf.

Mazzucato, M. 2015a. *The Entrepreneurial State: Debunking Public vs. Private Sector Myths*. London: Anthem Press.

Mazzucato, M. 2015b. "The Green Entrepreneurial State." In *The Politics of Green Transformations*, edited by I. Scoones, M. Leach, and P. Newell, 134–152. London: Routledge.

Meadowcroft, J. 2005. "From Welfare State to Ecostate." In *The State and the Global Ecological Crisis*, edited by J. Barry and R. Eckersley, 3–24. Cambridge, MA: MIT Press.

Meadowcroft, J. 2012. "Greening the State?" In *Comparative Environmental Politics: Theory, Practice, and Prospects*, edited by P. F. Steinberg and S. D. VanDeveer, 63–88. Cambridge, MA: MIT Press.

Meadows, D. H., J. Randers, D. L. Meadows, and W. W. Behrens. 1972. *The Limits to Growth: A Report for the Club of Rome's Project on the Predicament of Mankind*. New York: Universe Books.

Melloan, G. 2009. "Why 'Stimulus' Will Mean Inflation." *The Wall Street Journal*, February 6. https://www.wsj.com/articles/SB123388703203755361.

METI and MLITT (Japan). 2010. "Regarding the Environmentally Friendly Car Purchase and Trade-in Subsidy Program: Supplementary Edition." http://www.meti.go.jp/policy/mono_info_service/mono/automobile/100329sankoushiryou.pdf.

Mian, A. and A. Sufi. 2010. "The Effects of Fiscal Stimulus: Evidence from the 2009 'Cash for Clunkers' Program." Working Paper 16351, Cambridge, MA: National Bureau of Economic Research. http://www.nber.org/papers/w16351.

Michaels, R. and R. Murphy. 2009. *Green Jobs: Fact or Fiction?* Washington, DC: Institute for Energy Research.

Milkis, S. M. and J. M. Mileur. 2002. *The New Deal and Triumph of Liberalism*. Amherst, MA: University of Massachusetts Press.

Milne, C. 2009. "Greens Secure Energy Efficiency in Local Green Jobs Package." News Release, February 13. https://greensmps.org.au/articles/greens-secure-energy-efficiency-local-green-jobs-package.

Min, H. 2015. "Korea's Cash-for-Clunkers Program: Household-Level Evidence." *Asian Economic Journal* 29 (4): 347–363.

Miyazaki, T. 2015. "Fiscal Stimulus Effectiveness in Japan: Evidence from Recent Policies." Discussion Paper no. 1508, Kobe: Graduate School of Economics, Kobe University.

Mizobuchi, K. and K. Takeuchi. 2015. "Did the Purchase Subsidy for Energy-Efficient Appliances Ease Electricity Shortages After Fukushima?" In *Environmental Subsidies to Consumers: How Did They Work in the Japanese Market?*, edited by S. Matsumoto, 111–138. New York: Routledge.

MLTM (Japan). 2012. *Four Rivers Restoration Project*. Seoul: MLTM.

Moe, E. 2012. "Vested Interests, Energy Efficiency and Renewables in Japan." *Energy Policy* 40: 260–273.

MOE (Japan). n.d. "Green Appliances Eco Points: Regarding the Eligible Appliances." Last accessed April 1, 2016. https://www.env.go.jp/policy/ep_kaden/buy/index.html.

MOE, METI, MIAC (Japan). n.d. "Regarding the Policy Impact of the Home Appliance Eco Point Program." Last accessed October 19, 2016. https://www.env.go.jp/council/02policy/y020-60/mat03.pdf.

MIAC (Japan). 2010. "Regarding the Improvement of Environmentally Friendly Domestic Appliance Diffusion Through the 'Eco Point' System." February 19. http://www.soumu.go.jp/menu_kyotsuu/important/topics100219.html.

Monbiot, G. 2009a. "G20 Forgets the Environment." *The Guardian*, April 3. http://www.theguardian.com/environment/georgemonbiot/2009/apr/02/1.

Monbiot, G. 2009b. "Scrap It." *The Guardian*, March 10, 2009. http://www.monbiot.com/2009/03/10/scrap-it/.

Moores, N. 2013. "Critics Claim Four Rivers Project 'A Bottomless Pit' and a 'Fraud'. What About Saemangeum?" Birds Korea (blog), October 2. http://www.birdskorea.org/Habitats/4-Rivers/BK-HA-4R-Bottomless-Pit-and-Fraud.shtml.

Morris, A. C., P. S. Nivola, and C. L. Schultze. 2012. "Clean Energy: Revisiting the Challenges of Industrial Policy." *Climate and Energy Economics Discussion Paper.* Washington, DC: The Brookings Institution.

Morriss, A. P., W. T. Bogart, A. Dorchak, and R. E. Meiners. 2009. "Green Jobs Myths." Law & Economics Research Paper no. LE09–001, Chicago: University of Illinois.

Mueller, T. and F. O. Wolf. 2009. "Green New Deal: Dead End or Pathway Beyond Capitalism?" *Turbulence* 5, December. Last accessed January 16, 2018. http://www.turbulence.org.uk/index.html@p=351.html.

Mundaca, L. and J. L. Richter. 2015. "Assessing 'Green Energy Economy' Stimulus Packages: Evidence From the U.S. Programs Targeting Renewable Energy." *Renewable and Sustainable Energy Reviews* 42: 1174–1186.

Mundy, S. 2015. "South Korea Aims for Creative Economy to End Reliance on Chaebol." *Financial Times*, June 23.

Mutter, J. 2015. *The Disaster Profiteers: How Natural Disasters Make the Rich Richer and the Poor Even Poorer.* New York: St. Martin's Press.

Nakano, S. and A. Washizu. 2017. "Changes in Consumer Behavior as a Result of the Home Appliance Eco-Point System: An Analysis Based on Micro Data From the Family Income and Expenditure Survey." *Environment Economics and Policy Studies* 19 (3): 459–482.

Nam, J.-Y. 2011. "Experts of Government-Affiliated Institute Say the Impacts of Deteriorated Water Quality Have Removed the Economic Basis Used to Justify the Project." *The Hankyoreh*, March 22. http://english.hani.co.kr/arti/english_edition/e_national/469236.html.

Nanto, D. K. 2009. "The Global Financial Crisis: Analysis and Policy Implications." CRS Report for Congress. Collingdale, PA: DIANE Publishing.

National Academy of Sciences, National Academy of Engineering, and Institute of Medicine. 2007. *Rising Above the Gathering Storm: Energizing and Employing America for a Brighter Economic Future.* Washington, DC: The National Academies Press. https://doi.org/10.17226/11463.

National Energy Technology Laboratory. 2017. "FutureGen 2.0." https://www.netl.doe.gov/File%20Library/Research/Coal/major%20demonstrations/futureGen/FE0001882-FE0005054.pdf.

National Highway Traffic Safety Administration. 2009. *Consumer Assistance to Recycle and Save Act of 2009.* Report to the House Committee on Energy and Commerce, the Senate Committee on Commerce, Science, and Transportation and the House and Senate Committees on Appropriations, US Department of Transportation. http://www.cars.gov/files/official-information/CARS-Report-to-Congress.pdf.

National Roundtable on the Environment and the Economy. 2011. *Response of the National Round Table on the Environment and the Economy to its Obligations Under the Kyoto Protocol Implementation Act.* Ottawa: ON.

Natural Capital Finance Alliance. 2012. "The Natural Capital Declaration." Presented at Rio+20 Earth Summit, United Nations. http://www.naturalcapitalfinancealliance.org/the-declaration/.

Newell, P. 2015. "The Politics of Green Transformation in Capitalism." In *The Politics of Green Transformations*, edited by I. Scoones, M. Leach and P. Newell, 68–85. Abington, UK: Routledge.

Niman, M. 2009. "Cash for Clunkers?" *ColdType (Canada)* http://works.bepress.com/niman/99/.

Nixon, R. 2014. "$11 Billion Later, High-Speed Rail is Inching Along." *The New York Times*, August 6. https://www.nytimes.com/2014/08/07/us/delays-persist-for-us-high-speed-rail.html?_r=0.

Normille, D. 2010. "Restoration or Devastation?" *Science* 327 (5973): 1568–1570.

Northwest Powerline Coalition. 2009. "Delivering Green Power to Northern British Columbia: Northwest Powerline Coalition." *Market Wired*, May 29. http://www.market wired.com/press-release/delivering-green-power-to-northern-british-columbia-north west-powerline-coalition-996823.htm.

NRCAN. 2009. *Grant Table for ecoENERGY Retrofit–Homes*. Ottawa: Government Canada. http://publications.gc.ca/collections/collection_2013/rncan-nrcan/M144-149-1-2009-eng.pdf.

NRCAN. 2010. *Evaluation of Energy Efficiency for Industry, Housing and Buildings*. Ottawa: Government of Canada. http://www.nrcan.gc.ca/evaluation/reports/2010/832.

NRCAN. 2011. *Improving Energy Performance in Canada: Report to Parliament Under the Energy Efficiency Act for the Fiscal Year 2010–2011*. Ottawa: Government of Canada.

NRCAN. 2013. "Clean Energy." In NRCAN Departmental Sustainable Development Strategy. Last accessed August 16, 2017. http://www.nrcan.gc.ca/plans-performance-reports/sustainable-development/departmental-strategy/433.

NRCAN. 2014. *Evaluation of the Clean Energy Fund (CEF)*. Ottawa: Government of Canada. http://www.nrcan.gc.ca/evaluation/reports/2014/16534.

NRCAN. 2016a. "Clean Energy Fund – Background." Government of Canada. Last accessed August 16, 2017. http://www.nrcan.gc.ca/energy/funding/current-funding-pro grams/17905.

NRCAN. 2016b. "Shell Canada Energy Quest Project." Government of Canada. Last accessed August 16, 2017. http://www.nrcan.gc.ca/energy/funding/current-funding-pro grams/18168.

NRCAN. 2016c. "Renewable Energy and Clean Energy Systems Demonstration Projects." Government of Canada. Last accessed August 16, 2017. http://www.nrcan.gc.ca/energy/funding/current-funding-programs/cef/4953.

NRCAN. (n.d.). "Frequently-Asked Questions (FAQ) about eco-ENERGY Retrofit-Homes." Last accessed August 16, 2017. http://www.nrcan.gc.ca/energy/efficiency/hous ing/home-improvements/5019.

Nugent, J. P. 2011. "Changing the Climate: Ecoliberalism, Green New Dealism, and the Struggle Over Green Jobs in Canada." *Labor Studies Journal* 36 (1): 58–82.

Obama, B. 2009. "Remarks on Transportation Infrastructure." April 16, 2009. The American Presidency Project. http://www.presidency.ucsb.edu/ws/?pid=86015.

O'Brien, R. and Williams, M. 2013. *Global Political Economy: Evolution and Dynamics*. 5th ed. New York: Palgrave Macmillan.

OECD. n.d.a. "Financing Climate Change Action." Last accessed August 1, 2014. http://www.oecd.org/env/cc/financing.htm.

OECD. n.d.b. "What is Green Growth and How Can It Help Deliver Sustainable Deve-lopment?" Last accessed July 1, 2017. http://www.oecd.org/general/whatisgreengrowt handhowcanithelpdeliversustainabledevelopment.htm.

OECD. 2002. *Indicators to Measure Decoupling of Environmental Pressure from Economic Growth*. Paris: OECD. http://www.oecd.org/environment/indicators-modelling-outlooks/1933638.pdf.

OECD. 2009a. *Policy Responses to the Economic Crisis: Investing in Innovation for Long-Term Growth*. Paris: OECD.

OECD. 2009b. "The Effectiveness and Scope of Fiscal Stimulus." In *OECD Economic Outlook*, 105–150. Paris: OECD.

OECD. 2009c. "Beyond the Crisis: For a Stronger, Cleaner, Fairer World Economy." Remarks by Angel Gurría at the China Development Forum, March 21, Beijing. http://www.oecd.org/china/beyondthecrisisforastrongercleanerfairerworldeconomy.htm.

OECD. 2009d. "2009 Ministerial Conclusions." Meeting of the Council at Ministerial Level, June 24–25. http://www.oecd.org/officialdocuments/publicdisplaydocumentpdf/?doclanguage=en&cote=C/MIN(2009)5/FINAL.

OECD. 2009e. "Strategies for Aligning Stimulus Measures with Long-Term Growth." Paris: OECD. https://www.oecd.org/economy/42555546.pdf.

OECD. 2009f. "Declaration on Green Growth." Meeting of the Council at Ministerial Level, June 24–25. https://www.oecd.org/env/44077822.pdf.

OECD. 2009g. *Responding to the Economic Crisis: Fostering Industrial Restructuring and Renewal*. Paris: OECD.

OECD. 2010. *Interim Report of the Green Growth Strategy: Implementing Our Commitment for a Sustainable Future*. Paris: OECD.

OECD. 2011. *Towards Green Growth*. Paris: OECD.

OECD. 2012a. *The Jobs Potential of a Shift Towards a Low-Carbon Economy*. Final Report for the European Commission. Paris: OECD. http://www.oecd.org/els/emp/thejobspotentialofashifttowardsalow-carboneconomy.htm.

OECD. 2012b. "Innovation in the Crisis and Beyond." *Science, Technology and Industry Outlook 2012*, 21–57. Paris: OECD.

OECD. 2015. "Local-Content Requirements in the Solar-and Wind-Energy Global Value Chains." In *Overcoming Barriers to International Investment in Clean Energy*, 47–87. Paris: OECD.

Office of the Auditor General of Canada. 2010. *Report of the Auditor General of Canada to the House of Commons*, Ottawa. http://www.oag-bvg.gc.ca/internet/English/parl_oag_201010_e_34282.html.

Office of the Premier. 2008. "B.C. to Move Forward with Northwest Transmission Line." News Release, September 26. https://archive.news.gov.bc.ca/releases/news_releases_2005-2009/2008OTP0238-001467.htm.

Oliver, M. and Pemberton, H. 2004. "Learning and Change in 20th-Century British Economic Policy." *Governance* 17 (3): 415–441.

Omarova, S. T. 2009. "The New Crisis for the New Century: Some Observations on the 'Big-Picture' Lessons of the Global Financial Crisis of 2008." *North Carolina Banking Institute* 13 (1): 157–165.

Osborne, M. 2017. "First PV Power Plant to Use 1366 Technologies High Performance Wafers." *PV Tech News*, June 29. https://www.pv-tech.org/news/first-pv-power-plant-to-use-1366-technologies-high-performance-wafers.

Ostrom, E. 1990. *Governing the Commons: The Evolution of Institutions for Collective Action (Political Economy of Institutions and Decisions)*. Cambridge, UK: Cambridge University Press.

Ostry, J., P. Loungani, and D. Furceri. 2016. "Neoliberalism: Oversold?" *Finance & Development*, June. Washington, DC: IMF. https://www.imf.org/external/pubs/ft/fandd/2016/06/pdf/ostry.pdf.

Overbeek, H. and B. van Apeldoorn, eds. 2012. *Neoliberalism in Crisis*. New York: Palgrave Macmillan.

Park, S. 2012. "Algal Blooms Hit South Korean Rivers." *Nature*, August 21. http://www.nature.com/news/algal-blooms-hit-south-korean-rivers-1.11221.

Parker, J. 2013. *Saving Neoliberalism: Rudd Labor's Response to the 2008 Global Economic Crisis*. PhD Thesis, University of Technology Sydney.

Parkinson, G. 2012. "Why the Federal Government Has Failed at Solar." *Crikey*, July 4. https://www.crikey.com.au/2012/07/04/why-the-federal-government-has-failed-at-solar/.

Peck, J. 2013. "Explaining (with) Neoliberalism." *Territory, Politics, Governance* 1 (2): 132–157.

Pembina. 2015. "Significant Canadian CCS Activities to Date." https://www.pembina.org/reports/canada-ccs-activities-table.pdf.

Penner, D. 2014. "Northwest Transmission Line Powered up, Critics and Proponents Wait to See if it Lives up to its Promise." *Vancouver Sun*, August 20. http://www.vancouversun.com/Northwest+Transmission+Line+powered+critics+proponents+wait+lives+promise/10135321/story.html#ixzz3LYj6y5c2.

Peterman, D. R., J. Frittelli, and W. J. Mallett. 2013. *The Development of High Speed Rail in the United States: Issues and Recent Events*. Washington, DC: Congressional Research Service.

Peters, B. 2011. "Governance Responses to the Fiscal Crisis—Comparative Perspectives." *Public Money & Management* 31 (1): 75–80.

Phillips, M. M. and D. Paletta. 2008. "Paulson Sees Credit Crisis Waning." *The Wall Street Journal*, May 7.

Plumer, B. 2015. "Energy Efficiency Can Be Incredibly Valuable – But We Do Need to Measure it Properly." *Vox*, June 26. https://www.vox.com/2015/6/26/8849695/weatherization-e2e-study-response.

PM & C (Australia). 2009. "Energy Efficient Homes – Ceiling Insulation in 2.7 Million Homes." News Release, February 3. http://www.homeinsulationroyalcommission.gov.au/Hearings/Documents/Evidence17March2014/AGS.002.021.1986.pdf.

Pollin, R., H. Garrett-Peltier, J. Heintz, and H. Scharber. 2008. *Green Recovery: A Program to Create Good Jobs and Start Building a Low-Carbon Economy*. Washington, DC: Center for American Progress and Political Economy Research Institute. https://cdn.americanprogress.org/wp-content/uploads/issues/2008/09/pdf/green_recovery.pdf.

Pollon, C. 2011a. "Northwest Power Line Grows, So Does Controversy." *The Tyee*, July 18. https://thetyee.ca/News/2011/07/18/NorthwestTransmissionLine/.

Pollon, C. 2011b. "Report from the Edge of BC's Copper Rush." *The Tyee*, January 13. https://thetyee.ca/News/2011/01/13/Stikine/print.html.

Pon, S. and A. Alberini. 2012. *What Are the Effects of Energy Efficiency Incentives? Evidence from the US Consumer Expenditure Survey*. Cleveland, OH: International Association for Energy Economics.

Posada, F., D. V. Wagner, G. Bansal, and R. Fernandez. 2015. *Survey of Best Practices in Reducing Emissions through Vehicle Replacement Programs*. White Paper. Washington, DC: International Council on Clean Transportation.

Prasad, E. and I. Sorkin. 2009. *Assessing the G-20 Stimulus Plans: A Deeper Look*. Washington, DC: Brookings Institution.

Presidential Committee on Green Growth. 2010. "Green Korea 2010 – Strengthening Global Green Growth Strategy and Green Economy" Conference Proceedings, September 9–10, The Korea Chamber of Commerce and Industry, Seoul.

Price, D. 2011. "G20 Version 2.0 Will Appease the Sceptics." *Financial Times*, March 31.

Primack, D. 2013. "Obama's Energy Loan Program is no Boondoggle After All." *Fortune*, June 13. http://fortune.com/2013/06/13/obamas-energy-loan-program-is-no-boondoggle-after-all/.

Raloff, J. 2009. "Cash for Clunkers II: Appliances." *Science News*, August 31. https://www.sciencenews.org/blog/science-public/cash-clunkers-ii-appliances?mode=blog&context=102.

Rampton, R. and M. Hosenball. 2011. "In Solyndra Note, Summers said Feds 'Crappy' Investor." *Reuters*, October 4. http://www.reuters.com/article/us-solyndra/in-solyndra-note-summers-said-feds-crappy-investor-idUSTRE7925C520111003.

Rauchway, E. 2008. *The Great Depression and the New Deal: A Very Short Introduction*. London: Oxford University Press.

Republic of Korea. n.d. The River Revitalization of Korea, Seoul (on file with author).

Richards, T. 2013. "Bait and Switch: Red Chris Mine, 'Green' Funding and the Northwest Transmission Line." *The Commonsense Canadian* (blog), April 29. http://commonsensecanadian.ca/bait-and-switch-red-chris-mine-green-funding-and-the-northwest-transmission-line/.

Rivers Without Borders. n.d. "About the Region: Overview of the Iskut-Stikine Watershed." Last accessed October 24, 2017. http://riverswithoutborders.org/about-the-region/iskutstikine.

Robins, N., R. Clover, and C. Singh. 2009a. *A Climate for Recovery*. London: HSBC Global Research. http://globaldashboard.org/wp-content/uploads/2009/HSBC_Green_New_Deal.pdf.

Robins, N., R. Clover, and C. Singh. 2009b. *Building a Green Recovery*. London: HSBC Global Research. https://www.unglobalcompact.org/docs/issues_doc/Environment/Building_a_Green_Recovery.pdf.

Røpke, I. 2016. "Complementary System Perspectives in Ecological Macroeconomics: The Example of Transition Investments During the Crisis." *Ecological Economics* 121: 237–245.

Rotman, D. 2009. "Can Technology Save the Economy?" *Technology Review* 112: 44–52.

Royal Commission into the HIP. 2014a. *Submission on Behalf of the Honourable Kevin Rudd*, June 4. http://www.homeinsulationroyalcommission.gov.au/Documentation/Documents/the-honourable-kevin-rudd.pdf.

Royal Commission into the HIP. 2014b. *Witness Statement of Beth Brunoro (Riordan)*, March 17. http://www.homeinsulationroyalcommission.gov.au/Hearings/Documents/Evidence18March2014/STA.001.002.0001.pdf.

Royal Commission into the HIP. 2014c. *Witness Statement of Ross Carter*, March 17. http://www.homeinsulationroyalcommission.gov.au/Hearings/Documents/Evidence20March2014/STA.001.001.0340.pdf.

Royal Commission into the HIP. 2014d. *Witness Statement of Gregory Ivan Combet AM*, April 30. http://www.homeinsulationroyalcommission.gov.au/Documentation/Pages/default.html.

Royal Commission into the HIP. 2014e. *Witness Statement of Peter Robert Garrett*, May 8. http://www.homeinsulationroyalcommission.gov.au/Documentation/Pages/default.html.

Royal Commission into the HIP. 2014f. *Witness Statement of Kevin Keeffe*, March 28. http://www.homeinsulationroyalcommission.gov.au/Documentation/Pages/default.html.

Royal Commission into the HIP. 2014g. *Witness Statement of Robyn Kruk AM*, March 26. http://www.homeinsulationroyalcommission.gov.au/Documentation/Pages/default.html.

Royal Commission into the HIP. 2014h. *Witness Statement of Matt Levey*, March 18. http://www.homeinsulationroyalcommission.gov.au/Hearings/Documents/Evidence21March2014/STΛ.001.003.0001.pdf.

Royal Commission into the HIP. 2014i. *Witness Statement of Mike Mrdak*, March 24. http://www.homeinsulationroyalcommission.gov.au/Hearings/Documents/Evidence27March2014/STA.001.009.0001.pdf.

Royal Commission into the HIP. 2014j. *Witness Statement of Kevin Rudd*, May 14. http://www.homeinsulationroyalcommission.gov.au/Hearings/Documents/Evidence15May2014/STA.001.080.0001.pdf.

Royal Commission into the HIP. 2014k. *Testimony of James Fricker in Proceedings of the Royal Commission into the Home Insulation Program*, March 24. http://www.homeinsulationroyalcommission.gov.au/Hearings/Documents/Transcript24March2014.pdf.

Royal Commission into the HIP. 2014l. *Witness Statement of Mary Wiley-Smith*, March 15. http://www.homeinsulationroyalcommission.gov.au/Hearings/Documents/Evidence17March2014/STA.001.001.0271.pdf.

Rudd, K. 2007. Speech at the National Climate Change Summit. YouTube, August 6. http://www.youtube.com/watch?v=CqZvpRjGtGM.

Rudd, K. 2009. "The Global Financial Crisis." *The Monthly*, February. https://www.themonthly.com.au/issue/2009/february/1319602475/kevin-rudd/global-financial-crisis.

Ruffin, R. .2010. "South Korea's Four Rivers Dam Construction Rolls Over Opposition." *Environmental News Service*, August 16.

Rydge, J., M. Jacobs, and I. Granoff. 2015. *Ensuring New Infrastructure is Climate-Smart*. New Climate Economy Working Paper. London: The Global Commission on Economy and Climate.

Sachs, J. 2009. "Dig for Victory." *The Guardian*, March 23. https://www.theguardian.com/commentisfree/2009/mar/20/g20-globalrecession.

Sachs, J. 2013. "Professor Krugman and Crude Keynesianism." *The Huffington Post Australia*, May 9. http://www.huffingtonpost.com.au/entry/professor-krugman-and-cru_b_2845773.

Salleh, A. 2010. "Green New Deal or Globalisation Lite?" *Arena* 105: 15–19.

Santisi, J. 2013. "The Cash for Clunkers Conundrum." *The Environmental Magazine*, January 2. https://emagazine.com/the-cash-for-clunkers-conundrum/.

Saskatchewan Research Council. 2017. *Case Study: Cowessess First Nation, Saskatchewan*. Saskatoon: Saskatchewan Research Council. http://www.src.sk.ca/sites/default/files/files/resource/HighWind_Apr17.pdf.

Schepelmann, P., M. Stock, T. Koska, R. Schüle, and O. Reutter. (2009). *A Green New Deal for Europe*. Green New Deals Series vol. 1, Green European Foundation. https://cz.boell.org/sites/default/files/study_-_green_new_deal_for_europe_en.pdf.

Schmelzer, M. 2016. *The Hegemony of Growth. The OECD and the Making of the Economic Growth Paradigm*. Cambridge, UK: Cambridge University Press.

Schwartzman, D. 2011. "Green New Deal: An Ecosocialist Perspective." *Capitalism Nature Socialism* 22: 49–56.

Sekiguchi, S. 2015. "Environmental Tax and Subsidy in Japan: Past and Present." In *Environmental Subsidies to Consumers: How Did They Work in the Japanese Market?*, edited by S. Matsumoto, 27–60. New York: Routledge.

Seib, G. F. 2008. "In Crisis, Opportunity for Obama." *The Wall Street Journal*, November 21. https://www.wsj.com/articles/SB122721278056345271.

Sharan, S. 2010. "The Green Jobs Myth." *The Washington Post*, February 26.

Shell Canada. 2017. "Shell Divests Oil Sands Interests in Canada for Net Consideration of US$7.25 Billion." News Release, March 9. http://www.shell.ca/en_ca/media/news-and-media-releases/news-releases-2017/shell-divests-oil-sands-interests-in-canada.html.

Shim, D. 2010. "Green Growth: South Korea's Panacea?" In *Korea, 2010: Politics, Economy and Society*, edited by F. Rudiger, J. Hoare, P. Kollner, and S. Pares, 165–188. Leiden: Brill.

Shin, H. 2011. "Global Forum Touts Green Growth Paradigm." *The Korea Herald*, June 20. http://www.koreaherald.com/view.php?ud=20110620000810.

Shiraishi, D. 2010. *Eco Car Program CO2 Savings 0.1% of Japan's National Emissions— In Reality Just a Program Promoting Replacement Vehicles, Concerns of Value for Money Also Arise*. Tokyo: Japan Centre for Economic Research. https://www.jcer.or.jp/environment/pdf/rep100902.pdf.

Simms, A., V. Johnson, and P. Chowla. 2010. *Growth Isn't Possible: Why We Need a New Economic Direction*. London: New Economics Foundation.

Simpson, S. 2007. "Collapse of the Galore Mine Project Leaves Transmission Line in Limbo." *The Vancouver Sun*, November 28. https://www.pressreader.com/canada/vancouver-sun/20071128/282209416510015.

Skidelsky, R. 2009. *Keynes: The Return of the Master*. London: Public Affairs.

Slaughter, S. 2013. "Debating the International Legitimacy of the G20: Global Policy Making and Contemporary International Society." *Global Policy* 4: 43–52.

Slaughter, S. 2015. "The G20's Role in Legitimating Global Capitalism: Beyond Crisis Diplomacy?" *Contemporary Politics* 21 (4): 384–398.

Sleight, C. 2013. "Price-Fixing Charges on US$20.5 Billion Four Rivers Project." *International Construction*, September 24. https://www.khl.com/news/price-fixing-charges-on-us-205-billion-four-rivers-project/88539.article.

Snell, D. and P. Fairbrother. 2013. "Just Transition and Labour Environmentalism." In *Trade Unions in the Green Economy: Working for the Environment*, edited by N. Rathzel and D. Uzzell, 146–161. London: Earthscan.

Sofer, K. 2016. "Climate Politics in Japan: The Impacts of Public Opinion, Bureaucratic Rivalries, and Interest Groups on Japan's Environmental Agenda." *Sasakawa USA Forum*, Issue 1, Washington, DC: Sasakawa Peace Foundation USA.

Solty, I. 2011. "After Neoliberalism: Left versus Right Projects of Leadership in the Global Crisis." In *Global Crises and the Crisis of Global Leadership*, edited by S. Gill, 199–215. Cambridge, UK: Cambridge University Press.

Sorrell, S. 2007. *The Rebound Effect: An Assessment of the Evidence for Economy-Wide Energy Savings from Improved Energy Efficiency*. London: UK Energy Research Centre.

Sorrell, S. 2009. "Jevons' Paradox Revisited: The Evidence for Backfire from Improved Energy Efficiency." *Energy Policy* 37: 1456–1469.

Spies-Butcher, B. and F. Stilwell. 2009. "Climate Change Policy in Economic Recession." *Journal of Australian Political Economy* 63: 108–125.

Spratt, S., A. Simms, E. Neitzert, and J. Ryan-Collins. 2009. *The Great Transition: A Tale of How It Turned Out Right*. London: New Economics Foundation. http://www.ourfutureplanet.org/newsletters/resources/nef%20The_Great_Transition.pdf.

Starke, P., A. Kaasch, and F. Van Hooren. 2013. *The Welfare State as Crisis Manager: Explaining the Diversity of Policy Responses to Economic Crises*. New York: Palgrave Macmillan.

Stedman, L. 2013. "Audit Claims Extensive Four Rivers Project Problems." *Water* 21, January 22. London: IWA Publishing. https://www.iwapublishing.com/?name=news1448.

Steffen, W., K. Richardson, J. Rockström, S. E. Cornell, I. Fetzer, E. M. Bennett, R. Biggs, S. R. Carpenter, W. de Vries, C. A. de Wit, and C. Folke. 2015. "Planetary Boundaries: Guiding Human Development on a Changing Planet." *Science* 347(6223): 1259855.

Stein, S. 2011. "McCain on 'Black Monday': Fundamentals of our Economy are Still Strong." *The Huffington Post Australia*, May 26. http://www.huffingtonpost.com.au/entry/mccain-fundamentals-of-th_n_126445.

Steinberg, D., G. Porro, and M. Goldberg. 2012. *Preliminary Analysis of the Jobs and Economic Impacts of Renewable Energy Projects Supported by the 1603 Treasury Grant Program*. Colorado: DOE.

Steinberg, P. F. and S. D. VanDeever. 2012. *Comparative Environmental Politics: Theory, Practice, and Prospects*. Cambridge, MA: MIT Press.

Stevens, B., P. A. Schieb, and Andrieu, M. 2006. "A Cross-Sectoral Perspective on the Development of Global Infrastructures to 2030." In *Infrastructure to 2030: Telecom, Land Transport, Water and Electricity*, 13–50. Paris: OECD.

Stewart, K. 2012. "Shell's Carbon Capture Plan for the Tar Sands Has Some Holes." Greenpeace (blog), September 6. http://www.greenpeace.org/canada/en/blog/Blogentry/shells-carbon-capture-plan-for-the-tar-sands-/blog/42026/.

Stiglitz, J. E. 2003. *Globalization and Its Discontents*. New York: W. W. Norton & Company.

Stone, C. and K. Cox. 2008. *Principles for Fiscal Stimulus Economic Policy in a Weakening Economy*. Washington, DC: Center on Budget and Policy Priorities. https://www.cbpp.org/research/principles-for-fiscal-stimulus-economic-policy-in-a-weakening-economy.

Strand, J. and M. Toman. 2010. *'Green Stimulus' Economic Recovery, and Long-Term Sustainable Development*. Policy Research Working Paper no. 5163, Washington, DC: World Bank.

Strange, S. 1996. *"The Retreat of the State: The Diffusion of Power in the World Economy*. Cambridge: Cambridge University Press.

Styles, J. and A. Talberg. 2009. "Budget 2009–10: Climate Change and Energy." In *Budget Review 2009–10*, Canberra: Parliament of Australia. http://www.aph.gov.au/About_Parliament/Parliamentary_Departments/Parliamentary_Library/pubs/rp/BudgetReview200910/ClimateEnergy.

Summers, L. 2008. "Lawrence Summers Presents Case for Economic Stimulus to House Budget Committee." http://www.hks.harvard.edu/news-events/news/testimonies/summers-testimony-house-budget-committee.

Sustainable Development Commission. 2009. *A Sustainable New Deal*. London: Sustainable Development Commission. http://www.sd-commission.org.uk/data/files/publications/SND_booklet_w.pdf.

Sustainable Prosperity. 2009. *Building a Green Economic Stimulus Package for Canada*. Ottawa: Sustainable Prosperity.

Sutts, Strosberg LLP. 2009. "$500 Million Class Action Lawsuit Alleges the Government of Canada was Negligent in Licensing Inspectors who Recommend RetroFoam be

Used to Meet the Requirements of Natural Resources Canada's Eco-Energy Retrofit Program." *Canada News Wire*, February 17.

Suzuki, D. 2013. "Tahltan's Sacred Headwaters Defence has Deep Roots." *Science Matters*, September 19. Vancouver: David Suzuki Foundation. http://www.davidsuzuki.org/blogs/ science-matters/2013/09/tahltans-sacred-headwaters-defence-has-deep-roots/.

Swan, W. 2009. "Budget Speech 2009–10." May 12. http://www.budget.gov.au/2009-10/ content/speech/html/speech.htm.

Swan, W. and K. Rudd. 2009. "$42 Billion Nation Building and Jobs Plan." News Release, February 3. https://ministers.treasury.gov.au/DisplayDocs.aspx?doc=pressreleases/2009/ 009.htm&pageID=003&min=wms&Year=&DocType=0.

Taiju, K. 2013. *Disguised Protectionism? Environmental Policy in the Japanese Car Market*. Discussion Paper Series 13-E-059. Tokyo: The Research Institute of Economy, Trade and Industry.

Tait, C. 2012. "Alberta's Carbon Capture Efforts Set Back." *The Globe and Mail*, April 26.

Talberth, J. 2010. "Measuring What Matters: GDP, Ecosystems and the Environment." World Resources Institute (blog), April 14. http://www.wri.org/blog/2010/04/measur ing-what-matters-gdp-ecosystems-and-environment.

Tapper, J. 2012. "Federal Government Pulls Plug on EcoENERGY Retrofit Program." *The Star*, January 30. https://www.thestar.com/news/canada/2012/01/30/federal_government_ pulls_plug_on_ecoenergy_retrofit_program.html.

Taylor, L. and D. Uren. 2010. *Shitstorm: Inside Labor's Darkest Days*. Melbourne: Melbourne University Press.

Teräväinen-Litardo, T. 2014. "Negotiating Green Growth." In *Rethinking the Green State: Environmental Governance Towards Climate and Sustainability Transitions*, edited by K. Bäckstrand and A. Kronsell, 174–189. London: Routledge.

Tessaro, L. 2013. "Red Chris Mine." EcoJustice (blog), February 10. http://www. ecojustice.ca/cases/red-chris.

The Chosun Ilbo. 2013. "Probe Finds Massive Underhand Dealings in 4 Rivers Project." July 11. http://english.chosun.com/site/data/html_dir/2013/07/11/2013071101465.html.

The Dong-a Ilbo. 2011. "Nat'l Defense Bridge Collapses on Korean War Anniversary." June 27. http://english.donga.com/List/3/all/26/401586/1.

The Economist. 2010. "Picking Winners, Saving Losers." August 5. http://www.economist. com/node/16741043.

The Economist. 2011. "Rick Scott Deep-Sixes Florida High-Speed Rail." February 19. https://www.economist.com/blogs/gulliver/2011/02/high-speed_rail_florida.

The Economist. 2016. "Taxpayers Could Pay Dearly for California's High-Speed-Train Dreams." March 27. https://www.economist.com/news/science-and-technology/2169 5237-taxpayers-could-pay-dearly-californias-high-speed-dreams-biting-bullet.

The Hankyoreh. 2012. "Four Rivers Project Deemed Illegal." February 11. http://www. hani.co.kr/arti/english_edition/e_national/518581.html.

The Huffington Post. 2010. "Illinois Offers to Take High-Speed Rail Money Rejected by Wisconsin's Incoming Governor Scott Walker." May 25. http://www.huffingtonpost. com/2010/11/09/illinois-offers-to-take-h_n_781120.html.

Thematic Groups. 2012. "Another Future is Possible." Paper presented at Rio+20. http:// rio20.net/en/iniciativas/another-future-is-possible/.

The Province. 2007. "Northwest Transmission Line Ok'd." October 2. http://www.pre- ssreader.com/canada/the-province/20071002/281990373151841.

The Wall Street Journal. 2009. "Clunkers in Practice: One of Washington's All-Time Dumb Ideas." October 4. https://www.wsj.com/articles/SB100014240527487036283045 74453280766443704.

Tienhaara, K. 2014. "Varieties of Green Capitalism: Economy and Environment in the Wake of the Global Financial Crisis." *Environmental Politics* 23 (2): 187–204.

Tienhaara, K. 2015. "Green Stimulus and Pink Batts: The Environmental Politics of Australia's Response to the Global Financial Crisis." *Journal of Australian Political Economy* 76: 54–78.

Tienhaara, K. 2016. "Governing the Global Green Economy." *Global Policy* 7: 481–490.

Time Magazine. n.d. "Top 10 Unfortunate Political One-Liners." http://content.time.com/time/specials/packages/article/0,28804,1859513_1859526_1859517,00.html.

Tollefson, J. 2015. "US Government Abandons Carbon-Capture Demonstration." *Nature*, February 5.

Tonn, B., D. Carroll, E. Rose, B. Hawkins, S. Pigg, D. Bausch, G. Dalhoff, M. Blasnik, J. Eisenberg, C. Cowan, and B. Conlon. 2015. *Weatherization Works II – Summary of Findings From the ARRA Period Evaluation of the U.S. Department of Energy's Weatherization Assistance Program*. Oakridge: Oakridge National Laboratory.

Toshimitsu, T. 2010. "On the Paradoxical Case of a Consumer-Based Environmental Subsidy Policy." *Economic Modelling* 27: 159–164.

Tutton, M. 2011. "How Green is High-Speed Rail?" *CNN*, November 19. http://edition.cnn.com/2011/11/18/world/how-green-is-hsr/.

Tyrrell, M. and J. C. Dernbach. 2011. "The 'Cash for Clunkers' Program: A Sustainability Evaluation." *University of Toledo Law Review* 42: 467–491.

UNCSD. 2012. "The Future We Want." Rio+20 Outcome Document, Rio de Janeiro, June 20–22. http://www.un.org/disabilities/documents/rio20_outcome_document_complete.pdf.

UNEP. 2009a. *Learning from Cyclone Nargis: Investing in the Environment for Livelihoods and Disaster Risk Reduction*. Nairobi: UNEP. https://wedocs.unep.org/bitstream/handle/20.500.11822/14116/myanmar_cyclonenargis_case_study.pdf?sequence=1&isAllowed=y.

UNEP. 2009b. *UNEP Year Book 2009: New Science and Developments in Our Changing Environment*. Nairobi: UNEP.

UNEP. 2009c. *Global Green New Deal*. Policy Brief. Geneva: UN. http://www.unep.org/greeneconomy/sites/unep.org.greeneconomy/files/publications/a_global_green_new_deal_policy_brief.pdf.

UNEP. 2009d. *Overview of the Republic of Korea's Green Growth National Vision: An Interim Report*. Nairobi: UNEP.

UNEP. 2010a. *Green Economy: Developing Country Success Stories*. Geneva: UN.

UNEP. 2010b. *Overview of the Republic of Korea's National Strategy for Green Growth*. Geneva: UN. http://www.cdn.giweh.ch/2015/9/21/1-15-24-1-1.pdf.

UNEP. 2011a. *Towards a Green Economy: Pathways to Sustainable Development and Poverty Eradication. A Synthesis for Policy Makers*. Geneva: UN.

UNEP. 2011b. *Towards a Green Economy: Pathways to Sustainable Development and Poverty Eradication*. Geneva: UN.

UNFCCC. 2015. *The Paris Agreement*. Adopted in Paris, December 12, 2015, in force November 4, 2016. http://unfccc.int/paris_agreement/items/9485.php.

United States Treasury. 2017. "Overview and Status Update of the §1603 Program." April 1. https://www.treasury.gov/initiatives/recovery/Documents/STATUS%20OVERVIEW.pdf.

Unmüßig, B., W. Sachs, and T. Fatheuer. 2012. *Critique of the Green Economy: Toward Social and Environmental Equity*. Berlin: Heinrich Böll Foundation.

Urban Land Institute. 2009. "Infrastructure 2009: Pivot Point." http://uli.org/wp-content/uploads/ULI-Documents/Infrastructure-2009.pdf.

Utting, P. 2012. "Green Economy: The New Enemy?" *Road Logs Rio + 20* (blog). July 21. http://roadlogs.rio20.net/green-economy-the-new-enemy/.

Van de Graaf, T. and K. Westphal. 2011. "The G8 and G20 as Global Steering Committees for Energy: Opportunities and Constraints." *Global Policy* 2: 19–30.

Vartabedian, R. and K. Bensinger. 2009. "Why 'Clunkers' Won't Take Some of the Most-Polluting Cars." *Los Angeles Times*, August 13. http://articles.latimes.com/2009/aug/13/business/fi-clunkers13.

Vestergaard, J. and R. Wade. 2012. "Establishing a New Global Economic Council: Governance Reform at the G20, the IMF and the World Bank." *Global Policy* 3: 257–269.

Victor, P. 2008. *Managing Without Growth: Slower by Design, Not Disaster.* Cheltenham, UK: Edward Elgar.

Vivid Economics. 2013. *Analysis of Electricity Consumption, Electricity Generation Emissions Intensity and Economy-Wide Emissions.* Report prepared for the Climate Change Authority, October. http://climatechangeauthority.gov.au/files/files/Target-Progress-Review/Analysis-of-electricity-consumption-electricity-generation-emissions-intensity-and-economy-wide-emissions/Australia%20electricity%20and%20emissions%20final%20report%202013%2010%2018.pdf.

Webb, R., S. Kompo-Harms, and Styles, J. 2009. *Bills Digest: Appropriation (Nation Building and Jobs) Bill (No. 1) 2008–09.* Canberra: Parliamentary Library.

Wei, M., S. Patadia, and D. M. Kammen. 2010. "Putting Renewables and Energy Efficiency to Work: How Many Jobs can the Clean Energy Industry Generate in the US?" *Energy Policy* 38: 919–931.

Westin, J. and P. Kågeson. 2012. "Can High Speed Rail Offset its Embedded Emissions?" *Transportation Research Part D* 17: 1–7.

Wessner, C. W. and A. W. Wolff. 2012. *Rising to the Challenge: U.S. Innovation Policy for the Global Economy.* Washington, DC: National Research Council.

Wettenhall, R. 2011. "Global Financial Crisis: The Australian Experience in International Perspective." *Public Organization Review* 11: 77–91.

White, D., A. Rudy, and B. Gareau. 2016. *Environments, Natures and Social Theory: Towards a Critical Hybridity.* New York: Palgrave Macmillan.

Wild Border Watersheds. n.d. "Project: Northwest Transmission Line." Last accessed October 24, 2017. http://wildborderwatersheds.org/projects/northwest-transmission-line.

Wilkins, R. 2008. *Strategic Review of Australian Government Climate Change Programs.* Canberra: Commonwealth of Australia.

Williams, N. 2009. "G20 Fears." *Current Biology* 19: 306–307.

Williams, T. 2011. "Florida's Governor Rejects High-Speed Rail Line, Fearing Cost to Taxpayers." *The New York Times*, February 16. http://www.nytimes.com/2011/02/17/us/17rail.html.

Winfield, M. 2012. *Blue-Green Province: The Environment and the Political Economy of Ontario.* Vancouver: UBC Press.

Wintour, P., D. Adam, and D. Carrington. 2009. "Climate Change Experts Call on G20 Members to Commit to Action." *The Guardian*, March 31.

Woods, N. 2006. *The Globalizers: The IMF, the World Bank, and Their Borrowers.* Ithaca: Cornell University Press.

World Commission on Environment and Development. 1987. *Our Common Future.* Oxford: Oxford University Press. http://www.un-documents.net/our-common-future.pdf.

World Water Network. 2012. *Wetland Globes, Category: Grey Globe Award Asia.* http://www.worldwetnet.org/docs/files/awards_2012/4_Rivers_poster.pdf.

WTO. n.d. "Dispute Settlement." *Trade Topics*. Last accessed July 7, 2017. https://www. wto.org/english/tratop_e/dispu_e/dispu_e.htm.

WTO. 2011. *Harnessing Trade for Sustainable Development and a Green Economy*. Geneva: WTO.

Wurzel, Rüdiger. 2012. "The Environmental Challenge to Nation States: From Limits to Growth to Ecological Modernisation." In *The Withering of the Welfare State: Regression*, edited by J. Connelly and J. Hayward, 137–154. New York: Palgrave Macmillan.

Wurzelmann, S. 2012. *Advanced Research Projects Agency-Energy (ARPA-E): Innovation through the U.S. Department of Energy*. Arlington, VA: Center for Climate and Energy Solutions.

WWF. 2008. Living Planet Report. Gland, Switzerland: WWF. http://wwf.panda.org/ about_our_earth/all_publications/living_planet_report_timeline/lpr_2008/.

Xu, G., T. Miwa, T. Morikawa, and T. Yamamoto. 2015. "Vehicle Purchasing Behaviors Comparison in Two-Stage Choice Perspective Before and After Eco-Car Promotion Policy in Japan." *Transportation Research Part D* 34: 195–207.

Yamaguchi, K., S. Matsumoto, and T. Tasaki. 2015. "Effect of an Eco-Point Program on Consumer Digital TV Selection." In *Environmental Subsidies to Consumers: How Did They Work in the Japanese Market?*, edited by S. Matsumoto, 76–90. New York: Routledge.

Yoshida, Y., Y. Inahata, M. Enokibori, and R. Matsuhashi. 2010. "Estimating CO2 Emission Reduction in Eco-Point Program for Green Home Appliances in Japan." *Procedia Environmental Sciences* 2: 605–612.

Yun, S., M. Cho, and D. von Hippe. 2011. "The Current Status of Green Growth in Korea: Energy and Urban Security." *The Asia-Pacific Journal* 9 (44): 4.

Zhaokun, W. 2016. "China Plans to Invest $538 Billion in Railway in 5 Years: Report." *China Daily*, January 4. http://www.chinadaily.com.cn/china/2016-01/04/content_2292 6538.htm.

Zoback, M. D. and S. M. Gorelick. 2012. "Earthquake Triggering and Large-Scale Geologic Storage of Carbon Dioxide." *Proceedings of the National Academy of Sciences* 109 (26): 10164–10168.

Zomer, A. 2009. "Tracking Environmental Impact Assessment Rollbacks." WRI (blog), June 4. http://www.wri.org/blog/2009/06/tracking-environmental-impact-assessment-rollbacks.

Index

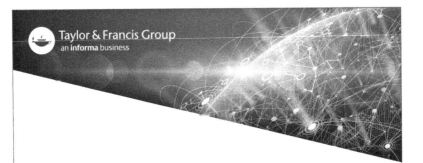

For Product Safety Concerns and Information please contact our EU
representative GPSR@taylorandfrancis.com
Taylor & Francis Verlag GmbH, Kaufingerstraße 24, 80331 München, Germany

www.ingramcontent.com/pod-product-compliance
Ingram Content Group UK Ltd.
Pitfield, Milton Keynes, MK11 3LW, UK
UKHW020953180425

457613UK00019B/666